BARRON'S

READING WORKBOOK
for the
NEW SAT*

Brian W. Stewart, M.Ed.

President

BWS Education Consulting

Columbus, Ohio

BARRON'S

Dedication

Dedicated to my wife Caitlin, my son Andrew, and my daughter Eloise—without your love and support, this book would not have been possible. I would like to especially thank my mom, my dad, Andy, Mitchell, Mercedez, Hannah, Alaina, Andrew, and Doug for their help with this undertaking. I am grateful to everyone at Barron's.

Thanks so much to all of my students over the years—I have learned far more from you than you have learned from me.

About the Author

Brian W. Stewart is the founder and president of BWS Education Consulting, Inc., a boutique tutoring and test preparation company based in Columbus, Ohio. He has worked with thousands of students to help them improve their test scores and earn admission to selective schools. Brian is a graduate of Princeton University (A.B.) and The Ohio State University (M.Ed.). You can connect with Brian at *www.bwseducationconsulting.com.*

All inquiries should be addressed to:
Barron's Educational Series, Inc.
250 Wireless Boulevard
Hauppauge, New York 11788
www.barronseduc.com

ISBN: 978-1-4380-0576-8

Library of Congress Control Number: 2015953336

PRINTED IN THE UNITED STATES OF AMERICA

9 8 7 6 5 4 3 2 1

10%
POST-CONSUMER WASTE
Paper contains a minimum of 10% post-consumer waste (PCW). Paper used in this book was derived from certified, sustainable forestlands.

Contents

Contents

Introduction

FAQs ABOUT THE NEW SAT READING TEST

How does the Reading section factor into the overall new SAT?

The new SAT has two required sections—(1) Math and (2) Evidence-Based Reading and Writing. Each section will be scored between 200–800, making for a potential total score of between 400-1600. The Reading section and the Writing and Language section will contribute in equal measure to your overall Evidence-Based Reading and Writing score.

What is the general format of the new SAT Reading section?

It is a single section with these features:

- First test section
- 65 minutes long
- 52 questions (10 Fiction, 21 Social Studies, 21 Science).

What will the reading passages be like?

- 5 passages total—each passage between 500 and 750 words for a total of around 3,250 words.

  - One fiction passage—a selection from U.S. or world literature
  - Two social studies passages—one from social science and one from a U.S. founding document or a selection from the "Great Global Conversation" (e.g., a historical speech or essay)
  - Two science passages

- One of the passages will comprise two smaller passages that you will need to compare and contrast in the questions.
- Two graphs accompany the reading that you will need to analyze.
- The passages range in difficulty from early high school level to early college level.

What are the questions like?

- 10 Words in Context questions

  Example: *As used in line 30, the word "advance" most closely means . . .*

- 10 Command of Evidence questions

  Example: *Which option gives the best evidence for the answer to the previous question?*

- 32 Analysis questions

Examples:

- *What statement best summarizes the passage?*
- *The paragraph in lines 21–37 primarily serves to . . .*
- *The narrator's statement in lines 48–51 ("The primary . . . forecast") most clearly implies that . . .*

- The questions for a given passage generally appear in the same order as the material in the passage (e.g., Question 1 is about lines 1–5, Question 2 is about lines 6–9, etc.).
- The questions are arranged in a random order of difficulty.
- There are 10–11 questions per passage.

How is the new SAT Reading Test different from the old SAT Critical Reading Test?

Old SAT Critical Reading Test	New SAT Reading Test
A completely separate section for scoring purposes	Combined with the Writing and Language section for the overall "Evidence-Based Reading and Writing" score
3 shorter test sections	1 large test section
Sentence Completion questions—necessary to know lots of difficult vocabulary words	Words in Context questions—more important to be able to determine appropriate word meaning in a given situation
No graphs; no "evidence" questions	Graphs to analyze; demonstrate command of text through evidence-based questions
Questions require considerable reading time	Easier to determine what is being asked
A quarter point guessing penalty	NO guessing penalty

How can I use this book to prepare?

- **IF YOU HAVE ONE DAY**, look over the reading strategies, become familiar with the test directions and format, and try a couple of passages under time constraints.
- **IF YOU HAVE ONE WEEK**, complete the diagnostic test, read the strategy chapter, and do targeted practice on the types of passages and questions that give you difficulty.
- **IF YOU HAVE A MONTH OR MORE,** do everything in this book. Start with the diagnostic, read the strategy chapter very carefully, and complete the practice exercises under time constraints, carefully reflecting on your approach as you practice further.

What can I do beyond this book to prepare?

- Practice with the other Barron's books that have excellent sample reading tests, such as *Barron's New SAT*, *Barron's 6 Practice Tests for the New SAT*, and *Barron's Strategies and Practice for the New PSAT.*

- Take rigorous courses in school, such as A.P. English Language and Composition, A.P. U.S. History, and International Baccalaureate Literature.
- Make reading a daily habit—talk to your local librarian about books that may suit your interests, read well-written online journals and blogs, and download an e-reader to your smartphone so you can read good books no matter where you are.
- If you are ambitious, read publications that you find more challenging. *The Best American* series is good for a wide variety of texts. If you have trouble with fiction, seek out books by authors like Emily Dickinson, James Joyce, and Charles Dickens. If you struggle with social studies, read historical documents and publications like *The Economist* or *The Atlantic*. And if you find science challenging, read publications like *Science News* and *Scientific American*, and check out online resources like *Pubmed.gov*.
- Use the free official practice resources available at *KhanAcademy.org*.

The SAT Reading Test is a test of your reading skill, not any specific knowledge. You will do well on this test if you improve your overall reading comprehension ability, which is exactly what this text is designed to do. Let's get started!

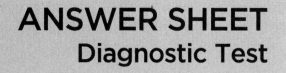

ANSWER SHEET
Diagnostic Test

Reading

1. Ⓐ Ⓑ Ⓒ Ⓓ
2. Ⓐ Ⓑ Ⓒ Ⓓ
3. Ⓐ Ⓑ Ⓒ Ⓓ
4. Ⓐ Ⓑ Ⓒ Ⓓ
5. Ⓐ Ⓑ Ⓒ Ⓓ
6. Ⓐ Ⓑ Ⓒ Ⓓ
7. Ⓐ Ⓑ Ⓒ Ⓓ
8. Ⓐ Ⓑ Ⓒ Ⓓ
9. Ⓐ Ⓑ Ⓒ Ⓓ
10. Ⓐ Ⓑ Ⓒ Ⓓ
11. Ⓐ Ⓑ Ⓒ Ⓓ
12. Ⓐ Ⓑ Ⓒ Ⓓ
13. Ⓐ Ⓑ Ⓒ Ⓓ

14. Ⓐ Ⓑ Ⓒ Ⓓ
15. Ⓐ Ⓑ Ⓒ Ⓓ
16. Ⓐ Ⓑ Ⓒ Ⓓ
17. Ⓐ Ⓑ Ⓒ Ⓓ
18. Ⓐ Ⓑ Ⓒ Ⓓ
19. Ⓐ Ⓑ Ⓒ Ⓓ
20. Ⓐ Ⓑ Ⓒ Ⓓ
21. Ⓐ Ⓑ Ⓒ Ⓓ
22. Ⓐ Ⓑ Ⓒ Ⓓ
23. Ⓐ Ⓑ Ⓒ Ⓓ
24. Ⓐ Ⓑ Ⓒ Ⓓ
25. Ⓐ Ⓑ Ⓒ Ⓓ
26. Ⓐ Ⓑ Ⓒ Ⓓ

27. Ⓐ Ⓑ Ⓒ Ⓓ
28. Ⓐ Ⓑ Ⓒ Ⓓ
29. Ⓐ Ⓑ Ⓒ Ⓓ
30. Ⓐ Ⓑ Ⓒ Ⓓ
31. Ⓐ Ⓑ Ⓒ Ⓓ
32. Ⓐ Ⓑ Ⓒ Ⓓ
33. Ⓐ Ⓑ Ⓒ Ⓓ
34. Ⓐ Ⓑ Ⓒ Ⓓ
35. Ⓐ Ⓑ Ⓒ Ⓓ
36. Ⓐ Ⓑ Ⓒ Ⓓ
37. Ⓐ Ⓑ Ⓒ Ⓓ
38. Ⓐ Ⓑ Ⓒ Ⓓ
39. Ⓐ Ⓑ Ⓒ Ⓓ

40. Ⓐ Ⓑ Ⓒ Ⓓ
41. Ⓐ Ⓑ Ⓒ Ⓓ
42. Ⓐ Ⓑ Ⓒ Ⓓ
43. Ⓐ Ⓑ Ⓒ Ⓓ
44. Ⓐ Ⓑ Ⓒ Ⓓ
45. Ⓐ Ⓑ Ⓒ Ⓓ
46. Ⓐ Ⓑ Ⓒ Ⓓ
47. Ⓐ Ⓑ Ⓒ Ⓓ
48. Ⓐ Ⓑ Ⓒ Ⓓ
49. Ⓐ Ⓑ Ⓒ Ⓓ
50. Ⓐ Ⓑ Ⓒ Ⓓ
51. Ⓐ Ⓑ Ⓒ Ⓓ
52. Ⓐ Ⓑ Ⓒ Ⓓ

Diagnostic Test

65 MINUTES, 52 QUESTIONS

> **Directions:** Each passage or pair of passages is accompanied by several questions. After reading the passage(s), choose the best answer to each question based on what is indicated explicitly or implicitly in the passage(s) or in the associated graphics.

Questions 1–10 are based on the following reading selection.

The following is an excerpt from Jane Austen's Mansfield Park, *1814. The novel's protagonist, Fanny Price, returns home after many years of living with her wealthy relatives at Mansfield Park.*

William was gone: and the home he had
left her in was—Fanny could not conceal it
from herself—in almost every respect the
Line very reverse of what she could have wished.
(5) It was the abode of noise, disorder, and
impropriety. Nobody was in their right place,
nothing was done as it ought to be. She could
not respect her parents as she had hoped.
On her father, her confidence had not been
(10) sanguine, but he was more negligent of his
family, his habits were worse, and his man-
ners coarser, than she had been prepared for.
He did not want abilities; but he had no curiosity, and no information beyond his profes-
(15) sion; he read only the newspaper and the
navy-list; he talked only of the dockyard, the
harbour, Spithead, and the Motherbank; he
swore and he drank, he was dirty and gross.
She had never been able to recall anything
(20) approaching to tenderness in his former
treatment of herself. There had remained
only a general impression of roughness and
loudness; and now he scarcely ever noticed
her, but to make her the object of a coarse
(25) joke.

Her disappointment in her mother was
greater: *there* she had hoped much, and
found almost nothing. Every flattering
scheme of being of consequence to her soon
(30) fell to the ground. Mrs. Price was not unkind;
but, instead of gaining on her affection and
confidence, and becoming more and more
dear, her daughter never met with greater
kindness from her than on the first day of
(35) her arrival. The instinct of nature was soon
satisfied, and Mrs. Price's attachment had no
other source. Her heart and her time were
already quite full; she had neither leisure nor
affection to bestow on Fanny. Her daughters
(40) never had been much to her. She was fond
of her sons, especially of William, but Betsey
was the first of her girls whom she had ever
much regarded. To her she was most inju-
diciously indulgent. William was her pride;
(45) Betsey her darling; and John, Richard, Sam,
Tom, and Charles occupied all the rest of her
maternal solicitude, alternately her worries
and her comforts. These shared her heart;
her time was given chiefly to her house and
(50) her servants. Her days were spent in a kind

GO ON TO THE NEXT PAGE

of slow bustle; all was busy without getting on, always behindhand and lamenting it, without altering her ways; wishing to be an economist, without contrivance or regularity;
(55) dissatisfied with her servants, without skill to make them better, and whether helping, or reprimanding, or indulging them, without any power of engaging their respect.

Of her two sisters, Mrs. Price very much
(60) more resembled Lady Bertram than Mrs. Norris. She was a manager by necessity, without any of Mrs. Norris's inclination for it, or any of her activity. Her disposition was naturally easy and indolent, like Lady Bertram's;
(65) and a situation of similar affluence and do-nothingness would have been much more suited to her capacity than the exertions and self-denials of the one which her imprudent marriage had placed her in. She might have
(70) made just as good a woman of consequence as Lady Bertram, but Mrs. Norris would have been a more respectable mother of nine children on a small income.

Much of all this Fanny could not but be
(75) sensible of. She might scruple to make use of the words, but she must and did feel that her mother was a partial, ill-judging parent, a dawdle, a slattern, who neither taught nor restrained her children, whose house was
(80) the scene of mismanagement and discomfort from beginning to end, and who had no talent, no conversation, no affection towards herself; no curiosity to know her better, no desire of her friendship, and no inclination
(85) for her company that could lessen her sense of such feelings.

Fanny was very anxious to be useful, and not to appear above her home, or in any way disqualified or disinclined, by her foreign
(90) education, from contributing her help to its comforts, and therefore set about working for Sam immediately, and by working early and late, with perseverance and great despatch, did so much, that the boy was shipped off at
(95) last, with more than half his linen ready. She had great pleasure in feeling her usefulness,

but could not conceive how they would have managed without her.

1. What best describes what happens in the passage as a whole?

   (A) A character discusses her troubled thoughts with close family and friends.
   (B) A character analyzes her observations relative to her experiences and expectations.
   (C) A character reflects on how she could be a better contributor to her immediate family.
   (D) A character considers her economic station in a strongly hierarchical society.

2. Fanny's overall attitude toward her parents is best described as

   (A) justified affection.
   (B) unjustified jealousy.
   (C) unwarranted disrespect.
   (D) warranted disappointment.

3. The first paragraph characterizes Fanny's father's intellectual interests as

   (A) relevant and interesting.
   (B) coarse and joking.
   (C) overly pragmatic.
   (D) arrogantly erudite.

4. As used in line 35, the phrase "instinct of nature" most closely means

   (A) maternal feeling.
   (B) desire for survival.
   (C) thirst for acceptance.
   (D) sense of justice.

GO ON TO THE NEXT PAGE

5. The more that Fanny is around her mother, the more her mother treats her with

   (A) abuse.
   (B) affection.
   (C) inattention.
   (D) encouragement.

6. Which option gives the best evidence for the answer to the previous question?

   (A) Lines 19–21 ("She . . . herself")
   (B) Lines 33–35 ("her . . . arrival")
   (C) Lines 55–58 ("without . . . respect")
   (D) Lines 61–63 ("She . . . activity")

7. When Fanny returns to live with her parents, she is eager to be

   (A) an idealistic martyr.
   (B) an economical innovator.
   (C) an empowering mentor.
   (D) a helpful contributor.

8. Which option gives the best evidence for the answer to the previous question?

   (A) Lines 5–8 ("It . . . hoped")
   (B) Lines 37–43 ("Her heart . . . regarded")
   (C) Lines 69–73 ("She might . . . income")
   (D) Lines 87–91 ("Fanny . . . comforts")

9. As used in line 46, the word "occupied" most closely means

   (A) stayed.
   (B) resided.
   (C) dwelled.
   (D) engaged.

10. The third paragraph (lines 59–73) suggests that Mrs. Norris is

    (A) more capable than Mrs. Price.
    (B) similar in personality to Mrs. Price.
    (C) more lethargic than Mrs. Price.
    (D) less respectable than Mrs. Price.

Questions 11–20 are based on the following reading selection and accompanying material.

The Downfall of Democracy?

"The future of this republic is in the hands of the American voter."

—*Dwight D. Eisenhower*

The statement above, made by the 34th President of the United States, paints a dismal picture when one considers the trends
Line of the American youth. Those under the age
(5) of 35, in general, do not vote, do not participate in politics, and frankly, have no interest or trust in the government itself. The retreat of youngsters from the political realms can be seen in election turnouts surely, but it
(10) can also be noted in the miniscule numbers of young Americans who identify as either Democrats or Republicans. It is not only disinterest but also distaste that keep the next generation of representatives far from
(15) the poll booths and even further from office. In fact, a recently published book *Running From Office: Why Young Americans Are Turned Off to Politics* found that only about ten percent of high school and university
(20) students would even consider running for public office, with disdain for federal positions at the highest.

It might be easy to chalk up the younger generation as careless and unconcerned
(25) and altogether misdirected, but that's the easy way out, and it is flawed. Students are largely civic-minded; they volunteer, worry about public policies, and even congregate to debate solutions to everything from environ-
(30) mental issues to human rights to healthcare. Significant events like the war in Iraq or Barack Obama running for President or gay marriage rights may generate an influx in youth participation, but overall, young voters
(35) are disengaged from American democracy and looking at other ways of tackling society's problems. It is not that they are merely apa-

GO ON TO THE NEXT PAGE

thetic, but instead that they have lost faith in electoral politics and are highly suspicious of
(40) party labels.

If it is distrust and suspicion that keep youngsters away, the U.S. must ask what has changed to trigger this worrying trend. One doesn't have to prepare extensive research
(45) methods to find that today's millennials view themselves as in an altogether worse situation than that of their parents or grandparents. Widespread opinion has them in a bitter, unrewarding job market bankrupted
(50) by the university and crushed underneath a stifling national debt. Their path is difficult and uncertain at best; behind these obstacles lies an inefficient and wasteful government that they are less than anticipatory to inherit.
(55) The aforementioned book found that 25% of student-aged Americans showed absolute indifference to politics. More worrying were the 60% who held negative views of politics, avoided the subject at all costs, and
(60) thought of all politicians as devious and

untrustworthy. More and more Americans are shunning away from the loaded labels of "conservative" and "liberal," instead finding themselves somewhere in the middle,
(65) socially liberal but fiscally conservative. Alienated by the two-party system, young Americans would rather not be included in either disagreeable side.

Disinterested in a bleak future of more
(70) debt and less freedom, and wary of aligning themselves within partisanship, today's youth are doubtful of a government that promises few of the assurances it once pledged. Naturally, this trend is disquieting
(75) for a nation that depends on its voters and an interest in representation, both of which are in a state of deterioration. Yet, some may applaud the veer from partisanship—a phenomena that has left more undone
(80) than accomplished. Still, if democracy is to survive, something must be done to align the cynical millennials with a system that desperately needs their interference.

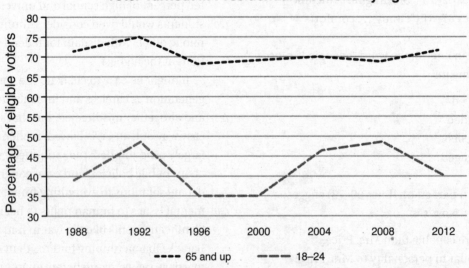

Voter Turnout in Presidential Elections by Age

Source: 2012 U.S. Census Bureau: *http://www.census.gov/prod/2014pubs/p20-573.pdf.*

GO ON TO THE NEXT PAGE

11. What is the overall point of the essay?

    (A) To argue against the continuation of the two-party political system
    (B) To raise specific concerns about the lack of millennial political engagement
    (C) To suggest that mandatory voting would alleviate much of the skepticism towards the political process
    (D) To explain why millennials are more interested in pursuing political office than people from past generations

12. The tone of the essay is best described as

    (A) panicked.
    (B) wavering.
    (C) concerned.
    (D) optimistic.

13. As used in line 23, the phrase "chalk up" most closely means

    (A) ascribe.
    (B) draw.
    (C) blame.
    (D) dispute.

14. The author most strongly suggests that those Americans under age 35 are most likely to take what approach to solving societal problems?

    (A) Active participation in the political process
    (B) General apathy and lack of activity
    (C) Attacking problems outside of a governmental paradigm
    (D) Focusing on their own individual interests above all

15. Which option gives the best evidence for the answer to the previous question?

    (A) Lines 1–4 ("The statement . . . youth")
    (B) Lines 34–37 ("young . . . problems")
    (C) Lines 43–48 ("One . . . grandparents")
    (D) Lines 77–80 ("Yet . . . accomplished")

16. As used in line 36, the word "tackling" most closely means

    (A) beginning.
    (B) discovering.
    (C) solving.
    (D) dismissing.

17. The primary purpose of the paragraph in lines 55–68 is to

    (A) give evidence pertaining to the lack of interest in politics on the part of young Americans.
    (B) explain the inherent flaws with the American two-party political system.
    (C) describe the specific reasons why young people find party labels distasteful.
    (D) analyze why older Americans are more likely to participate in the political process than younger Americans.

18. What is the purpose of the sentence in lines 77–80 ("Yet . . . accomplished.")?

    (A) To state the thesis of the essay
    (B) To give details about the pitfalls of partisanship
    (C) To acknowledge a contrasting viewpoint
    (D) To cite an expert point of view

GO ON TO THE NEXT PAGE

19. According to the information in the graph, during what year were the voter turnout rates of Americans ages 65 and older and Americans ages 18–24 closest to one another?

   (A) 1992
   (B) 2000
   (C) 2004
   (D) 2008

20. The variation in the ages 18–24 voter turnout can most directly be accounted for by what selection from the passage?

   (A) Lines 4–7 ("Those . . . itself")
   (B) Lines 31–34 ("Significant . . . participation")
   (C) Lines 57–61 ("More . . . untrustworthy")
   (D) Lines 74–77 ("Naturally . . . deterioration")

Questions 21–31 are based on the following reading selection and accompanying material.

Microbiomes

Germs make us sick. It's an elementary truth that we teach to our children. It's why we wash our hands before eating. It's why we
Line pasteurize our milk, and refrigerate our food.
(5) When they do make us sick, our ability to safely exterminate them is nothing short of a modern miracle. Beginning with penicillin in 1928, antibiotics forever transformed the way we both treat and prevent infectious disease.
(10) Today, moreover, one can stroll down any cleaning supply aisle at a supermarket, and discover a bevy of products boasting of their broad-spectrum antimicrobial activity.

For better or for worse, our culture of
(15) "germophobia" was hard-won by its proponents. From the time it was first proposed in the 16th century, the germ theory of disease faced three hundred years' worth of influential naysayers, and it was not until the
(20) late 1800's that the theory began to gain the pervasive public vindication it enjoys today. However, an emerging body of research indicates that we have been perhaps overzealous in our crusade to eradicate the germs that
(25) live within us.

The "human microbiome" refers collectively to the microscopic organisms that naturally colonize the human body, and the application of dynamic ecological theories
(30) to this biome represents a rapidly expanding field of study. Comprised of fungi, viruses, archaea, and perhaps 1,000 species of bacteria, the population of this microbiome is thought to outnumber our own cells by as
(35) much as ten to one. What's more, much like our own cells, a significant portion of these organisms play crucial roles in our metabolic and immunological processes.

GO ON TO THE NEXT PAGE

For example, *Oxalobacter formigenes*, (40) which colonizes the colon, is a primary source of the enzyme oxalyl-CoA decarboxylase, which allows us to safely eliminate dietary oxalate. Without this enzyme, calcium oxalate salts tend to accumulate in the (45) kidney tubules, and eventually precipitate as renal stones. Other colonic bacteria catalyze the reduction of bilirubin into urobilinogen: a reaction critical to our digestion of fats, and absorption of fat-soluble vitamins. (50) Interestingly, many bacteria within our gastrointestinal tracts also directly synthesize several vitamins in excess of their own metabolic needs, and, as a result, represent an important source of both vitamin B12, which (55) is necessary for the production of new red blood cells, and vitamin K, which is a cofactor in the synthesis of several blood clotting factors.

The benefits we gain from a balanced, (60) thriving microbiome are diverse, and we are only just beginning to appreciate their true complexity, though perhaps no single function it serves is more significant than its role in regulating our immune systems. There are (65) numerous mechanisms by which the microbiome helps protect us from disease. Some species, for instance, secrete special proteins, known as "bacteriocins," that are directly toxic to pathogenic bacteria, but harmless (70) to our own cells. One particularly impressive member of the microbiome, *Lactobacillus*, produces a powerful bacteriocin called reuterin, as well as lactic acid and hydrogen peroxide, which inhibit the growth of dis-(75) ease-causing organisms by lowering local pH and damaging lipid membranes respectively.

Of no less importance, there are a number of more indirect, ecologically-oriented ways in which the microbiome confers protec-(80) tion to its host. Abundant colonization of our bodies by benign microorganisms, for example, inhibits the overgrowth of more dangerous ones through the sheer depletion of microbial nutrients. This notion of ecologi-(85) cal balance has been of particular interest to scientists studying the microbiome, as it hinges upon both the variable diversity of species that colonize an individual, as well as factors that affect the dynamism of a micro-(90) biotic population. Age, geography, diet, and stress have all been implicated in influencing both the composition and balance of the microbiome. None, however, has been shown to have so drastic an effect as the use of anti-(95) biotics, which, unlike bacteriocins, tend to be just as deadly to disease-causing bacteria as they are to those that colonize us naturally.

Admittedly, antibiotics save lives. Yet our decision to use them must be weighed (100) carefully, as artificially upsetting the ecological balance of our bodies can have dire consequences. There is perhaps no greater example of this than *Clostridium difficile*, a colonic bacterium that is both highly resis-(105) tant to antibiotics, and an increasing cause of hospital-acquired disease. When properly counterbalanced by its neighboring species, *C. difficile* is harmless to humans. However, following the administration of antibiot-(110) ics, and the elimination of its ecological competitors, *C. diff* proliferation proceeds unchecked, resulting in a frequently fatal infection for which very few effective treatments exist.

GO ON TO THE NEXT PAGE

The table illustrates variations in microbiota for individuals following either vegetarian or omnivorous diets across three geographical demographics.

Diversity of Human Microbiomes

Microorganism	Geographical Location					
	United States		Vietnam		Ireland	
	Vegetarian diet (%)	Omnivorous diet (%)	Vegetarian diet (%)	Omnivorous diet (%)	Vegetarian diet (%)	Omnivorous diet (%)
Actinobacteria	7.3	8.1	5.5	4.9	6.3	6.4
Bacteroides	23.4	22.9	18.8	19.2	26.1	24.7
Bifidobacteria	16.9	17.0	27.0	30.4	4.6	8.9
Clostridia	13.1	14.8	7.7	7.5	23.0	22.5
Enterococci	26.8	29.2	27.5	29.0	26.9	28.8
Lactobacilli	7.9	5.0	8.1	5.4	8.6	6.0
Methanogens	0.0	0.0	0.6	0.3	0.0	0.0
Yeasts	4.6	3.0	4.8	3.3	4.5	2.7

21. The general structure of the passage is best described as

    (A) a broad introduction followed by specific illustrations.
    (B) a logical, point-by-point argument.
    (C) an interesting look followed by in-depth persuasion.
    (D) a sequence of technical examples.

22. As used in line 1, the word "elementary" most closely means

    (A) scholastic.
    (B) medical.
    (C) healthy.
    (D) fundamental.

23. The paragraph in lines 14–25 most directly serves to

    (A) articulate that while society has now embraced germ theory, taking the theory too far may be detrimental.
    (B) argue that germophobia has continued to be a major obstacle to scientific progress.
    (C) point out the shortcomings of germ theory by presenting the valid concerns of germophobics.
    (D) present the many ways that germ theory has concrete applications to everyday life.

GO ON TO THE NEXT PAGE

24. What is the overall purpose of the paragraph in lines 39–58?

  (A) To recommend specific bacteriological treatments to common gastrointestinal illnesses
  (B) To provide concrete examples of the utility of some bacteria to our metabolic and immunological processes
  (C) To address the objections of those who are inherently skeptical towards the existence of bacteria
  (D) To explain the metabolic processes whereby bacteria lead to the creation of vitamins B12 and K

25. Which of the following does the passage explicitly state illustrates the potential danger in overusing antibiotics?

  (A) *Oxalobacter formigenes*
  (B) Bilirubin
  (C) *Lactobacillus*
  (D) *Clostridium difficile*

26. Which option gives the best evidence for the answer to the previous question?

  (A) Lines 39–43 ("For . . . oxalate")
  (B) Lines 46–49 ("Other . . . vitamins")
  (C) Lines 70–76 ("One . . . respectively")
  (D) Lines 108–114 ("However . . . exist")

27. As used in line 87, the word "hinges" most closely means

  (A) fulcrums.
  (B) analyzes.
  (C) depends.
  (D) joints.

28. The information in the table would be most helpful to the study of which of the following concepts mentioned in the passage?

  (A) Germophobia
  (B) Ecological balance
  (C) Blood clotting
  (D) Pathogenic bacteria

29. Which option gives the best evidence for the answer to the previous question?

  (A) Lines 14–21 ("For better . . . today")
  (B) Lines 50–58 ("Interestingly . . . factors")
  (C) Lines 66–76 ("Some . . . respectively")
  (D) Lines 84–93 ("This . . . microbiome")

30. Based on the information in the table, analysis of the variations of which two microorganisms would be most helpful in roughly determining the country of residence of a randomly selected human test subject?

  (A) *Actinobacteria* and *Bacteroides*
  (B) *Bifidobacteria* and *Clostridia*
  (C) *Enterococci* and *Lactobacilli*
  (D) Methanogens and Yeasts

31. Based on the information in the table, knowing the percentage of each of the following microorganisms would be useful in determining whether someone had a vegetarian or omnivorous diet, no matter his or her geographical location, EXCEPT:

  (A) *Bacteroides.*
  (B) *Enterococci.*
  (C) *Lactobacilli.*
  (D) Yeasts.

GO ON TO THE NEXT PAGE

Questions 32–42 are based on the following reading selection.

Adapted from a 1981 speech to Congress, Ronald Reagan states his reasons for a new program for economic recovery.[1]

Mr. Speaker, Mr. President, distinguished Members of Congress, honored guests, and fellow citizens:

Line   Only a month ago I was your guest in this
(5) historic building, and I pledged to you my cooperation in doing what is right for this Nation that we all love so much. I'm here tonight to reaffirm that pledge and to ask that we share in restoring the promise that is
(10) offered to every citizen by this, the last, best hope of man on Earth.

All of us are aware of the punishing inflation which has for the first time in 60 years held to double-digit figures for 2 years in a
(15) row. Interest rates have reached absurd levels of more than 20 percent and over 15 percent for those who would borrow to buy a home. All across this land one can see newly built homes standing vacant, unsold because of
(20) mortgage interest rates.

Almost 8 million Americans are out of work. These are people who want to be productive. But as the months go by, despair dominates their lives. The threats of layoff
(25) and unemployment hang over other millions, and all who work are frustrated by their inability to keep up with inflation.

One worker in a Midwest city put it to me this way: He said, "I'm bringing home more
(30) dollars than I ever believed I could possibly earn, but I seem to be getting worse off." And he is. Not only have hourly earnings of the American worker, after adjusting for inflation, declined 5 percent over the past 5
(35) years, but in these 5 years, federal personal taxes for the average family have increased 67 percent. We can no longer procrastinate and hope that things will get better. They will not. Unless we act forcefully—and now—the
(40) economy will get worse.

Can we, who man the ship of state, deny it is somewhat out of control? Our national debt is approaching $1 trillion. A few weeks ago I called such a figure, a trillion dollars,
(45) incomprehensible, and I've been trying ever since to think of a way to illustrate how big a trillion really is. And the best I could come up with is that if you had a stack of thousand-dollar bills in your hand only 4 inches high,
(50) you'd be a millionaire. A trillion dollars would be a stack of thousand-dollar bills 67 miles high. The interest on the public debt this year we know will be over $90 billion, and unless we change the proposed spending for the
(55) fiscal year beginning October 1st, we'll add another almost $80 billion to the debt.

Adding to our troubles is a mass of regulations imposed on the shopkeeper, the farmer, the craftsman, professionals, and
(60) major industry that is estimated to add $100 billion to the price of the things we buy, and it reduces our ability to produce. The rate of increase in American productivity, once one of the highest in the world, is among the low-
(65) est of all major industrial nations. Indeed, it has actually declined in the last 3 years.

Now, I've painted a pretty grim picture, but I think I've painted it accurately. It is within our power to change this picture, and we can
(70) act with hope. There's nothing wrong with our internal strengths. There has been no breakdown of the human, technological, and natural resources upon which the economy is built.
(75)   […]

This, then, is our proposal—America's new beginning: a program for economic recovery. I don't want it to be simply the plan of my administration. I'm here tonight to ask you
(80) to join me in making it our plan. Together we can embark on this road.

[1]**Citation:** Ronald Reagan: "Address Before a Joint Session of the Congress on the Program for Economic Recovery," February 18, 1981. Online by Gerhard Peters and John T. Woolley, The American Presidency Project. *http://www.presidency.ucsb.edu/ws/?pid=43425.*

GO ON TO THE NEXT PAGE

32. The overall point of this passage is to

(A) present scholarly research.
(B) survey popular opinion.
(C) argue for a call to action.
(D) persuade economic thinkers.

33. The speaker's tone is best described as

(A) direct and empathetic.
(B) haughty and dismissive.
(C) pessimistic and grave.
(D) erudite and urbane.

34. As used in line 12, the word "punishing" most closely means

(A) sad.
(B) confined.
(C) disciplined.
(D) severe.

35. The speaker most directly suggests that unemployed Americans

(A) would much rather not be in that situation.
(B) clearly understand the economic causes of their troubles.
(C) wish that foreign aid could provide needed relief.
(D) hope that they can receive unemployment benefits for an extended period.

36. Which option gives the best evidence for the answer to the previous question?

(A) Lines 18–20 ("All . . . rates")
(B) Lines 21–24 ("Almost . . . lives")
(C) Lines 28–31 ("One . . . off")
(D) Lines 57–62 ("Adding . . . produce")

37. The quotation in lines 29–31 ("I'm . . . off") serves to

(A) give concrete statistics.
(B) provide anecdotal evidence.
(C) separate fact from opinion.
(D) acknowledge likely objections.

38. The speaker most strongly suggests that the underlying structure of the U.S. economy is

(A) inflationary.
(B) unsound.
(C) solid.
(D) focused.

39. Which option gives the best evidence for the answer to the previous question?

(A) Lines 12–15 ("All . . . row")
(B) Lines 21–24 ("Almost . . . lives")
(C) Lines 37–40 ("We . . . worse")
(D) Lines 70–74 ("There's . . . built")

40. The speaker primarily uses the paragraph in lines 41–56 to

(A) share relevant first-hand observations.
(B) concretely illustrate the severity of a problem.
(C) verbalize the incomprehensible complexity of a concept.
(D) highlight the widespread interest in a particular solution.

41. Lines 58–60 ("shopkeeper . . . industry") are intended to illustrate the

(A) widespread impact of government regulations.
(B) specific jobs that have been lost in the recession.
(C) those who will most benefit from the proposed programs.
(D) primary members of the audience the speaker is addressing.

42. As used in line 66, the word "declined" most closely means

(A) decreased.
(B) decayed.
(C) failed.
(D) wilted.

GO ON TO THE NEXT PAGE

DIAGNOSTIC TEST 17

Two scientists present their views on corn syrup.

PASSAGE 1

Since coming to a head in 2004, the high
fructose corn syrup crisis and its role in the
emergent obesity epidemic has faced unwav-
Line ering denial from the food industry; yet the
(5) efforts to defend the additive on scientific
grounds have been dubious at best. We are all
familiar with the pitiful syllogism: corn syrup
comes from corn, and corn is natural; corn
syrup, therefore, is natural. However true this
(10) may be, it provides no proof whatsoever as
to corn syrup's safety for human consumption. Solanine, for example, is easily extracted
from potatoes, and while harmless in smaller
amounts, once concentrated it becomes a
(15) potent and potentially deadly neurotoxin.
But I digress. Let us not look to the source
of corn syrup to determine its nutritional
demerit, but turn instead to its direct metabolic effects on our bodies.
(20) Under ideal circumstances, the vast
majority of sugar in our blood is derived
from starch, which is broken into glucose
before being released to the bloodstream.
Glycolysis is the name applied to ten
(25) sequential chemical reactions that allow us
to either liberate energy from glucose, or
transform it into fats for storage in adipose
tissue. Gluconeogenesis, meanwhile, is an
opposite process in which glucose is derived
(30) from non-carbohydrate substances, and a
close and efficient regulation of the balance
between glycolytic and gluconeogenic
processes in response to the changing
concentrations of glucose in the blood is
(35) necessary for the maintenance of healthful
homeostasis.
By far the most critical point in this regulation occurs at the third step of glycolysis: in
the hormonally-controlled phosphoryla-
(40) tion of fructose-6-phospate into fructose-
1,6-bisphospate. When glucose is abundant,
pancreatic insulin induces the forward
glycolytic catalysis of this reaction, allowing
the production of fructose-1,6-bisphospate,
(45) which in turn is cleaved into glyceraldehyde-
3-phosphate and dihydroxyacetone phosphate. When glucose is scarce, pancreatic
glucagon blocks glycolysis, and induces
the gluconeogenic production of fructose-
(50) 6-phosphate, which is subsequently isomer-
ized into glucose-6-phosphate, and released
into the blood.
The primary problem, therefore, with
deriving major amounts of dietary sugar
(55) directly from fructose rather than from
starch lies in the fact that the degradation of
fructose—which, upon entry into the cell,
is split immediately into dihydroxyacetone
phosphate and glyceraldehyde—completely
(60) bypasses the first four steps of glycolysis,
including the most critical regulatory reaction in the entire process. Thus, how our
bodies handle the usage of fructose is utterly
dissociated from the hormonal controls
(65) of insulin and glucagon, which, over time,
invariably predisposes one to obesity, diabetes mellitus, and a host of other dangerous
metabolic disorders.

PASSAGE 2

The media frenzy and public outcry
(70) that have surrounded the use of high fructose corn syrup as a food additive are as
unfounded as the similarly nonsensical
indignations that erupted in response to the
advent of commercially available genetically
(75) modified crop seeds. Despite ongoing proof
that genetically modified crops are not only
perfectly safe for consumption, but that they
have in fact saved an estimated 600 million
people from starvation over the past two
(80) decades, fears and skepticism toward them

GO ON TO THE NEXT PAGE

persist simply because they are popularly perceived as "unnatural," and thus, somehow, unhealthy.

These same misguided apprehensions have been at the forefront of the crusade against high fructose corn syrup. Yet, in real-
(85) ity, the process of producing corn syrup is strikingly similar to the carbohydrate metabolism that occurs naturally within the human body. First, corn starch is broken down into glucose by bacterial amylase enzymes, and
(90) glucose is subsequently converted to fructose via glucose isomerase. Overall, the recipe is hardly as sinister as its opponents would have us believe.

We must acknowledge, of course, that
(95) research has identified several serious health risks associated with the chronic overconsumption of sugar, and perhaps of fructose in particular. These risks, however, are by no means limited to foodstuffs containing high
(100) fructose corn syrup. Depending on the formula, corn syrup contains between 42% and 55% fructose by volume. For comparison, cane sugar, honey, and agave nectar—three popular sweeteners touted as "natural", and
(105) therefore, more healthful—contain 50%, 52%, and 85% fructose, respectively. Thus, while it is true that fructose should be consumed only in moderation, the singling out of products that contain high fructose corn
(110) syrup is not merely insufficient action to curb the fructose-associated obesity epidemic in our country, it's also patently misleading to consumers.

43. What is the primary purpose of lines 12–15 ("Solanine . . . neurotoxin.")?

(A) To present practical applications
(B) To refute a particular line of thinking
(C) To clarify an unfamiliar term
(D) To draw attention to a harmful process

44. As used in line 16, the word "digress" most closely means

(A) stray.
(B) analyze.
(C) contradict.
(D) reexamine.

45. According to lines 37–52, bodily regulation of glucose levels is best summarized as

(A) artificial.
(B) dynamic.
(C) arbitrary.
(D) static.

46. The author of passage 1 most directly suggests that the long-term consumption of fructose will lead to

(A) an increasingly well-regulated hormonal balance.
(B) a significant increase in neurotoxins in the blood supply.
(C) a greater likelihood of developing health ailments.
(D) no significant changes to bodily processes.

47. Which option gives the best evidence for the answer to the previous question?

(A) Lines 13–15 ("while . . . neurotoxin")
(B) Lines 41–47 ("When . . . phosphate")
(C) Lines 47–52 ("When . . . blood")
(D) Lines 62–68 ("Thus . . . disorders")

GO ON TO THE NEXT PAGE

48. As used in line 81, the word "persist" most closely means

    (A) persevere.
    (B) mislead.
    (C) continue.
    (D) affect.

49. The author of passage 2 most likely uses lines 100–106 ("Depending . . . respectively") in order to

    (A) demonstrate that corn syrup is especially harmful to consumers.
    (B) show that corn syrup is undeservingly singled-out for criticism.
    (C) argue that fructose is but one reason that corn syrup is maligned.
    (D) illustrate that many foodstuffs contain great quantities of sugar.

50. It can most reasonably be inferred that the two authors would disagree with those who declared a food to be healthy simply because it is

    (A) "engineered."
    (B) "genetically modified."
    (C) "natural."
    (D) "metabolized."

51. Which option gives the best evidence for the answer to the previous question?

    (A) Lines 6–12 ("We are . . . consumption") and lines 75–83 ("Despite . . . unhealthy")
    (B) Lines 16–19 ("Let . . . bodies") and lines 84–88 ("Yet . . . body")
    (C) Lines 24–28 ("Glycolysis . . . tissue") and lines 98–102 ("These . . . volume")
    (D) Lines 47–52 ("When . . . blood") and lines 88–91 ("First . . . isomerase")

52. The authors of Passage 1 and Passage 2 primarily analyze examples from what general areas to make their respective cases?

    (A) Passage 1 analyzes examples internal to the human body, and Passage 2 analyzes examples external to the human body.
    (B) Passage 1 analyzes examples external to the human body, and Passage 2 analyzes examples internal to the human body.
    (C) Both focus on examples internal to the human body.
    (D) Both focus on examples external to the human body.

STOP

If you finish before time is called, you may check your work on this section only. Do not turn to any other section.

ANSWER KEY
Diagnostic Test

Reading

1.	**B**	14.	**C**	27.	**C**	40.	**B**
2.	**D**	15.	**B**	28.	**B**	41.	**A**
3.	**C**	16.	**C**	29.	**D**	42.	**A**
4.	**A**	17.	**A**	30.	**B**	43.	**B**
5.	**C**	18.	**C**	31.	**A**	44.	**A**
6.	**B**	19.	**D**	32.	**C**	45.	**B**
7.	**D**	20.	**B**	33.	**A**	46.	**C**
8.	**D**	21.	**A**	34.	**D**	47.	**D**
9.	**D**	22.	**D**	35.	**A**	48.	**C**
10.	**A**	23.	**A**	36.	**B**	49.	**B**
11.	**B**	24.	**B**	37.	**B**	50.	**C**
12.	**C**	25.	**D**	38.	**C**	51.	**A**
13.	**A**	26.	**D**	39.	**D**	52.	**A**

Number Correct _____

Number Incorrect _____

SELF-ASSESSMENT GUIDE

Use this table to determine which types of questions will demand more of your attention:

Question Type	Question Numbers
Words in Context	4, 9, 13, 16, 22, 27, 34, 42, 44, 48
Graph Analysis	19, (20), 28, 30, 31
Command of Evidence	6, 8, 15, (20), 26, 29, 36, 39, 47, 51
Sentence-level Analysis	5, 7, 14, 18, 25, 35, 37, 41, 43, 49
Paragraph-level Analysis	3, 10, 17, 23, 24, 38, 40, 45, 46
Whole Passage Analysis	1, 2, 11, 12, 21, 32, 33, 50, 52

SCORING APPROXIMATION

This table gives you an estimate of how your performance on the Reading section will contribute to your overall Evidence-Based Reading and Writing score. Keep in mind that each test *will be curved*, making the number of questions needed for a particular score dependent on the test that day. This is the best estimate we can give you based on (1) previous SAT curves and (2) the fact that guessing is now permitted on the SAT.

Questions out of 52 answered correctly	Estimated overall section score (between 200–800)
52	800
49	750
46	700
43	650
40	600
37	550
33	500
30	450
26	400
20	350
13	300
7	250
0	200

ANSWERS EXPLAINED

1. **(B)** Generally, this passage contrasts Fanny's expectations of her parents to the realities she finds upon returning home, making choice (B) correct. Her discussion is *of* her family rather than with her family and friends as in (A). (C) is a detail of the passage, but not its main idea. Furthermore, although she contemplates her mother's incongruity with her economic circumstance, this is neither the main point of the passage nor does she extend the deliberation to herself, making (D) incorrect.

2. **(D)** Fanny finds home "the very reverse of what she could have wished," and finds her parents unaffectionate and slovenly. The best option is choice (D) since her attitude towards them can be described as *disappointment*, and she provides several reasons to support her feelings. She is not affectionate, jealous, or disrespectful toward them.

3. **(C)** Lines 11–18 depict Fanny's father as a man without ambition, curiosity, or knowledge "beyond his profession," making *overly pragmatic* the correct answer. *Pragmatic* means "practical and realistic, uninterested in ideas or theories," so her father's simple-mindedness fits this description. She finds him dull rather than interesting as in (A). (B) describes his personality, but not his intellectual interests. And *erudite* means "cultured" or "well-educated," making (D) the opposite of Fanny's description of her father.

4. **(A)** The sentence before indicates that Mrs. Price never showed Fanny more kindness than she did on that first day. The sentence after states that "she had neither leisure nor affection to bestow." So, it can be inferred that the "instinct of nature" that had to be satisfied was her *maternal feeling*. It is not related to survival, acceptance, or justice.

5. **(C)** Lines 31–35 give evidence that she did not offer more affection or kindness to Fanny. Lines 83–86 support the idea that she did not try to get to know her or befriend her in any way. So, (C) is the best choice. (B) and (D) are opposite of Mrs. Price's treatment of Fanny. There is no evidence of (A).

6. **(B)** Lines 33–35 provide direct support that Mrs. Price did not increase her tenderness toward Fanny. (A) refers to her relationship with her father rather than her mother. (C) refers to her mother's household mismanagement rather than her relationship with Fanny. (D) compares Mrs. Price to her sister and again refers to her disorder and inefficiency.

7. **(D)** Based on the final paragraph, Fanny is "anxious to be useful," so it would be appropriate to say she is eager to be a "helpful contributor." Choice (A) is too extreme. Choices (B) and (C) incorrectly describe characteristics which she mistakenly hoped to find in her mother.

8. **(D)** These lines successfully illustrate Fanny's desire to contribute at home. None of the other choices are applicable to her aspirations within her parents' household. Instead (B) and (C) refer to Fanny's unfavorable depiction of her mother, and (A) states Fanny's disappointment toward her home in general.

9. **(D)** *Engaged* accurately refers to Mrs. Price's absorption with her sons. It is appropriate to say they "engaged," or preoccupied, her attention. None of the other words fit; the sons neither "stay," "reside," nor "dwell" her worry or care.

10. **(A)** Lines 59–73 compare Mrs. Price to her sisters, indicating that Mrs. Price is more inclined to the idleness of Lady Bertram than the vigor of Mrs. Norris, so choice (A)

is correct. Choice (B) falsely implies that Mrs. Price and Mrs. Norris are comparable, choice (C) suggests that Mrs. Price is the assiduous one, and choice (D) wrongly indicates that Mrs. Price's negative qualities make her more respectful.

11. **(B)** The purpose of this passage can be said to raise awareness and address the issues surrounding a politically disinclined youth in America. While the generation is skeptical of the two-party system, the author does not argue to end it. Likewise, the passage doesn't give support for mandatory voting measures. Finally, (D) is incorrect because the passage provides evidence that millennials are actually avoiding political office.

12. **(C)** *Concerned* is the best word to describe the narrator's tone. (A) is too extreme. (B) is too neutral. And (D) is far too positive.

13. **(A)** *Ascribe* is a verb that can be defined as "attribute to," and is the precise word meaning. Here, the passage is saying that it would be misguided to attribute the generation's political indifference to an essentially unconcerned disposition. It is not accurate to "draw," "blame," or "dispute" the younger generation as careless.

14. **(C)** Given the context of the passage, it is safe to assume that the author believes the younger generation is concerned with solving social issues, but prefers to do so outside of political spheres. The passage argues against (A). Choices (B) and (D) are refuted in lines 26–40.

15. **(B)** Lines 34–37 specifically state that American youth are "looking at other ways of tackling society's problems," providing direct evidence for the previous question. (A) gives the lines that introduce the focus of the passage. (C) refers to the declining opinion toward the American quality of life. (D) considers the opinion that avoidance of the two political parties is a positive trend.

16. **(C)** *Solving* fits here since this line refers to efforts to tackle problems. It is misleading to state that the youth are *beginning* or *discovering* society's problems. Likewise, it opposes the narrator's position to say they are *dismissing* the problems.

17. **(A)** Lines 55–68 provide statistics and recent evidence to substantiate the author's claim, making (A) the correct choice. Choice (C) is tempting, but is only a detail of the paragraph. Choices (B) and (D) are not addressed within the passage.

18. **(C)** Lines 77–80 serve as the author's acknowledgement of a possible objection that would find a move away from partisanship a positive trend in American politics, so (C) is accurate. These lines show an opposing view, ruling out (A), and do not go into details as in (B). Finally, choice (D) is incorrect since the lines do not include a citation.

19. **(D)** The lines are closest to one another in 2008, so (D) is correct. The other choices provide years where the deviation between voters is greater than it is in 2008.

20. **(B)** In lines 31–34, the author accounts for particular events that "generate an influx in youth participation," providing evidence that the candidacy of Barack Obama most likely accounts for an increase in young voter turnout in 2008. Choices (A), (C), and (D) all indicate a declining trend of voter turnout in the millennials, and so would not account for the 2008 increase.

21. **(A)** This passage opens with a preface on germs and antibiotics generally before moving into specific examples of beneficial bacteria and of instances when antibiotics have

been harmful rather than helpful. Choice (A) is the only option that captures that structure. (B) and (D) fail to recognize the introduction, while (C) doesn't consider the use of exemplification.

22. **(D)** Line 1 refers to an "elementary truth," so *fundamental* is the correct choice. *Scholastic* would indicate that the truth was concerned with education, while (B) and (C) are not synonymous with elementary.

23. **(A)** The second paragraph expresses a turning point within the introduction where the author suggests that we have been too adamant in our germophobia, making (A) correct. There is no evidence for (B). Choice (C) is contradictive because the valid concerns of germophobics would support rather than refute germ theory. And choice (D) would inaccurately indicate that the purpose of this paragraph was to show the everyday instances of germ theory; in fact, this paragraph gives a historical reminiscence of germ theory before positing the argument that the elimination of all germs is not necessarily the best approach to human health.

24. **(B)** Lines 39–58 furnish a direct example of the statement made in lines 35–38 that points out the metabolic and immunological advantages of some natural bacteria. Hence, (B) is correct. (A) and (D) misunderstand details of the passage. (C) is appealing because it is true that this example could be used to address an objection toward all germ theory, but this paragraph is more interested in giving that illustrative example rather than responding to objections.

25. **(D)** This is most clearly seen in lines 102–106 where *Clostridium difficile* is given as a real-life example of the "dire consequences" that occur when antibiotics disrupt our body's natural ecological balance. Choices (A), (B), and (C) provide examples of beneficial bacteria, but aren't used to illustrate the dangers of antibiotics.

26. **(D)** These lines specifically address the artificial upsetting of our body's ecological balance that occurs with an overuse or misuse of antibiotics; therefore, they serve as direct evidence to the previous question. They serve to allow the reader to understand a potentially fatal condition that emerges when "good bacteria" have been wiped out. The other choices give evidence for beneficial bacteria in digestive health and in fighting disease, allowing the reader to understand the crucial role of our body's natural microbiome. However, they don't directly address the potential harms of antibiotics.

27. **(C)** *Depends* works best here since the line refers to ecological balance being contingent on two things. It would be improper to say the balance *fulcrums, analyzes,* or *joints* on two things.

28. **(B)** From the table, we can see variations in microbiota based on their diets and locations. Since ecological balance depends on the diversity of one's microbiome and the factors that influence that population, it makes sense that this table would be helpful in studying that balance. *Germophobia* refers to a fear of germs, which is not what the table is about. From the passage, we know that our gastrointestinal bacteria help with "blood clotting," but there is no evidence that this table could help to study this topic, since it is not the focus of the table. The table doesn't address beneficial bacteria versus "pathogenic bacteria" or infectious bacteria.

29. **(D)** Lines 84–93 directly give the factors that affect ecological balance, and therefore provide the evidence for the previous question. Since the table shows the variable diversity of microbiota, and ecological diversity depends on the variable diversity of microbiota, we can infer that this table would be useful. The other choices fail to mention concepts that are dependent on the diversity of one's microbiome.

30. **(B)** The best approach to this question is to examine the table for where the numbers are very different between the indicated countries. A quick look has noticeable variations in two microorganisms: *Bifidobacteria* and *Clostridia*. Therefore, choice (B) is correct because the percentages alone could be used to differentiate persons by country of residence.

31. **(A)** To approach this question, we should examine the table for instances where diet choice does not make a significant difference in the percentage of particular microorganisms. Of the four choices given, the smallest variation in percentages occurs in *Bacteroides* where there is a 0.5%, 0.4%, and 1.4% change, respectively.

32. **(C)** The purpose of Reagan's speech can be said to argue for a new economic policy and immediate action, so (C) is the correct choice. Although he uses research and statistics for evidence, his purpose is not to present those findings, but to use them logically to persuade Congress. Finally, he is neither surveying a popular audience nor directing his persuasion toward economists only.

33. **(A)** *Haughty*, or "arrogant," and *dismissive* don't describe Reagan's firm sense of urgency. (C) isn't appropriate because he affirms that "we can act with hope." And while Reagan is certainly *erudite*, or "knowledgeable," his attitude is not *urbane*, or "suave." So, the correct answer is (A), with *empathetic* meaning the ability to understand another's experiences and emotions.

34. **(D)** *Severe* is the appropriate definition since Reagan is referring to a "punishing" rise in the price of goods and services. (B) and (C) are opposite of how Reagan might describe the unchecked increase. As for (A), though the effects of the inflation may be *sad*, inflation itself is better described as a critical condition.

35. **(A)** In regard to unemployment, Reagan states that millions of Americans "who want to be productive" are out of work. There is no evidence for choices (C) and (D). While (B) is tempting, Reagan also mentions that inflation is hard to keep up with, so (B) is not likely.

36. **(B)** Reagan poses unemployment as a reason behind the need for a new economic plan in lines 21–24, so (B) is the correct answer. These lines indicate that the unemployed are not without work by choice. Options (A), (C), and (D) all refer to other rationales for the proposed plan: interest rates, earning, and regulations, respectively.

37. **(B)** In lines 29–31, Reagan quotes an American worker to illustrate the incongruity of the hourly wage. Since *anecdotal* means an "account based on personal story or experience," (B) is accurate. These lines specifically do not contain "statistics" or address a counterargument. Moreover, choice (C) is wrong because rather than separating them, Reagan uses facts directly after the quote to support the personal testimony.

38. **(C)** Be sure to read the question closely. While the current situation could be described as both *inflationary* and *unsound*, the underlying structure of the economy, according

to lines 70–74, is still intact. So, (C) is correct. Likewise, Reagan suggests that the economy needs to refocus and reprioritize, so (D) wouldn't fit.

39. **(D)** These lines directly indicate Reagan's belief that, "There has been no breakdown of the human, technological, and natural resources upon which the economy is built." Thus, they provide evidence to his thoughts regarding the economy's foundation. Choices (A) and (B) refer to the current problematic situation rather than the underlying structure of the nation's economy. (C) is Reagan's call to action.

40. **(B)** The best approach to a question like this is to consider the purpose of lines 41–56 in the context of the entire passage. Reagan speaks directly to Congress here, providing visuals and empirical evidence of just how bad the current situation is. So, (B) is the only choice that indicates his intention to illustrate severity.

41. **(A)** Choice (A) is accurate because Reagan's listing of several facets of the American workforce shows that regulations are affecting everyone. This paragraph is addressing regulation rather than unemployment as in (B). Reagan is proposing that the effects are harmful rather than beneficial as in (C). Additionally, the audience, as described in the introduction, is Congress rather than representatives from the workforce as in (D).

42. **(A)** *Decreased* works here because this line indicates that American productivity has "declined." (B) and (D) are synonymous, but suggest a "rotting" that isn't as precise. And (C) would imply that productivity has failed altogether, which is not the point the speaker is making.

43. **(B)** Look at the surrounding context. The author states that just because corn syrup is natural does not mean it is safe, and then goes on to talk about another example of a natural component which proves harmful. So, (B) is correct since these lines refute the idea that whatever is natural must be safe. Corn syrup is already sensible, so we wouldn't need to introduce a practical application as in (A). The author isn't using *solanine* to define something else as in (C). And while the lines do draw attention to a harmful element of potatoes, it is only to prove that nature can be toxic.

44. **(A)** *Digress* means to deviate from the topic, so "stray" is the closest meaning. In line 16, the author is referring to the fact that he or she has strayed from the topic, and then transitions back into corn syrup. Since the potato example is neither an analysis nor a contradiction, we can rule out (B) and (C). Choice (D) might be tempting, but the contrasting conjunction *but* should hint that we are referring to what was just mentioned rather than what is coming.

45. **(B)** Lines 37–52 discuss the third step of glycolysis and how it works in tandem with the body's current levels of glucose. So, *dynamic*, or in a "state of constant activity and change," is appropriate. *Artificial* means "fake," while *arbitrary* means "random." *Static*, or "unchanging," is the opposite of *dynamic*.

46. **(C)** According to the first author, consuming your sugars from fructose eventually causes obesity and other health issues. Thus, (C) is correct because it is the only choice that considers the long-term effects of fructose according to the first passage.

47. **(D)** Lines 62–68 state that our body's use of fructose "predisposes one to obesity, diabetes mellitus, and a host of other dangerous metabolic disorders," and therefore, provide direct evidence for the previous question. (A) refers to the effects of solanine, not corn

syrup. And choices (B) and (C) describe the third step of glycolysis, which we know from the passage is actually bypassed by fructose.

48. **(C)** Here, the author is stating that fears and skepticism "persist" because unnaturalness is illogically linked to unhealthiness. So, they "continue" or carry on. "Persevere" is another meaning of *persist* that refers to a determination to continue despite difficulty. And (B) and (D) do not mean *persist*.

49. **(B)** In lines 98–113, Passage 2 states that the health risks are misdirected at corn syrup; realistically, they are associated with fructose, which is prevalent in "cane sugar, honey, and agave nectar" as well. So, (B) is correct. Corn syrup has comparable or even lesser amounts of fructose than the author's other examples, so (A) is not supported. (C) misunderstands the argument—fructose, not corn syrup, is problematic. And (D), although true, does not address the fact that the high amounts of fructose in other foodstuffs contradict the case against corn syrup.

50. **(C)** Both authors debunk the connection between natural and healthy, so (C) is correct. Only passage 2 explicitly considers (B), and implicitly considers (A), since "engineered" would be similar to genetic modification. And since metabolism is the name for how our bodies function, it is an imprecise choice.

51. **(A)** Lines 6–15 argue that just because corn syrup is natural does not mean it is safe for human consumption. Lines 75–83 extend the second author's aggravation at the popular misunderstanding that *unnatural* is synonymous with "unhealthy." Hence, both of these sets of lines indicate together that the authors would agree that a food is not necessarily healthy just because it is organic.

52. **(A)** The first author's argument is based on glycolysis and the processes of the body. Meanwhile, the second author considers the production of corn syrup and the fructose levels in other foodstuffs. So, (A) is the appropriate choice.

GO ON TO THE NEXT PAGE

Reading Strategies

1

Now that you have taken the Diagnostic Reading Test, let's review and practice some key strategies that will help you do your best on the SAT Reading Test. This chapter contains:

- 16 Key Strategies
- "Putting it All Together" with in-depth guidance on how to attack the different types of questions you will encounter
- Additional passages for further practice.

READING STRATEGIES

1 Realize that the SAT is not the type of test you are used to.

If you approach the SAT Reading section in the same way you approach a school-based assignment that assesses text recall, you will have some major difficulty. Here are some fundamental differences in how you should tackle typical tests and the SAT Reading Test:

Typical School-Based Reading Tests	SAT Reading Test
The tests are almost always **closed-book**, so you need to read and reread to be certain you remember everything that might be tested.	The SAT is **open-book**—you don't have to know anything ahead of time or memorize the passage. You can go back to the passage as often as you need.
Test questions are often about **specific facts**, so it is vital that you memorize details and definitions as you read.	Test questions are more often about **inference, purpose, and big ideas**, so focus on general paraphrasing instead of specific memorizing.
Occasionally, there are mistakes on a test with a **couple of right answers** to a question. It is easy for a teacher to simply give everyone a free point if there is an error.	SAT questions are *very* well written, and there will be **just one correct answer** to each question. The College Board does not want to throw out the results for hundreds of thousands of test-takers, so they invest tremendous resources into ensuring that the questions have answers that are 100% correct.

If you have told yourself that you are "a bad test-taker," ask yourself: "Am I taking the SAT in the same way I take a school-based test?" If so, the problem is not with *you* but with *your strategy*.

2 Take your time.

The SAT Reading Test has only about **3,250 words** of reading passages, and **52 questions**, but gives you a full **65 minutes** to finish. Most test-takers will find that the SAT Reading section is very manageable to complete—you need to read at a pace of about 150 words per minute, which is about as quickly as most people can talk. You will likely do your best if you use the full amount of time to read the passages well, and think through the questions carefully. Given the complexity of the questions, you will be better served if you *do the questions one time well* as opposed to rushing through them, making careless errors, and quickly "checking" over your work.

Since the passages all have 10–11 questions, you can pace yourself by taking about **13 minutes per passage**. This would involve taking about **5 minutes to read the passage** and about **8 minutes to do the accompanying questions**. Here is a table of how you might want to allocate your time for a typical Reading section as a whole (*you can adjust this based on your personal situation, but this breakdown will work for many students*):

A Total of 5 Passages, 52 Questions, 65 Minutes		
Passage 1, Fiction, **10 questions**	5 minutes reading	8 minutes answering questions
Passage 2, Social Science, **10–11 questions**	5 minutes reading	8 minutes answering questions
Passage 3, Science, **10–11 questions**	5 minutes reading	8 minutes answering questions
Passage 4, Social Studies (Great Document), **10–11 questions**	5 minutes reading	8 minutes answering questions
Passage 5, Science, **10–11 questions**	5 minutes reading	8 minutes answering questions

WHAT CAN YOU DO IF YOU HAVE DIFFICULTY FINISHING?

- **FOCUS ON THE PASSAGES THAT ARE EASIER FOR YOU.** Every question is worth the same, so pick your battles. If you know that Fiction is always more difficult for you, go ahead and guess on that passage and skip it. The same goes for Science or Social Studies. The test will always have 1 Fiction, 2 Social Studies, and 2 Science passages, so you can likely plan what you will skip before you take the test. You can also make a decision at the beginning of the test by *taking a quick look at the passage titles and descriptions*. Do the passages that seem easiest and most interesting first—save the ones that look difficult and boring for the end.

> Remember that there is NO GUESSING PENALTY on the new SAT, so if you are unsure about a question or you are running out of time, be sure to bubble in a letter.

■ **FOCUS ON THE QUESTIONS THAT ARE EASIER.** The questions that will likely take the least amount of time are the *Words in Context* questions (ask about the meaning of a word) and the *Command of Evidence* questions (ask about what lines give the best evidence in support of the previous question). Vocabulary questions take little time because you typically only need to consider the context immediately around the given lines. An evidence question is paired with the question that immediately comes before it—figure out the question that comes immediately before the evidence one, and pay close attention to where you found support in the text for your answer. That way, you will be able to answer two questions with about the same effort it takes to do one question.

3 Try reading the passages before doing the questions.

Most students will find it useful to read through the passages before doing the questions. Why? Because the majority of the questions involve *analysis* of the text. If the SAT Reading section involved mostly text recall questions, it would make sense to review the questions before reading the passage so you knew what to look for as you read. Since the SAT mainly has analytical questions involving inference, function, suggestion, tone, and purpose, it will be more helpful to put your energy into developing a strong initial understanding of what is written. Even questions that refer to a handful of lines will almost certainly require that you grasp how these lines fit into the passage as a whole. If, however, you have trouble staying focused when you read, you may want to quickly skim the questions first so you have a general idea of what to look for. Just be sure that if you do this, you are still paying attention to the big picture of the passage as you read. Whatever you do, decide before the day of the test which approach better suits you.

4 Focus on the overall meaning of the passage(s) as you read.

You should be able to restate the "gist" of what you have read—don't worry about memorizing details from the passage. You can change your focus depending on the passage type in order to maximize your comprehension:

■ **FICTION & LITERATURE**—Read the first paragraph or two a bit more carefully, and read the remainder of the passage normally. This can help you fully understand the characters and setting before you move into the rest of the story.

■ **NON-FICTION (SOCIAL STUDIES & SCIENCE)**—Read the first paragraph, first sentences of each paragraph, and last paragraph a bit more carefully, and the rest normally. Non-fiction is typically more structured than fiction, so these parts will typically give you more critical information, such as the thesis of the essay and general topics of each paragraph.

> You are NOT expected to have any background knowledge on any of the topics in the reading passages. Everything you need to answer the questions will be given to you in the text and, if applicable, the accompanying graphics.

■ **PASSAGE 1 & PASSAGE 2**—Read these with a focus on the overall meaning, but pay close attention to the *overall relationship* between the two passages. Why? Because there will be several questions that involve comparing the similarities and differences between the two reading selections.

Before each passage, there is a very brief summary that will give you some information about what you are about to read. Be sure to read this before reading the actual passage, as it will help you preview the general meaning of what follows. If any of the topics are unfamiliar or the passage language seems too lofty, don't be alarmed. If you carefully read the passages, you will have the information necessary to answer the questions well—the SAT makers do not expect you to be a master of all potential topics and potential writing styles.

5 Consider making small notes and annotations as you read the passage.

You are able to write all over your test booklet, so do not hesitate to jot down some brief notes as you read. Since you can take about five minutes to read the passage, some of this time can be devoted to making a short sentence that summarizes each paragraph. Do not feel compelled to do this if note-taking does little to help you focus. Just be mindful that it is something worth considering given the SAT Reading time constraints.

6 Come back to questions if they seem overly difficult.

The first questions after a passage will typically be about the overall meaning of the passage. If you have not fully grasped the overall meaning, come back to the general questions after having done more specific questions. If you find yourself stuck on a question, come back to it so that you can allow your subconscious mind to process the possibilities. Once you come back to the question with fresh eyes, you will often surprise yourself at how well you can think through it at that point.

> Careless mistakes are *still* mistakes! Don't allow carelessness to sabotage your performance.

7 Cover the answers as you read the questions.

On factual recall tests, checking out the answers before you have formulated an answer can help you narrow it down. With the critical thinking questions on the SAT, in contrast, you will often find yourself misled by persuasive but ultimately incorrect answers. Take control of the questions and don't let them control you.

8 Underline and circle key words as you read the questions.

Skipping a key word while reading a question will likely lead to a wrong answer. Instead of quickly reading through the question, and then having to reread it, read it one time well and underline and circle the most important words as you do so. This will ensure that you do not miss wording critical to understanding what the question is asking. Examples of these types of key words are *not, primary, infer, suggest*, etc. You are able to write on the SAT test pages, so take advantage of it!

9 Create your own general answer by considering the context.

The primary reading skill tested on the SAT is your ability to paraphrase (put in your own words) what you read. Prior to looking at the choices, create a broad idea of what the answer could be before you look. Whenever possible, take a look at the context related to the question so that you have all the relevant information available. For those questions where it is difficult to come up with an answer prior to considering the choices, do not "jump" to an answer or eliminate an answer without patiently thinking through all the possibilities.

10 Go back to the passage as often as you need.

Most tests we take are closed-book—the SAT Reading section is open-book. If you had an open-book test in school, you would surely use your textbook and notes to help you answer the questions. With so many SAT questions giving line references and key words, it makes sense to use the text whenever necessary.

11 Use passage evidence possibilities to help with the previous question.

> Since the questions are almost always in the order that they are in the passage, it is really easy to check back with the passage as you work through each problem.

There are 10 questions on the SAT Reading section that will ask you to select what evidence in the text supports the previous question. If you are having difficulty with a question that is followed by an evidence question, look at the lines of the passage to which the evidence question refers. Consider the following question.

> *Which option gives the best evidence for the answer to the previous question?*
>
> *(A) Lines 6–10 ("He introduced . . . lives")*
> *(B) Lines 37–40 ("While this . . . scientific")*
> *(C) Lines 47–50 ("Furthermore . . . space")*
> *(D) Lines 65–69 ("Despite . . . expensive")*

If the question that comes before this one is giving you trouble, look at the selected evidence lines in order to help you focus what you check out in the passage. The evidence you need for the previous question *will be* in one of these spots.

12 The answers will be either 100% correct or totally wrong.

A single word can contaminate an answer, making it completely wrong. When you narrow the choices down to two options, don't just look for the "best" answer—look for the "flawless" answer. Try to quickly debate with yourself the correctness or incorrectness of each answer, knowing that there is one that is definitely correct, and three that are definitely wrong. The College Board has put a great deal of effort into creating the questions you will see on the SAT, so you can safely assume they will be of the very highest quality.

13 Focus on meaning, not matching.

On ordinary school tests, we are often used to matching the choices with facts we recall from the assigned reading or the in-class lecture. On the SAT, the fact that an answer has wording that matches parts of the passage text is no guarantee that it is correct. There is nothing wrong with picking an answer because it *does* have wording that is in the passage; just don't pick an answer *only because* it has matching wording. Be certain the overall meaning of an answer gives the correct idea.

14 Work on picking up on context clues with word definitions.

The SAT reading section no longer has the sentence completion questions of the previous version. While memorizing vocabulary will still help you prepare, you should especially sharpen your skills in picking up on the meanings of words based on context. Even if you know the definitions of words, you will need to determine which definition is most applicable in the particular situation. For example, a word like "compromise" can mean very different things. If you are "compromising" with your friend about what to do over the weekend, that shows a willingness to meet someone halfway. If your immune system is "compromised," you are more likely to become sick. Build on this skill by making a habit of trying to pick up on the appropriate definitions of words given their context in books and articles. *For much more in-depth treatment of the word meaning questions, check out the separate in-depth exercise devoted to it on page 59.*

> The New SAT Reading focuses on picking up word meaning based on the surrounding context, not on memorizing hundreds of obscure word definitions. While having a great vocabulary is still helpful to test performance, it is not nearly as helpful as it once was.

15 Just because you do not know a word's meaning does not mean it is wrong.

One of the most frequent mistakes students make on word meaning and questions that happen to use elevated vocabulary is going with a word that "sort of works" simply because they know the meaning of the word. If you narrow the options down to two, one for which you know the meaning and doesn't quite fit, and the other for which you do *not* know the meaning, *go with the word you do not know* since it has the *potential* to be 100% correct.

16 When uncertain about your strategy, give the SAT the benefit of the doubt.

On poorly written tests, tricks and gimmicks can help you succeed—such shortcuts *will not* help you perform well on the new SAT. The new SAT is going to be an extraordinarily well-constructed assessment, given the amount of time and resources the College Board has devoted to its overhaul. As a result, do not waste your time and energy while taking the SAT looking for flaws in the test. Instead, give the SAT Reading section the benefit of the doubt and focus on how *you* can improve your reading comprehension and critical thinking skills.

PUTTING IT ALL TOGETHER

Now, let's put our strategies into practice with some sample passages and questions. The first passage is a **nonfiction Science passage**. While reading, do read all of the passage, but focus a bit more on the first paragraph, topic sentences (i.e., first sentence of each paragraph), and the last paragraph. Since it is non-fiction, these parts will likely take on greater significance in conveying the broad idea of the passage. You may also try annotating or underlining as you read to see if it improves your focus and comprehension. Try to take about 5 minutes to read this passage.

Time Travel

Time travel has long intrigued us; it's enough to spur a whole sub-genre of science fiction. It's mind-boggling to consider all of the implications of traveling through time and having free will. It's easy to see that the universe as we know it would be rather
Line unstable if, for instance, you could travel backwards in time and kill your own grandfa-
(5) ther. But is it possible?

To begin to understand the possibilities of time, we first need a brief introduction of spacetime. We're all familiar with our three-dimensional world, but we need to consider a fourth dimension as well—time. Time passes. Therefore, you can sit still in a chair not traveling in three-dimensions, but traveling in spacetime. We think of time as
(10) passing forward. Stephen Hawking explains this as three "arrows of time". The thermodynamic arrow of time points from a time of low entropy (high organization) to a time of high entropy (low organization/high chaos). It passes from a glass of water sitting on a table to a shattered glass and a puddle of water on the floor. There's a psychological arrow of time: we remember the past, but not the future. Finally, there's a cosmologi-
(15) cal arrow of time. The universe is expanding (though this arrow could reverse in the future).

We tend to think of time as an absolute: there are 60 seconds in every minute, and my 60 seconds should be the same as your 60 seconds. However, Einstein's theory of relativity defies this with time dilation. When a body approaches the speed of light,
(20) time effectively slows down. Therefore, if observers traveling at different fractions of the speed of light were to hold clocks, the clocks would be ticking at different speeds. Time is relative to the observer, rather than absolute. Consider what's referred to as the twin paradox: one identical twin stays on earth and the other travels near the speed of light in a spaceship. The twin aboard the spaceship will experience time dilation, and
(25) thus will age less quickly than the twin at home. Furthermore, if the twin's journey were long enough, the twin could return to earth to find that everyone he or she once knew was long dead. Essentially, this would be traveling into the future.

This isn't the exciting kind of time travel from the sci-fi books and movies, though. We would prefer our time travel to be instantaneous and not limited to the future. So
(30) far, we've examined only linear time travel in the form of slowing time down. But does time have to pass linearly? Is it possible that there could be loops in spacetime leading to the past and future? One possible candidate for such travel is the presence of worm-

holes. While wormholes also seem the stuff of sci-fi, their basis is actually in a paper written by Einstein and Nathan Rosen, where they refer to "bridges" in spacetime. They
(35) believed bridges to be extremely unstable and thus only temporary. The idea behind these bridges/wormholes is that there are theoretical tunnels between two far apart locations in spacetime. The distance of the wormhole wouldn't necessarily have to correspond to the distance between the two locations. There is evidence that such wormholes could theoretically exist, but that is beyond the scope of this paper. We'll suffice
(40) it to say that even if we find such wormholes, we'd have to figure out how to stabilize them in order to utilize them for time travel.

Stephen Hawking currently believes time travel into the past to be impossible for many reasons. One less than scientific reason is that humans tend to love "spilling the beans." If someone in the future had figured out how to time travel into the past, he or
(45) she likely would have traveled back and told us! So will we eventually be able to time travel without limit? I can't say; my psychological arrow of time doesn't point that way. Oh well, it's all relative anyway.

With each of these questions, take these general steps:

- Cover your answer choices as you consider the question.
- Underline and circle key words as you carefully read the question.
- Create an answer in your own words based on the context (or at least patiently consider the answers without jumping to anything or eliminating anything prematurely).
- Carefully evaluate the answers, picking only an answer that is 100% correct.

1. As used in line 10, the word "passing" most closely means
   (A) living.
   (B) moving.
   (C) throwing.
   (D) succeeding.

2. The author most strongly suggests that most people would react to Einstein's notions of time travel with

   (A) optimism.
   (B) derision.
   (C) disappointment.
   (D) bewilderment.

3. Which option gives the best evidence for the answer to the previous question?
   (A) Lines 13–14 ("There's a . . . future)"
   (B) Lines 19–21 ("When a . . . speeds")
   (C) Lines 25–27 ("Furthermore . . . future")
   (D) Lines 28–29 ("This isn't . . . future")

4. The primary theme of the passage is

    (A) informed contemplation.

    (B) skeptical dismissal.

    (C) imaginative musing.

    (D) factual presentation.

Answers Explained

1. **(B)** There will be 10 of these types of questions on the SAT Reading section. To answer this one, go back to line 10, and consider the context surrounding the word:

   *Time passes. Therefore, you can sit still in a chair not traveling in three dimensions, but traveling in spacetime. We think of time as **passing** forward. Stephen Hawking explains this as three "arrows of time".*

   Try to come up with your own synonym for the word before you examine the choices—that way, you won't be trapped by the highly persuasive wrong answers. *Passing* in this context means "going" or "progressing" since the sentence is expressing the nature of time. The best answer is *moving*, since it comes closest to meaning "going" or "progressing." It is not (A), *living*, because time is not a living thing, and is not described in this way—even metaphorically—in the surrounding sentences. It is not (C), because the type of movement that time undergoes is not a physical throw, but an abstract process. It is not (D), because although *succeeding* can mean "following," *passing* is describing an ongoing process, not a series of separate events.

2. **(C)** Start by going back to the paragraph that refers to Einstein's thoughts on time travel: the one that is in lines 17–27. This paragraph summarizes *his* views about time travel, but to see what *most people* would think, we should look at the beginning of the next paragraph. Lines 28–29 state:

   This isn't the exciting kind of time travel from the sci-fi books and movies, though. We would prefer our time travel to be instantaneous and not limited to the future.

   By using *We* and *our*, the author is implying that these sentences reflect the feelings that most people would have about Einstein's ideas about time travel. The author thinks that because Einstein's conception of time travel only involved travelling forward into time more gradually, it would not be as exciting as science fiction conceptions of time travel that entail travelling instantaneously into the distant past. So, most people would be "disappointed" with this idea of time travel. It is not (A) because this portion of the passage does not indicate hope or optimism about what would come from this sort of time travel. It is not (B) because *derision* has far too negative a connotation to be fitting here. It is not (D) because while concepts of time travel may be difficult to grasp, the text primarily indicates that most people would understand this idea, but would be disappointed that it didn't meet their hopes of what time travel would be.

3. **(D)** There will be 10 "Command of Evidence" questions on the SAT Reading test. Determine which of the choices presents textual evidence to support the answer to the previous question. Since these questions go hand-in-hand with the questions that precede them, give questions like #2 *plenty of focus* because if you miss #2, you are likely

to miss #3. If #2 is giving you trouble, check out the answers to #3 to see if any of the selected lines point you in the right direction. Lines 28–29 use inclusive language to indicate that the author believes that most people would be disappointed that Einstein's conceptions of time travel fall short of the dreams of science fiction. It is not (A) because lines 13–16 focus on Steven Hawking's views on time. It is not (B) because lines 19–21 provide explanatory information about Einstein's ideas but not on how people would react to them. It is not (C) because lines 25–27 also continue to give details about Einstein's thoughts, but not on those of the general public.

4. **(A)** For questions about the passage as a whole, be sure you choose an answer that is true for the passage in its entirety, not just for some small part of the passage. Incorrect answers on questions like these will often be true about specific components of the passage, making them very persuasive, but will fail to capture the big picture. "Informed contemplation" is the best of these descriptions, since the narrator speculates (contemplation) on the fascinating possibilities of time travel while grounding these thoughts in the theories of renowned scientific minds (informed). It is not (B) because the narrator presents a number of theories as being possible without dismissing any of them outright. It is not (C) because while there is some imaginative musing about the possibilities of time travel, there is a significant emphasis on what is realistically possible given the latest science. It is not (D) since while there is quite a bit of science, time travel is presented as much more theoretical than factual.

The next example is a **fiction passage**—this will be the first type of passage you will encounter on the SAT Reading Test. When reading this, take things more slowly at the beginning so you are clear on the setting, characters, and early part of the plot. You want to avoid getting half-way through the passage only to realize that you haven't understood what you have read up to that point. Reading more slowly can actually help you complete the task more quickly, so long as you understand things well the first time.

The following passage is from Irina Petrov's, More than Many Sparrows. *The setting is rural Russia 1917. Kolya is the heir to a large estate, upon which Anna and her family reside.*

Already, the fire was dying. Kolya watched, stonily, silently, as the warm, orange ribbons began to unravel, and vanish beneath the cinders. To feed the thing seemed pointless—almost cruel—and he wondered if perhaps it was better to stamp it out than to let it starve. He too, after all, was hungry. He too, after all, was cold.

Line
(5)   Already that winter, he had fed it half the books in his great grandfather's library. It had eaten up all the Napoleonic settees and tables that once adorned his ancestral home. He'd even offered it his mother's beloved mandolin, letting the strings on which she'd plucked his somber lullabies catch fire, snap, and turn to ash. He watched it happen, and felt nothing. Nothing, that is, but warm. It was winter, and sentimentality
(10)   was not in season—nor had it been for many months. Besides, no one still living in the house knew how to play it.

"Will this be enough?" Anna entered the barren parlor, shivering, and dragging a rococo cradle behind her, "It's not large, but I think it's dry."

Kolya nodded, watching her words turn to plumes of pale steam as she spoke. Much
(15)   like the lullabies, the cradle had long outlived its purpose. With pale hands, he broke free the first turned bar, and snapped it over his knee before condemning the splintered ends to the furnace. Anna sat, and warmed her hands.

She was right: the wood was dry. And dry wood, lately, was worth more to them than rubies. The rains, Kolya recalled, had come too early that autumn. Down in the village,
(20)   where Anna's family lived, he'd overheard the pilgrims in the street, with their silvery beards, and mud-caked sandals, speaking of a great *rasputitsa** to the south. They'd said it was an ill omen. They'd said there were stirrings in the capital. Kolya, at the time, had smiled. It pleased him to belong to so remote a province, cut off from the ugliness of cities and the southern roads.

* *'Sea of mud,' a semiannual occurrence when the unpaved roads of Russia become difficult to traverse*

(25)   But every day until they froze, the rains grew heavier, and the news still worse. A prince disappeared in Moscow. A farmer's wagon went missing in the mire. They found his horse the following morning, buried up to its bridle, though he, like a sailor lost at sea, had vanished. It wasn't long before the carts quit coming altogether, and in October, with the war on, the train quit coming as well. There was no timber from the

(30)   taiga, no grain from the steppes, nor sunflower seeds from the fertile, far-off south. And Kolya, for the first time, came to know the cost of living at the edge of the world.

"We're running out of tinder, you know," Anna turned to him. "How much longer do you really think we can stay here?"

Kolya frowned, "The entire house is tinder—we can tear out the rafters if we need

(35)   to," he said as he laid more wood on the fire, and hung a cast iron kettle over the coals. "So long as the root cellar holds, I think we can stay."

"But how long will that be?" Anna creased her brow.

She was anxious. Her father ought to have returned from his trapline four days ago, but the snows had been heavier than expected. Probably, he was just caught on the

(40)   other side of the pass until the storm cleared—probably. Kolya stirred the kettle slowly, mixing together the blood-red beets, and the ice-white cabbage. The nightly stews with which they'd started out the winter had given way to a thin, translucent soup. It would not be long, Kolya mused, before they were little more than seasoned water.

"I don't know," he replied, raising a rabbit bone from the bottom of the pot—the

(45)   only remnant of her father's last outing. He ladled out a bowl for Anna, "At least, no one will go hungry tonight."

She did not smile, but leaned back to gaze at the intricate millwork and murals overhead.

"When I was young, you know," she sighed, "I often dreamt of living here. Dolokhov

(50)   Palace—it seemed so mysterious up on the hill. I dreamt of lavish winter balls, of being courted by boys who would call me 'Countess'."

Kolya smirked grimly, taking a bowl for himself, and sat beside her.

"It is a dream come true, then, Countess Anna."

She shivered. Even now, she could neither smile, nor meet his gaze.

(55)   "Perhaps it is, Prince Nikolai. But now I'd much rather be awake."

1. The author uses the word "probably" in the sentence in lines 39–40 ("Probably . . . probably) to emphasize Anna's

   (A) confidence and self-assurance.
   (B) anxiety and uncertainty.
   (C) belligerence and hostility.
   (D) depression and lack of faith.

2. Kolya's point of view presented in the paragraphs in lines 18–31 can most fully be described as

   (A) generally optimistic.
   (B) consistently pessimistic.
   (C) shifting from appreciation to melancholy.
   (D) shifting from despair to hope.

3. What happens in the passage as a whole?

   (A) A young couple resolves to take measures to improve their lives.
   (B) Two thinkers share their views on contemporary politics and economics.
   (C) Two children muse on the status of their loved ones.
   (D) Two characters consider the past and their present situation.

Answers Explained

1. **(B)** Be certain to carefully read a question like this—the question asks you to determine *why the author is using* a particular word. To determine how the word is being used, we must consider sufficient context:

   *Anna was anxious. Her father ought to have returned from his trapline four days ago, but the snows had been heavier than expected. **Probably**, he was just caught on the other side of the pass until the storm cleared—**probably**. Kolya stirred the kettle slowly, mixing together the blood-red beets, and the ice-white cabbage.*

   Typically, "probably" is used to convey relative certainty. In the greater context of this paragraph, however, we see that Anna is anxious about whether her father will return from his trapline. She is repeating *probably* in a way that is quite telling about her uncertainty that he will come back. It is not (A) because if she were confident about his return, she wouldn't need this repetitive self-talk for reassurance. It is not (C) because there is no indication that she is feeling like fighting anyone or anything. It is not (D) because this is too extreme—she has not yet given up hope.

2. **(C)** Consider the evidence in the paragraphs that highlight Kolya's point of view. The point of view in the first of these paragraphs is most clearly seen in lines 23–24:

   It pleased him to belong to so remote a province; cut off from the ugliness of cities, and the southern roads.

   This is clearly a more appreciative point of view since he is pleased to be far away from distant troubles.

The point of view in the second of these paragraphs is most clearly seen in line 31:

And Kolya, for the first time, came to know the cost of living at the edge of the world.

This is a more melancholy point of view, because Kolya realizes, based on all the observations building up to this sentence, that his location keeps him from having many types of food that would make life much easier.

It is not (A) or (B) because the point of view *shifts* over the course of these two paragraphs and is not consistent throughout. It is not (D) because the first of these paragraphs is more positive in its outlook than the second.

3. **(D)** This question asks you to pick which choice gives the best plot summary of the passage. If this type of a question gives you difficulty, it can be very sensible to wait on it until after you have answered more specific questions. In the process of answering the specific questions, you will pick up on the overall plot of the passage, especially since the questions are generally in the order of where they are found in the text. (D) is the best answer because we have access to both Kolya and Anna's inner thoughts and their conversations. Their thoughts and conversations focus on their present state of affairs and also their experiences and thoughts in the past. It is not (A) because Anna and Kolya are more passive in their approach to the troubles they face. It is not (B) because this does not address what happens in the passage overall. It is not (C) because this too only comprises a small part of the passage.

Next up is a Passage 1 and Passage 2 selection—two authors will express their views on the same general topic. There will be one selection like this on the SAT Reading. You may want to read Passage 1 first and answer the questions about it, then read Passage 2 and answer the questions about it, and then answer the comparative questions that come at the end of the series of questions. If you read both passages before answering any of the questions, be sure that you consider *how the passages are similar and different from one another* because there will definitely be questions that will have you analyze the passages' relationship. This passage also has a graph that relates to the information in the passage—graphs will accompany two of the passages in the SAT Reading.

Two contemporary writers share their thoughts on the Electoral College of the United States.

PASSAGE 1

The electoral college has received much attention lately, primarily for being antiquated and absurd. However, I would argue that it's actually much more absurd than most realize. History class provides us with a rather fragmented understanding of the electoral college.

Line

(5)   We teach in schools that a presidential candidate must receive an absolute majority of the electoral college votes to win the presidential election, but we don't teach the mechanics of how a candidate actually receives these votes. A party's electors are chosen in a variety of ways, but they're typically reputable members of the party. When a citizen casts a vote during the presidential election, he or she is actually voting for

(10)   a particular party's electors to cast their votes for the presidential candidate to whom they have pledged.

What we certainly don't teach in schools is that these electors in many states aren't even legally obligated to actually choose the candidate with whom they're allied! As of 2000, there were 24 states without laws preventing this, for a total of a possible 257

(15)   rogue votes. In fact, there have been a minimum of 157 cases of such "faithless voting." Until 2008, Minnesota's electors voted anonymously, thus the number of faithless votes is almost certainly higher. Even in the states where there are penalties for faithless voting, the penalties tend to be minimal and aren't typically enforced. Thus, the only things keeping electors honest are the honor code and the desire to stay reputable

(20)   members of their parties.

Aside from faithless voting, there have also been cases where the electors died in between being chosen as electors and casting their votes. Obviously, this isn't a frequent occurrence, but still a problem that we wouldn't have to contend with in a popular vote system.

(25)   It's hard to understand why we maintain a system with so many glaring problems and very few redeeming qualities. Many cite tradition and the insight of our forefathers as reasons for preserving the electoral college, but the electoral college isn't even intact in its original form, since the second place candidate no longer serves as vice

president. It's way past time we cut our losses and admit that we've been defending a
(30) ridiculous arrangement for decades. If we weren't ashamed of it, maybe we'd actually
be teaching its intricacies in school.

PASSAGE 2

The iron fabric of Classic American Essence had a good run. It weathered its way
through the centuries, bending with the ebb of turmoil and stretching with the flow of
time that brought us to this point. But, the infrastructure was never meant to be a per-
(35) manent solution; it was a stopgap, a framework to be patched up and torn down and
remodeled as the country and its people grew. Somewhere along the line, though, we
turned our attention to other matters, and we forgot that basic premise of oxidation:
even iron, you see, corrodes.

Washington, Franklin, Jefferson, Adams: great men, one and all. Yet, only men—
(40) flawed and misinformed, limited by the pervasive misconceptions of the era and
hamstrung by the absence of electricity, Internet, Red Bull, and fish oil. Nonetheless,
with each monument built and mountain face carved, with each coin minted and
dollar bill printed, we came to see them less as mortals than demigods, until we came
to the point of no return when *our forefathers* became *Our Forefathers*. Now, seem-
(45) ingly every political debate hinges on the infallibility of these framers, and progress is
often thwarted by the unimaginative but omnipotent four-word objection—"but the
Constitution says...." as if anything written by quill and vellum inside lead-painted
walls could ever be indisputable in its absolute certainty.

More than 200 years of complacency have left us with something resembling less a
(50) federal government than a yard sale of antiquated institutions, with none more dusty
than the electoral college. Consider that it's theoretically possible to receive just 11
votes, have your opponent receive 200 million, and still *win the election* under the
electoral college.

Such is the nature of the "winner take all" system in which winning the 11 most
(55) populous states by as little as one vote is enough to overcome landslide defeats in the
other 39 states and the District of Columbia.

Whatever its initial purpose may have been, perhaps it's time to eschew the esoteric
in favor of simple arithmetic. Let us turn our attention to progress, lest our fervent
insistence on tradition leave us obsolete.

1912 U.S. Presidential Election Results

Presidential Candidate	Political Party	Number of Votes	Popular Vote Percentage	Number of Electoral Votes	Electoral Vote Percentage
Woodrow Wilson	Democratic	6,294,284	41.83%	435	81.9%
Theodore Roosevelt	Progressive	4,120,609	27.39%	88	16.6%
William Taft	Republican	3,487,937	23.18%	8	1.5%
Eugene Debs	Socialist	900,742	5.99%	0	0.0%
Eugene Chafin	Prohibition	208,115	1.38%	0	0.0%
Other		33,859	0.23%	0	0.0%
Total		15,045,546		531	

Source: *http://uselectionatlas.org/*

1. The relationship between the passages can best be described as which of the following statements?

   (A) Passage 1 and Passage 2 both cite political authority figures to make their cases.
   (B) Passage 1 focuses more on voting technicalities while Passage 2 focuses on historical foundations.
   (C) Passage 1 has more of a pious view of the Founding Fathers than does Passage 2.
   (D) Passage 1 focuses more on political dishonesty while Passage 2 focuses on economic repercussions.

2. Which statement from Passage 2 is most consistent with the style of argument primarily made in Passage 1?

   (A) Lines 36–38 ("Somewhere . . . corrodes")
   (B) Lines 41–44 ("Nonetheless . . . *Forefathers*")
   (C) Lines 46–47 ("anything . . . certainty")
   (D) Lines 51–53 ("Consider . . . College")

3. Someone who disagreed with both passage authors could make which of the following statements, based on information in the graph, most effectively to argue for her viewpoint?

   (A) The data shows that the electoral college is inherently flawed, since the winner need not even come close to winning the popular vote.
   (B) The electoral college ensures national unity even when there are widely different political views.
   (C) The electoral college prevents some candidates with significant support from having any voice in executive leadership.
   (D) The graph shows how electors can easily change their intended votes, sometimes with complete anonymity.

Answers Explained

1. **(B)** The relationships between the two passages will generally be more subtle—it is highly unlikely that the passages will be diametrically opposed to one another. As such, you will need to be thoughtful when it comes to determining the nature of the passages' relationship. These passages both argue that the electoral college is a bad idea, but they use different sorts of arguments to make their cases. (B) is correct because Passage 1 highlights the many risks of fraudulent voting that the electoral college may cause, and Passage 2 draws much more attention to the legacy of the Founding Fathers of the United States. The answer is not (A) because neither cites anyone as a political authority. It is not (C) because Passage 2 is more respectful toward the Founding Fathers, referring to them as "great men." It is not (D) because there is nothing in Passage 2 about economic consequences.

2. **(D)** The author of Passage 1 emphasizes problems with voting procedures in the electoral college process, and makes her case using more quantitative and analytical approaches. Review the text cited in choice (D):

   Consider that it's theoretically possible to receive just 11 votes, have your opponent receive 200 million, and still win the election under the electoral college.

   This statement is analytical and quantitative, making it stylistically most like what is found in Passage 1. Choice (A) is quite metaphorical, choice (B) is more historical, and choice (C) is rather ironic.

3. **(B)** Be sure you read the question carefully and pick up on the word *disagreed*. Since both passage authors oppose the electoral college system, someone who disagreed with both passage authors would want to cite information that most strongly *supported* the electoral college. (B) is the best option, since one consequence of electoral college voting is that in the 1912 election in which there were multiple candidates and no candidate won a majority of popular votes, the victorious candidate did receive a vast majority of electoral votes. This observation could be logically tied to the electoral college leading to more national unity than would otherwise be the case. The answer is not (A), (C), or (D) because these ideas would *support* the two passage authors, albeit to different degrees.

ADDITIONAL PRACTICE PASSAGES

The SAT Reading Test has more modern science and modern social science writing than it had in the past. Try these next two passages for additional practice with the types of passages and questions you are likely to encounter on test day.

A Natural Synthetic

In 1970, Norman Borlaug was awarded the Nobel Peace Prize and credited with saving over a billion people from starvation. In what is now called the Green Revolution, Borlaug led the research and development over a two-decade span
Line beginning in the 1940's to dramatically increase agricultural production worldwide.
(5) He introduced the synthetic farming methods already common in the United States and Britain to a global market, focusing particularly on the developing world, and succeeded in hiking food production and saving lives. Borlaug's initiative calls for celebration.

Yet, it is these same agricultural techniques—those associated with conventional
(10) farming—that have gotten a bad rap over the last twenty-five years, causing the organic food market to soar to a whopping $63 billion by 2012. These laborsaving, high-yielding techniques began in the late 18th century and were perfected for nearly two centuries before worry spread that they seriously harmed the soil and allowed toxic chemicals to enter the food supply. In the 1940's, while Borlaug was busy feeding
(15) the world's impoverished, Albert and Gabrielle Howard—both accomplished botanists—were developing organic agriculture. Organic farming is the process by which crops are raised using only natural methods to maintain soil fertility and control pests.

In the current food market, GMO's, or genetically modified organisms, turn noses faster than saturated fats and soda pop. Instead, organic farmers rely on crop rota-
(20) tion, green manure, and biological pest control, while excluding synthetic fertilizers, pesticides, and growth hormones. Organic agriculture is said to promote sustainability, openness, health, and safety, and its standards are closely regulated by the International Federation of Organic Agriculture Movements. The IFOAM bases the foundation of organic farming on the minimal use of off-farm inputs and on manage-
(25) ment practices that restore, preserve, and improve ecological harmony. While this strategy sounds more "conventional" and effortless than what is now coined conventional farming, organic agriculture is actually quite scientific.

Ecologically, organic farming is designed to promote and enhance biodiversity, so it must combine scientific knowledge and technologies to stimulate naturally occurring
(30) biological processes. For instance, organic farming uses pyrethrin, a natural pesticide found in the chrysanthemum flower, to deter pests, and potassium bicarbonate to control disease and suppress unruly weeds. Furthermore, where conventional farming focuses on mass production of each individual crop, organic farming encourages polyculture, or multiple crops being raised in the same space. To replace nutrients, organic
(35) farming relies on the natural breakdown of organic matter by microorganisms like

mycorrhiza, which forms a symbiotic relationship between fungi and plant roots. To replenish nitrogen, green manure is created by leaving uprooted crop parts to wither on a field, and is then used as a cover crop to fix nitrogen into the soil.

(40) The science doesn't stop with the crops. On farms with livestock, the field of agro-ecology—which includes organic agriculture—attempts to provide animals with natural living conditions and feed. Just like in plants, organic farming rejects any growth hormones or genetic engineering in animals. The USDA has specific regulations in regard to organic livestock, demanding that the animals receive only organic feed and are pastured rather than caged.

(45) Despite the popularity of organic foods, many argue that the concerns over conventional farming are a luxury of the rich. Organic farming yields far less than conventional methods, uses more land and more labor, and is, therefore, more expensive. When prices rise and production falls, it is the poor that suffer. With the United Nations reporting 870 million people worldwide suffering from chronic malnutrition, organic (50) farming faces a tough argument against the capital-intensive, prolific conventional means. Science has a lot more work to do before organic agricultural methods can feed the world.

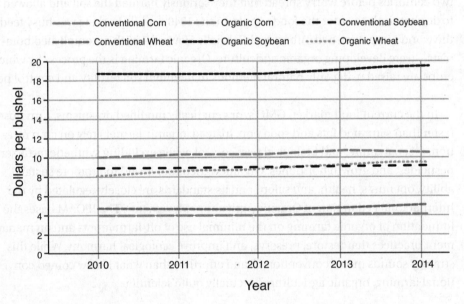

Average Cash Crop Prices

1. The author generally believes that synthetic agriculture is

   (A) an inferior alternative to the more sustainable organic agriculture.
   (B) the healthiest individual option for consumers, both wealthy and poor.
   (C) a misunderstood potential solution to global food shortages.
   (D) solidly grounded in science, unlike organic agricultural techniques.

2. As used in line 5, the word "common" most closely means

   (A) widespread.
   (B) lowly.
   (C) communal.
   (D) corporate.

3. An unstated assumption of the author is that

   (A) organic agriculture helps promote diversity of crops.
   (B) agriculture is the way that most people will acquire food.
   (C) many people in the world have a lack of sustenance.
   (D) organic agriculture is relatively popular.

4. Based on the passage, when compared to a non-organic farm field, an organic farm field will most likely be more

   (A) productive.
   (B) diverse.
   (C) mature.
   (D) centralized.

5. Which option gives the best evidence for the answer to the previous question?

   (A) Lines 5–7 ("He introduced . . . lives")
   (B) Lines 25–27 ("While this . . . scientific")
   (C) Lines 32–34("Furthermore . . . space")
   (D) Lines 45–47 ("Despite . . . expensive")

6. The paragraph in lines 28–38 functions to counter the claim that organic agriculture

   (A) lacks a scientific approach.
   (B) is relatively costly.
   (C) has nutritional merit.
   (D) causes widespread starvation.

7. As used in line 36, the word "symbiotic" most closely means

   (A) environmentally significant.
   (B) hierarchically predatory.
   (C) mutually beneficial.
   (D) agriculturally resilient.

8. Lines 39–41 serve to demonstrate that

   (A) animals that have been raised naturally are more content.
   (B) providing animals with unnatural feed is deleterious to their health.
   (C) agroecology is the first attempt to unify science with animal husbandry.
   (D) organic techniques have also been applied to raising animals.

9. Based on the graph, the difference in price between the organic version of a crop and the conventional version of the crop is greatest with

   (A) corn.
   (B) wheat.
   (C) soybeans.
   (D) none of these, as it depends on the particular year considered.

10. The information in the graph gives the most direct evidence in support of a claim made in

    (A) lines 9–11 ("Yet . . . 2012").
    (B) lines 19–21 ("Instead . . . hormones").
    (C) lines 21–23 ("Organic . . . Movements").
    (D) lines 46–47 ("Organic . . . expensive").

11. Generalizing based on the graph, one could estimate that organic produce is approximately

    (A) half as expensive as conventional.
    (B) one fourth as expensive as conventional.
    (C) twice as expensive as conventional.
    (D) four times as expensive as conventional.

Answers Explained

1. **(C)** "Synthetic" is the opposite of organic, so it refers to "conventional," manmade approaches to farming. The author shows both pros and cons of the synthetic approach, arguing that while it may not be as healthy or environmentally safe, it is much cheaper than the organic approach and can positively impact global hunger. (A) is incorrect because the author does not believe that synthetic agriculture is inferior to organic. (B) is incorrect because organic is healthier, but not accessible to the poor. And (D) doesn't work because the passage argues that both methods are scientific.

2. **(A)** Line 5 refers to Borlaug's contribution to worldwide poverty and hunger, stating that he extended the farming methods "already common in the United States and Britain." Since this is referring to their prevalence, *widespread* is the correct choice. *Lowly* means of low importance. *Communal* and *corporate* would imply that the methods were literally shared among members of a community.

3. **(B)** Since (A), (C), and (D) are all stated within the passage, choice (B) is the correct answer.

4. **(B)** According to the author, organic farming "encourages polyculture," so it produces more diversity. The passage states that conventional farming is more productive and centralized. There is no evidence for (C) either way.

5. **(C)** Lines 32–34 compare the individual focus of conventional farming to the multi-crop environment of organic farming, making it directly applicable to the previous question. (A) merely illustrates Borlaug's contribution via the Green Revolution. (B) suggests that organic farming uses science to mimic and provoke natural processes. (D) considers that the expense of organic agriculture doesn't allow it a comprehensive market.

6. **(A)** Lines 28–38 explain the science behind organic agriculture in response to the previous claim that it occurs naturally, so (A) is the best answer. (B) and (C) are done in other parts of the passage. And (D) is untrue.

7. **(C)** "Symbiotic" can be defined as the close association of two organisms in a mutually beneficial relationship. In line 36, we see that microorganisms form symbiotic relationships between fungus and plant roots to naturally break down organic matter and replace nutrients. Therefore, even without knowing the definition, we can infer that this relationship is favorable to all. (B) provides an opposite meaning from this. (A), while true, is not descriptive of the advantageous relationship. (D) is incorrect because there is no indication that these organisms have experienced a hardship that demands an agricultural resolution—they are simply helping out one another.

8. **(D)** These lines go on to show the science behind organic livestock, so (D) captures their purpose. Choices (A), (B), and (C) are all assuming.

9. **(C)** The question is asking you to find the greatest deviation between a crop's organic and non-organic price. Since, organic soybean is much more expensive than the other crop prices, we can see that this divergence is greatest.

10. **(D)** The graph shows crop prices, and in every case, organic prices are higher than conventional prices for that same crop. So, the graph supports lines 46–47, which state that organic farming is more expensive. (A) illustrates the recent growth of the organic market, while (B) and (C) give details of organic techniques.

11. **(C)** Since organic is clearly more expensive, we can rule out (A) and (B). Moreover, looking at the graph, the organic numbers are approximately double that of the non-organic numbers for the same crop. (D) is much too extreme for the data provided.

The Slums

You're driving and suddenly, out of nowhere, you end up in a very bad part of town. It looks very different from the neighborhoods you have just passed—the streets are rough and pot-holed, the windows are boarded up, most stores are closed down and the ones that aren't are covered in spray paint. You might turn the car around or lock your doors nervously or ask your iPhone to reroute. And your unease isn't unwarranted: these areas have the highest crime rates, the highest unemployment rates, the lowest graduation rates, the lowest median incomes, etc. But how did it get this way?

The answer may lie in residential segregation, or the sorting of population groups into areas to shape living environments. Residential segregation occurs on racial, ethnic, and income scales; but historically, African Americans are the most residentially segregated. The idea is to isolate neighborhood contexts to make certain areas more appealing to specific population groups. And while it may not be obvious how grouping "like" populations can create slums, it is proven to produce negative socioeconomic outcomes for minority groups.

Let us first consider the example of Baltimore, where a century of public policies segregated metropolitan landscapes and turned "black neighborhoods" into overcrowded slums. In 1910, residential segregation ordinances restricted African Americans to certain blocks and created federal housing subsidies that directed low income black families away from middle class suburbs. Additionally, favorable subsidies were denied to subdivisions that refused to exclude African Americans entirely. Real estate agencies began directing prospective buyers and/or renters to restrictive areas and banks began redlining, or failing to insure mortgages in black neighborhoods.

The result of these policies is clear. The federal government prohibited black families from accumulating housing equity and coerced blacks into homes with higher interest rates, while local jurisdictions forced public housing into designated areas and created overcrowded, under-resourced neighborhoods. The schools saw education deteriorate as teachers were overwhelmed with remediation and discipline, and unable to spend the necessary time on grade-level curriculum. Exclusionary zoning and discriminatory policies created communities of poverty with whites fleeing the area, businesses closing down, and future investments collapsing. Without employment opportunities, the poor became poorer, anxious, and more isolated.

In Chicago, a similar pattern occurred. Gentrification, or renovation to improve property values, forced the poor out of certain areas and steered them toward others. Homeowners were restricted from selling to blacks and when black families did purchase homes, it was at an average of one-third higher interest rate. The housing-starved African Americans were pushed into segregated neighborhoods via urban renewal plans, and municipal resources were reserved for white neighborhoods. Unemployment rates soared, public school systems had more students than their budgets allowed, understaffed police departments responded to violence with violence, and impoverished blacks turned to criminal activity to make money and gain protection.

St. Louis County has a history of state-sponsored segregation that is directly
(45) responsible for police-community hostility in its surrounding areas. Zoning rules have continuously classified white neighborhoods as "residential" and black neighborhoods as "commercial" or "industrial," leaving the latter starving for resources and ample law enforcement. Discrimination practices still allow landlords to refuse to accept tenants with subsidized rents, while relocation assistance programs offer incentives to families
(50) that comply with the city's population shifts. In essence, federal regulations enforce the continuance of "ghettos" or slums that are undoubtedly connected to distrust and violent protests.

Whether caused by exclusionary zoning, public housing enforcement, gentrification, white flight, or a combination of all these factors and more, a history of residen-
(55) tial segregation has purposely imposed areas of poverty, unemployment, and lack of necessary resources like healthcare, education, and security. The effects speak for themselves every time you accidentally drive into the slums. Moreover, once those policies turn neighborhoods into overcrowded slums, populations begin to associate the African Americans who live there with slum characteristics, erroneously mistaking
(60) the causes for the effects. Is it any wonder that the inhabitants find themselves angry, desperate, and distrustful?

1. The author's overall approach is best described as

    (A) presenting first-hand hypothetical situations to demonstrate the severity of a problem.
    (B) analyzing nationwide statistical data to generalize sociological patterns.
    (C) systematically addressing likely objections to a principal claim.
    (D) using specific case studies to help readers more deeply understand a subject.

2. Based on the first paragraph (lines 1–7), it is most reasonable to infer that the author believes her readers

    (A) do not themselves live in a slum-like neighborhood.
    (B) are naturally concerned about the welfare of the inner city.
    (C) are interested in potentially becoming involved in crime.
    (D) have cell phones that are not equipped with the latest software.

3. Lines 8–9 ("or the . . . environments.") most directly function to

    (A) give an example.
    (B) provide a concrete detail.
    (C) address an objection.
    (D) define a term.

4. The passage most strongly implies that slums were formed

   (A) accidentally.
   (B) belligerently.
   (C) intentionally.
   (D) randomly.

5. Which option gives the best evidence for the answer to the previous question?

   (A) Lines 5–7 ("And your . . . etc.")
   (B) Lines 31–32 ("Without . . . isolated")
   (C) Lines 53–56 ("Whether . . . security")
   (D) Lines 58–61 ("populations . . . distrustful")

6. As used in line 21, the word "prospective" most closely means

   (A) wealthy.
   (B) potential.
   (C) perceived.
   (D) privileged.

7. The passage suggests that slum-like neighborhoods are more likely to be what when compared to nicer neighborhoods?

   (A) heavily policed.
   (B) mixed-use.
   (C) zoned.
   (D) individualistic.

8. Which option gives the best evidence for the answer to the previous question?

   (A) Lines 1–4 ("You're . . . paint")
   (B) Lines 5–7 ("And your . . . way")
   (C) Lines 39–43 ("Unemployment . . . protection")
   (D) Lines 45–48 ("Zoning . . . enforcement")

9. As used in lines 40–41, the phrase "responded to violence with violence" most directly means

   (A) police responded to criminal acts with harsh reprisals.
   (B) police and citizens were engaged in open civil war.
   (C) an eye for an eye makes the whole world go blind.
   (D) the violence of both criminals and police negated one another.

10. Lines 53–56 ("Whether . . . security.") serve to underscore that the author believes that

   (A) a multitude of complex causes have led to a clear result.
   (B) a series of clear causes have led to a complex result.
   (C) a singular cause has led to a singular result.
   (D) a singular cause has led to a complex result.

Answers Explained

1. **(D)** The author uses particular geographical examples to illustrate the extensive ramifications associated with residential segregation. So, (D) is the correct answer. The author doesn't use first-hand (i.e., from the author's viewpoint) hypothetical situations or statistical data as in (A) and (B). Likewise, the passage doesn't address objections, but instead focuses on the butterfly effect of municipal, state, and federal regulations.

2. **(A)** Lines 1–7 introduce the topic of residential segregation by placing the reader into a hypothetical situation in which he or she is in the slums and feels uncomfortable. This is only an effective device if the reader can relate. Therefore, choice (A) is correct. The passage doesn't provide evidence for (C) or (D). Finally, the author does not confine her audience to those concerned about the inner cities, as in (B).

3. **(D)** Here, the author offers an explanation for the condition of the slum-like neighborhoods, i.e., residential segregation, and then defines it. Instances of (A) and (B) come later in the passage, and (C) is not sufficiently addressed in the passage.

4. **(C)** The author argues that historical racism and segregation purposefully "prohibited black families from accumulating housing equity," and the continuation of certain policies "enforce the continuance of 'ghettos.'" Therefore, the author would say that the slums were created (C), *intentionally*, rather than *randomly* or *accidentally*. *Belligerently* means "aggressively" and isn't as precise of a word choice.

5. **(C)** Lines 53–56 state that "a history of residential segregation has purposely imposed" slum-like conditions in designated areas. Thus, these lines give direct evidence of the author's opinion on how slums were formed. (A) discusses the sad living standards in low resourced areas. (B) considers the far-reaching consequences of exclusionary zoning. Finally, (D) posits that, as a result of residential segregation, those living in the slums are often mistaken to cause the undesirable conditions that they are themselves victims of.

6. **(B)** *Potential* is an accurate synonym since this line refers to "prospective" home buyers or renters. This word doesn't refer to their economic situation, as in (A) and (D). Nor is it definitive to say these buyers/renters were *perceived*, which means to become aware of.

7. **(B)** The author contends that one reason behind the lack of resources in designated neighborhoods is their tendency to be zoned as "commercial" or "industrial," while white neighborhoods are zoned as "residential." Therefore, we can assume slum-like neighborhoods are more likely to be used for things besides housing, as in (B).

8. **(D)** Lines 45–48 indicate that zoning categories influence available resources, and that black neighborhoods are often labeled "commercial" or "industrial," providing support for the previous question. Choice (A) refers to the author's opening visual of the slums. (B) is where the author poses the question that she hopes to shed light on. And (C) dives into the effects of urban renewal plans in Chicago.

9. **(A)** According to the context, urban renewal plans created an array of trouble for residentially segregated neighborhoods, including police departments who—without adequate staff and resources—"responded to violence with violence." We can infer that

this means the police felt unable to control certain circumstances and, instead, reacted aggressively.

10. **(A)** In the specified lines, the author refers to a number of causes that have overlapped with one another to create "areas of poverty, unemployment, and lack of necessary resources." So, while the causes are many and multifaceted, the result is clear: the slums. (B) is incorrect because the author believes it could be "a combination of all these factors and more." Likewise, (C) and (D) disregard the myriad of factors that may contribute to slum-like conditions.

Words in Context: Strategy and Practice

2

A substantial change to the redesigned SAT is the testing of word meaning within context rather than through a standard quizzing of vocabulary. There will be 10 questions on the Reading section that are like this. While this change avoids the esoteric and grandiose diction of past tests, it requires you to read closely and consider context around widely used words and phrases to interpret the most fitting meaning or implied meaning. This can be particularly challenging since the SAT will purposely use words with meanings that depend on how they are used. Yet, this can also be advantageous—a well-prepared student will have practiced using the surrounding context of a word to decipher its intended meaning. Moreover, the words will generally be simpler and more widely used. So, success no longer rests on whether you are familiar with the word. If you find this part of the test especially difficult, you should make use of a wide variety of scholarly magazines, articles, and journals as your command of language will only improve with a deeper understanding of how authors craft their arguments and which words they choose to employ. When you can think like a writer and use contextual evidence to derive meaning, you are best equipped for this part of the SAT.

This chapter includes:

- 8 Tips for Approaching Words in Context Questions
- Step-by-Step Practice of Easy, Moderate, and Difficult Problems
- 50 Practice Problems to Try Independently
- Answer Explanations That Explain Helpful Thinking Processes

STRATEGIES FOR APPROACHING THE SAT WORDS IN CONTEXT QUESTIONS

1 Consider Contextual Evidence

Read the sentence first, and then again, putting "blank" where the underlined word is. At the very least, look in the previous and following sentences for hints regarding the author's intended meaning.

2 Cover Answer Choices

It can be very distracting and use up more time if you consider the answer choices too early. Since the words tested will often be commonly used words with several different meanings, the answer choices will often be written in ways that can easily confuse you because you have most likely seen the indicated word used in a variety of contexts.

3 Create a General Synonym

Before looking at the choices given, replace the "blank" with your own general synonym. This can be broad or vague or simplified—don't worry too much about that. Instead, use this exercise to make sure you have some idea of the intended meaning before you jump into the choices given. This tool will be particularly useful in eliminating other or opposite meanings within the choices, and save you time.

4 Use Process of Elimination

Uncover the choices and eliminate those answers that sound nothing like your synonym. If there is a word you are not familiar with, leave it open for further consideration. You never want to negate an answer just because you don't know the definition of it. Likewise, if you get it down to a choice you are familiar with but is only "sort of right," and a choice that sounds appropriate but is unknown to you, you should go with the unfamiliar word since it has the potential to be 100% correct.

5 Read the Sentence with the Remaining Choices

The new format is not only going to test vocabulary, but usage as well. Especially when you cannot decide between two answers, reading the sentence with the answer choice replacing the original word(s) can often clear it up for you. It allows you to consider the meaning, but also to *hear* the sentence and decide if the usage is proper. Certainly, if the author is using a verb and you replace it with a noun that has a related meaning, mouthing the sentence out silently will help you notice that mistake.

6 Pick Your Answer Based on Meaning

Students make two common mistakes on these types of word choice problems. First, without covering their answers and creating a general synonym, they jump to "matching" words, or those that are associated with the underlined word, but don't fit the meaning of the sentence. Second, without paying attention to their own synonym, they become distracted by words that "make sense" in the sentence, but change the meaning of the indicated word. It is not enough to match words with their definitions, as the words tested will often derive their meaning from the contexts in which they are used. Additionally, it is not enough to pick a word that is logical in the sentence; it has to make sense *and* fit the meaning of the underlined word.

7 Read the Solutions in This Book

To make those finishing touches and eliminate careless mistakes, or to figure out why you continue to make the same type of mistake, refer to the answer explanations at the end of the exercise. This book is designed to be a unique resource for you, and acknowledging that you were incorrect is not nearly as important as understanding *why* you were incorrect. Go to the solutions so that you can improve your SAT-thinking.

8 Read, Read, Read

In the previous format, it made sense to study hundreds of obscure vocabulary words and hope that you would come upon that same rare, specialized language on the test. However, the new format is designed to test practical and widely used words that will continue to come up in college and/or your career. So, you can help yourself dramatically—for the test and life more generally—when you become familiar with these words and the ways they are used. Start with newspapers, magazines, and scholarly journals.

STEP-BY-STEP PRACTICE

Easy Examples

1. The vacation had the opposite effect on Jim. He despised the upcoming days and was depressed at the thought of his recent break-up. Although he marched into work fifteen minutes early on Monday morning, he was feeling very blue.
   (A) energetic
   (B) dispirited
   (C) indigo
   (D) rejuvenated

Correct Answer: **(B)**

To approach this question, consider the context clues. Vacation is supposed to replenish and relax you, but it had an opposite result. Words like *despised* and *depressed* make it easy to guess at Jim's condition. *Although* is a contrasting word, so how he feels must contradict his getting to work early and prepared. (C) refers to the actual color blue, so we can eliminate this. And then (A) and (D) are antonyms to what the writer is trying to convey.

2. Thad walked through the tunnel to loud applause. He mounted the pitching mound and breathed deeply to calm his nerves. He threw hard and fast, but was off his mark. The catcher had to run and retrieve the wild ball.

   (A) inaccurate
   (B) very nervous
   (C) not on the mound
   (D) careless

Correct Answer: **(A)**

The context allows us to understand that Thad is a nervous baseball player getting ready to throw the first pitch of the game. Since the ball was wild, we can infer that the intended meaning is (A), *inaccurate*. Choices (B) and (C) could be true about Thad, but don't represent the meaning of the indicated words. Choice (D) implies that he wasn't attentive or concerned, which we know is false.

3. The boss said to <u>call it a day</u>. The rain made the work impossible and half the materials hadn't been delivered on time. He was too frustrated to think!

    (A) do what you can
    (B) start the work
    (C) appreciate the sunlight
    (D) end the task

Correct Answer: **(D)**

This common idiom means to "declare the end of a task." The rain and lack of materials hint at the impossibility of getting the job done. Notice that (B) is the opposite meaning, (C) refers to daylight, and (A) could make sense, but doesn't fit the meaning. Remember it isn't enough that the sentence would read okay with this new meaning, it also has to fit the author's meaning.

Moderate Examples

1. When the speaker was done, the crowd rose and clapped vigorously. Yet, at the question and answer session, attentive spectators <u>raised</u> several points—particularly that the speech's moral lesson came off as condescending and was generally unfounded.

    (A) increased salary
    (B) elevated
    (C) put forward
    (D) nourished

Correct Answer: **(C)**

This line is referring to viewers who brought up, or presented, points that weakened the speaker's credibility. Therefore, the meaning is that they *put forward* several points. (A) is the type of raise one might get at a job. (B) is the definition for raise when it refers to lifting something up. And (D) indicates bringing up and caring for someone, like a mother might raise a child. Make sure to read the sentence with the choices replacing the underlined portion if you are struggling between two.

2. Ellen found the restaurant to be <u>a dime a dozen</u>. It lacked distinction and the food was merely average.

    (A) unique
    (B) expensive
    (C) common
    (D) below par

Correct Answer: **(C)**

Since the restaurant "lacked distinction" and was "merely average," we can infer that this restaurant was a lot like other mediocre places to eat. So, (A) is out right away since it implies that it is one-of-a-kind. (B) is wrong because this idiom does not actually refer to anything monetary. And in choosing between (C) and (D), remember that "average" is more like *common* than *below par* is.

3. In science class, the two friends frantically mixed their chemical solutions together. They had failed to meet over the weekend and their assignment was nowhere close to being finished. When they received a failing grade, the teacher remarked that the <u>solution</u> to their problem comes from adequate preparation.

    (A) resolution
    (B) mixture
    (C) choice
    (D) origin

Correct Answer: **(A)**

We can put our own synonym in here pretty easily. An "answer" to a problem is the intended meaning, so (A) works best. (B) refers to the first usage of solution, a mixture of liquids. (C) denotes an option. And (D) inaccurately signifies that the teacher is referencing the cause—a lack of preparation—rather than the solution, adequate preparation.

Difficult Examples

1. Sammy came home euphoric and thoroughly amused. From the parade to their animated dinner, she and Tanya had enjoyed every moment of their day together. That girl is <u>a riot</u>, she thought to herself, smiling at the fun they had had.

    (A) a loud protest
    (B) the one
    (C) an uproar
    (D) an entertaining person

Correct Answer: **(D)**

Riot is a word with several definitions, so be careful in your approach to this question. Choices (A), (C), and (D) are all meanings of *a riot*, but only (D) captures this sentence's precise meaning. (B) changes the meaning, and so is an inappropriate word choice. *Uproar* literally means "a loud disturbance or chaos."

2. Mr. Thompson decided to take the book off the syllabus permanently; he would have to replace it with another autobiography. The <u>book's</u> extreme views surpassed liberal and bordered on radicalism. He could already hear the parents arguing in his office.

    (A) non-fictional account's
    (B) author's
    (C) volume's
    (D) politician's

Correct Answer: **(B)**

Since this is referring to extreme views, we can infer that it is not the actual book being discussed. Furthermore, as it is autobiography, it is safe to assume these views are those of the author, as in (B). (A) and (C) both refer to the book itself, which is incapable of taking perspective. And (D) assumes the author is a politician and changes the meaning of the sentence.

3. Lee asserted that a movie like that <u>has a certain effect on</u> you. After watching it, he had not only joined the university's UNICEF chapter, but had also begun volunteering at the YMCA.

(A) is consequential
(B) creates a change in
(C) heals
(D) results in benefits for

Correct Answer: **(B)**

To approach this, look at contextual evidence. Lee is changed by the movie; it caused him to do things he might not normally have done. So, the line is referring to a consequential change in Lee. (B) fits the meaning and is used properly. (A) is incorrect because it is inappropriate to say a movie "is consequential you." And while it might do (C) and (D) for Lee, it doesn't have to in order to have an effect. So, these choices don't precisely reproduce that meaning.

PRACTICE EXERCISES

Instructions: Below are 50 questions representative of what you might see on the actual SAT. They vary in difficulty, but all require you to choose the appropriate meaning based on context and word choice. For each question, choose the answer that most closely fits the meaning of the underlined portion of the sentence.

1. To celebrate getting a new job at a law office, Mike decided to spend time with his family. They all went to the park and had a cookout. Mike had a youthful <u>nature</u> and loved playing with his nieces and nephews on the jungle gym.

(A) environment
(B) humor
(C) personality
(D) structure

2. Spencer was very interested in who all of her friends had a crush on. The <u>prying</u> girl asked them so many personal questions to try to figure it out.

(A) nosy
(B) interference
(C) curious
(D) lifting

3. Will's parents knew he was a very smart child. He mastered concepts in school much more quickly than other students. However, his grades did not reflect his intelligence. His lackadaisical nature was his downfall as he never completed his homework assignments on time. Perfect test scores were not enough to compensate for missing assignments.

(A) lazy
(B) drowsy
(C) moronic
(D) passionate

4. Johnny was afraid to jump off the diving board, so his sister called him a chicken. He knew he wouldn't get hurt but he was still scared, so he turned around and climbed back down the ladder.

(A) weakling
(B) fowl
(C) petrified
(D) coward

5. The proud boy talked about his accomplishments only when asked; he never boasted.

(A) haughty
(B) glorified
(C) conceited
(D) confident

6. The discounted dress fell apart the first time Emily tried to put it on. She couldn't believe the stitching was done so poorly. *Next time*, Emily thought, *I will go to a boutique.*

(A) rebated
(B) overlooked
(C) shabby
(D) cheap

7. Juan was surprised by what he heard, but discounted the information as lies. He knew many of his peers were jealous of his success, but he doubted they would stoop so low.

(A) reduced
(B) forgot
(C) concession
(D) dismissed

8. In chemistry class, we started a unit learning about pH. Acids often have a corrosive component to them. We had to mix some chemicals together and ended up with an acid that was so <u>strong</u> it burned a hole through the container!

   (A) weighty
   (B) potent
   (C) tenacious
   (D) athletic

9. When the reporter called the actress for a statement, her assistant said she <u>was not readily available.</u> The reporter doubted this as he later found out the actress had spent the day lounging around the pool.

   (A) could not be reached
   (B) was out of the country
   (C) was indisposed
   (D) would be cognizant

10. After she put a whoopee cushion under his seat at dinner, Joey set up a prank to <u>exact his revenge</u> on his older sister. It was time for her to feel embarrassed.

   (A) avenge
   (B) impose his retribution
   (C) enact his cruelty
   (D) tit for tat

11. In considering the prosecutor, the judge decided to <u>give leeway</u> on some mistakes as it was his first case. She could remember fumbling through her opening argument the first time she was in court.

   (A) provide room to grow
   (B) evoke carte blanche
   (C) tolerate a margin of freedom
   (D) grant amnesty

12. The audience waited with <u>bated breath</u> for the climax of the movie. The entire story had led up to the final battle between the villain and the hero. It was nerve wracking to see who would come out triumphant.

   (A) apprehension
   (B) impatiently
   (C) stagnant inhalation
   (D) cessation

13. Bennie and Jane liked to boat on the river on hot summer days. The <u>current</u> was powerful; it pulled the boat downstream incredibly quickly.

   (A) contemporary
   (B) waterway
   (C) flowing water
   (D) cutting-edge tide

14. Emily had <u>reservations</u> about being invited to Kayla's house. The last time they hung out it hadn't gone very well. In fact, Emily had stormed out angrily after Kayla made some rude comments.

   (A) detainments
   (B) territories
   (C) doubts
   (D) skeptical

15. While Mr. Davis, the art teacher, approved of creativity, he couldn't <u>sanction</u> the students expressing themselves in the form of graffiti. Stylistically, he could appreciate the pieces, but they were still vandalism.

   (A) endorse
   (B) consent with
   (C) confirm that
   (D) boycott

16. Andrew couldn't help it. He was still <u>harboring</u> bad feelings about his ex-girlfriend long after their breakup. There was simply no excuse for how she had treated him.

   (A) disregarding
   (B) camouflaging
   (C) entertaining
   (D) cherishing

17. Since Liz was trying to lose weight, she picked out <u>lean</u> turkey at the grocery store. She wrinkled her nose at the thought of how tasteless the meat would be compared to the beef she usually bought.

   (A) sinewy
   (B) slant
   (C) low-calorie
   (D) nutritious

18. Eloise was so excited about her birthday. She kept asking her parents about the party, but they carefully <u>skirted</u> her questions.

   (A) bordered
   (B) detoured about
   (C) evaded
   (D) avoidance of

19. Even though the homework was difficult, Maria <u>didn't mind</u> working on it. She knew in the long run it would help her be more prepared for college.

(A) was willingly
(B) took offense
(C) couldn't heed
(D) adhered

20. The pawn shop owner carefully inspected the ring. While the patron was convinced it was real silver, the owner determined it to be made of <u>base</u> metals.

(A) menial
(B) metallic
(C) artificial
(D) groundwork

21. The shining sun was a welcome <u>break</u> from the miserable weeks of winter. It had been gloomy and cloudy since September!

(A) dormancy
(B) obstruction
(C) fracture
(D) hiatus

22. Wren sleepily opened one eye and put a pillow over his ears. The birds were making such a <u>racket</u> it was impossible to stay asleep. He needed his sleep before the big tennis match.

(A) turmoil
(B) clamor
(C) roaring
(D) swindle

23. Melinda was on the left in <u>respect</u> to the stage. She gave a great performance and everyone was impressed with her talent.

(A) deference
(B) regard
(C) point
(D) admiration

24. Mel's <u>track record</u> was fraught with both awards and honors, but also countless references saying she was constantly late. When she showed up, her work was impeccable. However, her spacey nature generally made her distracted and she sometimes wouldn't even come into the office.

(A) indicator
(B) updated resume
(C) past performance
(D) achievement

25. Edwin's admission to the movie was <u>free</u> because he was still under the age of five. Once he was six or older, it would cost $5 for him to see movies.

   (A) without cost
   (B) comped
   (C) footloose
   (D) emancipated

26. Josiah <u>suffered at the hands of</u> the AP Exam. While he had been studying for months and felt as prepared as possible, it was still a very difficult test!

   (A) gave his best effort to
   (B) challenged willfully
   (C) experienced difficulty with
   (D) was wounded by

27. Even though he got a lot of his information from comedy news shows, Billy was always <u>up on</u> current events. The shows, surprisingly, presented a lot of accurate information with a punchline.

   (A) unseasoned with
   (B) at the summit of
   (C) up-to-date with
   (D) dashing on

28. The trial had been at a standstill for months. That was, until new evidence was <u>brought into play</u> for the jury to think about. Following this, the vote was nearly unanimous.

   (A) presented for consideration
   (B) became expositional
   (C) scrutinized for activity
   (D) contemplated

29. Grandpa Joe was very <u>set in his ways</u>. For the last twenty years, he had gotten up at 7:00 o'clock every morning, and gone to the local diner for coffee and eggs before work. Sidney doubted anything about this routine would change in the next ten years.

   (A) unwilling to change
   (B) steadily dependent
   (C) against modernity
   (D) disobliging to custom

30. The project was great in theory. However, outcomes are not always as quick as intended. The policy writers ran into difficulty with people being unreceptive to the new ideas. As such, their progress had plateaued.

    (A) fell into deep water
    (B) were provoked with objection
    (C) encountered resistance
    (D) confronted hostility

31. The plot was covered in weeds and other debris. It was going to take the family hours and hours to clear it.

    (A) storyline
    (B) space
    (C) graveyard
    (D) conspiracy

32. Three hundred people were present for the presentation on nuclear energy. Some of the speakers were in favor; others, opposed. It made for a very interesting set of speakers that covered almost every side of the issue.

    (A) introduced
    (B) in attendance
    (C) awarded
    (D) existing

33. The fight was about to begin. Every fiber in the boxer's muscles tensed in anticipation. This was going to be the fight of the century.

    (A) stressed out
    (B) swayed
    (C) arching
    (D) clenched

34. An education is usually thought to have intrinsic value rather than extrinsic. That is, its worth comes from the love of knowledge rather than something monetary. However, with the rising cost of tuition, one could maybe argue that there is a fiscal price related to education.

    (A) merit
    (B) price
    (C) principles
    (D) standard

35. Carl struggled to regain his balance, but it was too late. He <u>pitched</u> forward and tumbled down the hill.

   (A) inclined
   (B) stroked
   (C) fell
   (D) threw

36. While she really needed transportation, the low quality of the car <u>drove</u> Kelli to sell it. She simply couldn't afford the constant repairs it required. If she could take the bus for just a few months, she hoped she could save up for a nicer car.

   (A) steered
   (B) whirled
   (C) cruised
   (D) forced

37. The dog laid on her jeans and <u>panted</u> heavily. It was such a hot day; he was trying so hard to cool down!

   (A) gasped for air
   (B) drooled
   (C) fell asleep
   (D) lusted

38. Monica laughed at her cabin mate's ideas. While they were somewhat based on fact, her theories were essentially <u>bunk</u>. Pseudoscience is not a substitute for actual science.

   (A) indubitable
   (B) conflicted
   (C) cot
   (D) nonsense

39. Walker didn't mind mowing the grass. The <u>yard</u> for his tiny apartment was only about three feet by three feet. It only took ten minutes!

   (A) three feet
   (B) lawn
   (C) measurement
   (D) garden

40. Simon was <u>reared</u> in a small town by parents who were farmers. Simon's room was toward the back of the large, barn style house. He loved going back to visit the farm.

   (A) grown
   (B) raised
   (C) behind
   (D) discovered

41. <u>Live</u> comedy shows were always Hannah's favorite. She really enjoyed the idea that anything could happen during the lively banter!

    (A) subsist
    (B) premeditated
    (C) improvised
    (D) energetic

42. The storm was blowing the boat all over the place. "Roger! <u>Man</u> the helm!" the captain shouted over the loud wind. Roger ran to the steering wheel and righted the boat before it tipped over.

    (A) friend
    (B) hurry
    (C) operate
    (D) male

43. The <u>newspaper</u> printed false information in the daily headlines. As a result, the reporter in charge of the story was fired and forced to find other work.

    (A) journalist
    (B) article
    (C) publishing company
    (D) chronicle

44. Rossi needed to <u>book</u> a ticket to the author's tour. He had greatly enjoyed the novel; it was so different than anything else he had ever read.

    (A) fiction
    (B) present
    (C) reserve
    (D) arrest

45. The crowd started to ripple with excitement. The famous singer was stepping out of her car to enter the venue. Andre <u>craned</u> his neck to try to get a glimpse of her before she disappeared again.

    (A) stretched out
    (B) magnified
    (C) constricted
    (D) massaged down

46. The canoe was going too quickly toward the rapids. Yusef was <u>banking on</u> the shore to slow them down. While they hit the bank hard, it slowed the boat down enough that Yusef and his friend were able to jump out and pull the canoe off the water.

    (A) hitting off
    (B) counting on
    (C) running into
    (D) depositing

47. Emilia knew the car was in bad shape, but she was unprepared for the exorbitant <u>quote</u> to fix it. She would have to start working double shifts to cover the cost.

   (A) final cost
   (B) referenced excerpt
   (C) citation
   (D) estimated price

48. Pat had all the notes about the <u>case</u> in a suitcase that he carried with him everywhere. He was very nervous about what might happen if the information were to fall into the wrong hands.

   (A) baggage
   (B) trial
   (C) sampling
   (D) defendant

49. The extraordinarily strong man <u>might</u> be a good enough weight lifter to go to the Olympics! He had been training to do so since he was a young man.

   (A) used to
   (B) powerful force
   (C) dominated
   (D) may possibly

50. When the marching band won the competition, the drum line <u>beat</u> out a celebratory rhythm while the horn players chanted the school name.

   (A) played
   (B) pummeled
   (C) subdued
   (D) exhausted

Answer Key

1. **C**	11. **C**	21. **D**	31. **B**	41. **C**
2. **A**	12. **A**	22. **B**	32. **B**	42. **C**
3. **A**	13. **C**	23. **B**	33. **D**	43. **C**
4. **D**	14. **C**	24. **C**	34. **A**	44. **C**
5. **D**	15. **A**	25. **A**	35. **C**	45. **A**
6. **D**	16. **C**	26. **C**	36. **D**	46. **B**
7. **D**	17. **C**	27. **C**	37. **A**	47. **D**
8. **B**	18. **C**	28. **A**	38. **D**	48. **B**
9. **A**	19. **A**	29. **A**	39. **B**	49. **D**
10. **B**	20. **A**	30. **C**	40. **B**	50. **A**

Answers Explained

1. **(C)** Here, *nature* refers to Mike's character or disposition, making (C) the closest word choice. (A) and (D) are other meanings of *nature*. (B) is an appealing choice, but usually refers to a temporary mood rather than a combination of characteristics that make up one's persona.

2. **(A)** *Nosy* is the most precise choice given. Since she is asking many personal questions, we can infer that *nosy* is more accurate than *curious*. Choice (B) wouldn't work because this meaning is referring to an adjective, while this choice is a noun; it would have to be "interfering" to be considered. And (D) refers to another definition of pry or lever.

3. **(A)** Will never completes his assignments on time, so we can infer that the intended meaning is *lazy* as in choice (A). (B) refers more to sleepiness than idleness. (C) would indicate that Will was unintelligent, and is not a meaning of *lackadaisical*. (D) is a near antonym, since it refers to eagerness and intensity.

4. **(D)** Another name Johnny's sister might call him is *coward*. (A) is tempting, but refers to his physical strength more than his courage. (B) refers to another definition of *chicken*. And while Johnny may be *petrified*, *chicken* is referring to his lack of courage rather than his fear.

5. **(D)** Since the boy is not boastful, we can eliminate (A) and (C) which refer to arrogance. *Glorified* refers to something being idolized, often overly so. Instead, it is appropriate to say that the boy is *confident* or "self-assured."

6. **(D)** Approach this carefully; the dress is made poorly and Emily wishes she went somewhere more sophisticated like a boutique. Therefore, we can infer that it is a "cheap" dress, perhaps both in price and composition. (A) refers to a refund or a payback after purchase. (B) is another meaning of *discount*: to overlook or dismiss. (C) is true of the dress, but is not a meaning of *discounted*.

7. **(D)** Here, *discounted* means "discredited" or "dismissed." (A) refers to a lower price. (B) is not a meaning of *discount*. (C) is a noun where we need a verb.

8. **(B)** *Strong* is referring to the concentration of the acid, so (B) is correct. (A) and (D) refer to other common uses of *strong*. (C) means persistent or determined.

9. **(A)** It is accurate to say that the actress "could not be reached." (B) doesn't reflect meaning, but adds assumption. (C) indicates that the actress was indecent. *Cognizant* means "to be aware of."

10. **(B)** This line says "Joey set up a prank to exact his revenge on his older sister," so the closest meaning for the underlined portion is (B). (A) is "to inflict harm on behalf of," so it would only be appropriate to say, "Joey set out to avenge himself." (C) adds assumption, namely that Joey is cruel. (D) is a slang term for revenge, but it isn't precise to say "tit for tat on his older sister."

11. **(C)** *Leeway* means "freedom for error" or "flexibility." So, the judge is allowing some liberty that she might not normally allow on the grounds that the prosecutor is new. (C) evokes this same intended meaning. (A) speaks more of an opportunity than a lenience. *Carte blanche* means "free rein or full authority." And *amnesty* is a pardon for past convictions.

12. **(A)** *Apprehension* means "anticipation or suspense" and is the appropriate word meaning. It doesn't make sense to say "waited with impatiently." (C) indicates literal breathing troubles. And *cessation* is defined as "the end or termination of something."

13. **(C)** Here, *current* is referring to the fast-moving river water, so (C) is appropriate. (A) and (D) evoke other meanings of *current*. And while (B) is true, it refers to the river as a whole rather than to the moving water.

14. **(C)** Use context clues—Emily is nervous about her invitation because of her last encounter with Kayla. So, she has "doubts." (A) and (B) refer to other meanings of *reservations*. And (D), while appealing, is wrong because you cannot "have skeptical"; rather you would "be skeptical."

15. **(A)** Mr. Davis cannot approve of, or "endorse," the students' new medium of expression. (B) indicates that he cannot make an agreement "with the students" and is, therefore, poorly worded and imprecise. (C) and (D) are not meanings of *sanction*.

16. **(C)** This one can be tricky. (C) is correct because this usage of *entertaining* means "thinking of often or deeply." Choice (B) does not work since it is unlikely that he would have the self-control to keep these feelings secret. Choices (A) and (D) are the opposite of what the sentence might convey.

17. **(C)** Here, *lean* refers to the meat's reduced calories or reduced fat. (A) means tough; (B) refers to being angled. And while (D) is quite true of the meat, it is not what the author is saying; "nutritious" is not a meaning of *lean*, but a possible implication of it.

18. **(C)** *Evaded* means "avoided" and is the best meaning. (A) is another meaning of *skirted*. (B) assumes a roundabout route. (D) has the correct idea, but it is improper to say "they carefully avoidance of her questions."

19. **(A)** Here, Maria is willing to do the difficult work because she sees the long-term results, making (A) correct. (B) and (C) indicate near opposite meanings. And (D) would have to be "adhered to" in order to be considered. Still, it would mean that she acted in the way required, but not signify a personal willingness.

20. **(A)** The context tells us that the ring is not silver, but "made of base metals," so you might be thinking *inferior*. (A) means "lowly" or "inferior." While it might be correct to

say the ring is "metallic" or "artificial," those are not meanings of *base*. And (D) refers to another definition of base, as in a foundation.

21. **(D)** *Break* means a pause or gap, so (D) is correct. (A) indicates inactivity. And choices (B) and (C) represent other meanings of *break*.

22. **(B)** According to the context, the birds are being so loud that Wren is having trouble sleeping. So, (B) is correct. (A) refers to confusion and upheaval. (C) is a specific pro-longed sound that is imprecise here. (D) means "fraud or deception."

23. **(B)** For this question, read the line with each answer. It refers to Melinda's location, so (B) is correct. (A) and (D) imply the other meaning of *respect*, as in "respecting and show-ing reverence for someone or something."

24. **(C)** Here, *track record* refers to "past performance" as in (C). It would be inaccurate to say Mel's "indicator" or "achievement" was fraught with awards and honors. And while a resume could consist of those things, it refers to a specific document one uses for net-working and hiring.

25. **(A)** This meaning of *free* is indicating the absence of cost, so (B) *comped* implies that someone else paid for it, or it was given away for a special reason. (C) and (D) reference other meanings of *free*.

26. **(C)** We can say that Josiah "experienced difficulty with" the test. (A) and (B) would change the intended meaning, and (D) would imply that the test actually caused harm to Josiah.

27. **(C)** We know that Billy has "accurate information," so *up on* refers to choice (C). (A) is an opposite meaning. (B) means that he was actually standing on or positioned on the events. And (D) would either imply that he was "running on current events" or "fashion-able on them," neither representative of the intended meaning here.

28. **(A)** Think about the meaning. Evidence was introduced so that it could be taken into account. (A) captures that meaning best. Choices (C) and (D) are close, but not correct. We need both ideas—that it was put forward and that it was considered—to be precise.

29. **(A)** Grandpa has a routine that he is "unwilling to change." Choices (B) and (D) are op-posite meanings of what the sentence is trying to convey. (C) implies that he is morally opposed to contemporary social customs.

30. **(C)** Here, the writers experienced resistance when people were uncomfortable with change, so (C) is the best word meaning. (A) and (B) change the meaning of the sen-tence, while (D) is too extreme since it denotes violence.

31. **(B)** "Space" is the intended meaning. Choices (A) and (D) refer to other meanings of *plot*. And while the spaces in a cemetery are called "plots," the graveyard itself is not. Additionally, there is no evidence that this type of space is what the author intends.

32. **(B)** Substitute your own synonym for *present*; you might say "there" or "in attendance" as in (B). (A) implies that the three hundred viewers were all introduced. (C) relates to *present* when it involves a gift or reward, and again changes the meaning to signify that the viewers were all given awards. (D) refers to *present* as in "the current time rather than past or future."

33. **(D)** *Clenched* is the appropriate word choice. Choices (A) and (C) are other definitions of *tense*. Meanwhile, choice (B) invokes a back and forth motion.

34. **(A)** *Merit* means "value or worth," and is the correct choice here. *Price* would refer to the extrinsic value rather than the intrinsic. Choices (C) and (D) refer to a set of values or moral standards.

35. **(C)** Here, *pitched* just means that Carl's body is falling forward as in (C). Choices (A) and (D) use other meanings of *pitch*. (B) could either involve hitting something or a condition of brain damage caused by interruption of blood flow. Either way, it is not a meaning of *pitched*.

36. **(D)** Kelli was caused to act, or "forced" to sell. Choices (A), (B), and (C) all refer to other meanings of *drove* related to operating a vehicle.

37. **(A)** Choices (B) and (C) could both be true of the dog, but are not meanings of *panted*. (D) is a meaning of *panted*, but does not fit the context.

38. **(D)** Be sure to consider context. Monica's roommate has ideas that are vaguely based on fact, but then are exaggerated or mistaken so that they cannot be tested or rationalized. Therefore, they are *nonsense*. *Indubitable* means "impossible to doubt." (B) is much too mild. And (C) refers to a bunk bed, which is not the intended meaning of the sentence.

39. **(B)** Here, *lawn* is precise. (A) and (C) are indications of *yard* as a unit of length. (D) is inaccurate; it can be part of a yard, but is not synonymous with yard. Also, it would be unusual to mow a garden.

40. **(B)** Substitute a general answer before looking at the choices. Simon was brought up, or "raised," in a small town is what the line is intended to convey. It does involve his growing up, but he was not "grown" like a crop. (C) is another meaning of *rear*. (D) changes the meaning of the sentence.

41. **(C)** A "live" show indicates that it was not pre-recorded, but televised as it happened in real time. Choice (C) is the closest meaning since it refers to a spontaneous or not prepared-ahead-of-time performance. (A) is a different definition of *live*, as in "survival." (B) is an opposite meaning. (D) refers to *live*, as in lively or vigorous. Even if you didn't know the meaning of *improvise*, you could likely eliminate the other answers.

42. **(C)** Here, the captain is telling Roger to go to and "operate" the steering wheel of the boat. Choices (A) and (D) inaccurately imply that the captain is calling Roger a "man." And (B) is not a meaning of *man*.

43. **(C)** This one can be tricky. If you read carefully, you can see that the sentence is referring to the newspaper company, rather than the paper itself. While the information could have been within an article and written by a journalist, neither of those "print" the paper, and so are imprecise. (D) is a written account and a common name for newspapers, but again, is not indicating the company.

44. **(C)** Substitute your own synonym here. Rossi needed to "get" or "reserve" a ticket. (A) and (D) are different meanings of *book*, while (B) is not a meaning of it.

45. **(A)** Here, Andre is elongating his neck to see farther, so (A) is the most accurate word meaning. (B) would mean that he is actually causing magnification, as with a micro-

scope. (C) is an opposite meaning. And choice (D) is not a meaning of *craned* and changes the meaning of the sentence entirely.

46. **(B)** According to the context, Yusef is hoping the shore will slow down the boat's speed. So, (B) is appropriate. (A) and (C) are what will eventually happen, but not what he is doing at this point of the sentence.

47. **(D)** A *quote* is "an estimated figure given for the completion of a project or service." So, (D) is correct. (A) can be appealing, but quotes are not the same and sometimes vary greatly from actual expense. Choices (B) and (C) denote other meanings of *quote*.

48. **(B)** Here, *the case* is referring to "an occurrence that is being tried in court," so (B) is correct. (A) and (C) are other meanings of *case*, and *defendant* is related to the trial, but is certainly not the trial itself. And while it would make sense to say the notes were concerning the *defendant*, it would ultimately change the meaning of the sentence.

49. **(D)** Here, *might* refers to potential so (D) is correct. (B) and (C) point to other meanings of *might*. (A) would alter the meaning to involve past performance or events.

50. **(A)** Put in your own synonym. We can see from the context that *beat* refers to the drummers hitting their instruments to play a rhythm. So, (A) is the best choice. (B) is far too violent and extreme in its connotation, using a word associated not with music but with physical fighting. (C) and (D) signify other meanings of *beat*—"defeating an opponent" and "being tired out," respectively.

Graph Analysis: Strategy and Practice

3

Another major change to the redesigned SAT is assessing your ability to analyze quantitative information as portrayed in graphs, tables, and charts. The SAT now has quantitative analysis as a part not just of the math, but of the entire Evidence-Based Reading and Writing section. Five of the questions on the Reading section will be graph interpretation. The skills assessed in these questions are applicable not just in the physical sciences, but in social sciences, finance, computer science, and anything else that involves using statistics and numbers as evidence. While you will not need any background knowledge to answer these questions, taking rigorous courses in the sciences and social sciences will help you do your best.

This chapter includes:

- 5 Tips for Approaching Graph Analysis Questions
- 32 Practice Problems to Try Independently
- Answer Explanations That Break the Questions Down Step-By-Step

STRATEGIES FOR APPROACHING THE SAT GRAPH ANALYSIS QUESTIONS

1 Use only the evidence provided

Since you are not required to use background knowledge on questions, do not allow yourself to pick anything that is not directly supported by the information in the graph. Even if a choice may be true based on your memory, do not choose it unless there is evidence right in front of you.

2 Be certain that your answer is 100% correct

As in the SAT as a whole, there simply will not be partially right answers. If an answer is mostly correct but has some small part incorrect, throw it out and consider the other possibilities.

3 Carefully consider the graph labels and axes

The information presented depends greatly on the starting points and scales on the axes. Take the time to be sure you know exactly what is being presented—graph labels and descriptions are essential to doing this.

4 Don't jump to your answer

Since the questions are well-crafted and the answers are quite persuasive, take the time necessary to break the questions down. The SAT is not a rapid recall test that you must finish quickly—it is a critical thinking test that demands patience and care.

5 Refer back to the text when necessary

Many of the graph analysis questions will ask you to connect information in the graph to information in the text. Be aware that you will often need to go back and forth between the text and the graph.

PRACTICE EXERCISES

Below are 32 questions representative of what you might see on the actual SAT. They vary in difficulty, but all require you to choose the appropriate answer based on what is given in the graph. For each question, choose the answer that is best supported by the information provided.

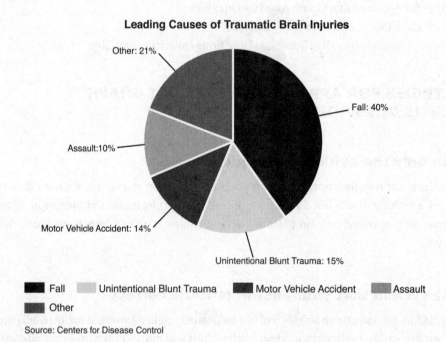

Leading Causes of Traumatic Brain Injuries

Other: 21%
Fall: 40%
Assault:10%
Motor Vehicle Accident: 14%
Unintentional Blunt Trauma: 15%

■ Fall ■ Unintentional Blunt Trauma ■ Motor Vehicle Accident ■ Assault
■ Other

Source: Centers for Disease Control

1. Based on the evidence in the graph, which of the following is true?

(A) People are four times as likely to be involved in a fall than assaulted.

(B) Increased seat belt use would decrease the number of traumatic brain injuries from motor vehicle accidents.

(C) 21% of the causes of traumatic brain injury are unknown.

(D) "Other" and "Assault" account for approximately one-third of traumatic brain injuries.

2. According to the graph, 15 out of 100 traumatic brain injuries are caused by

(A) motor vehicle accidents.
(B) unintentional blunt trauma.
(C) assault.
(D) falls.

Likelihood a Job Will Be Done by a Machine

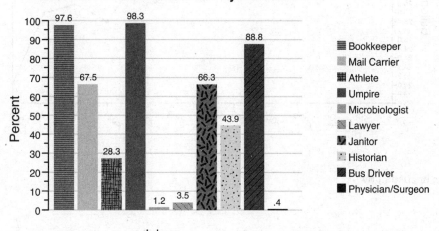

Source: Npr.org

3. Which job is most likely to be done by a machine according to the graph?

(A) Umpire
(B) Bookkeeper
(C) Microbiologist
(D) Bus Driver

4. Using the information in the graph, which statement is true?

(A) GPS and automation will lead to bus drivers being obsolete.
(B) Careers with a high likelihood of a machine performing the job have poor employment outlooks.
(C) A historian is less likely to have their job performed by a machine than a janitor is.
(D) More people are employed as umpires than any other profession.

5. Fill in the blank: The job of a/an _____ is three times as likely to be performed by a machine as that of a/an _____.

(A) umpire, athlete
(B) microbiologist, physician/surgeon
(C) historian, bookkeeper
(D) microbiologist, lawyer

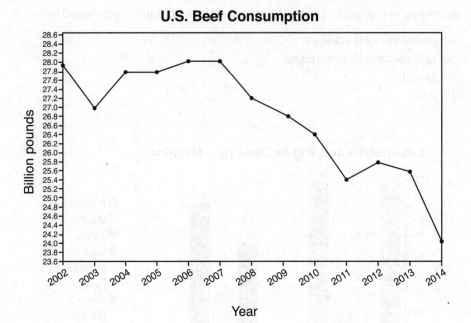

U.S. Beef Consumption

Year

Source: ers.usda.gov

6. A "best fit line" of the data presented in the graph would show that U.S. consumption of beef over time has

   (A) increased.
   (B) decreased.
   (C) remain unchanged.
   (D) peaked in 2007.

7. Americans consumed the fewest pounds of beef in

   (A) 2003.
   (B) 2014.
   (C) 2011.
   (D) 2006.

8. Based on the information in the graph, what can be said about U.S. consumption of beef between 2006 and 2007?

   (A) Americans consumed substantially less beef.
   (B) Americans consumed substantially more beef.
   (C) Consumption was nearly unchanged.
   (D) Due to an increase in population, each American consumed less beef.

World's Tallest Mountains

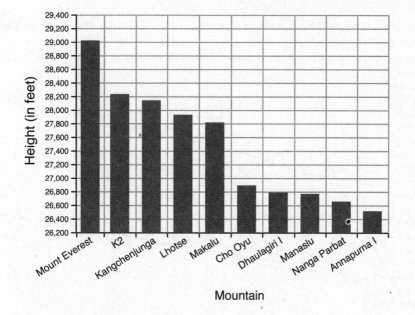

9. _____ is approximately three times as tall as _____.

   (A) Mount Everest, Cho Oyu
   (B) Lhotse, Dhaulagiri I
   (C) K2, Makalu
   (D) None of the above

10. Which statement is best supported by the evidence in the graph?

   (A) The world's tallest mountains are in Tibet.
   (B) 30% of mountain names also contain a number.
   (C) Nanga Parbat is a less dangerous mountain to climb than Lhotse.
   (D) Mount Everest is the world's tallest mountain.

Average Cost of Higher Education in the United States

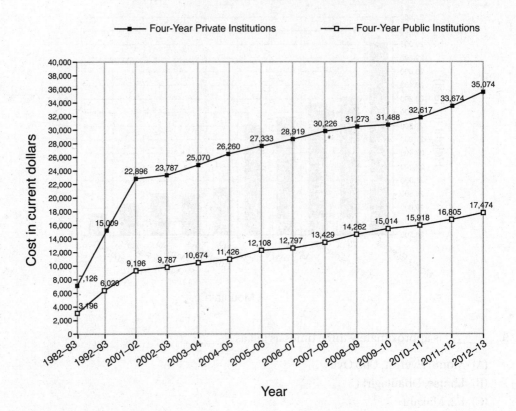

Source: Nces.ed.gov

11. The cost difference between four-year public and four-year private institutions was the smallest during which years?

    (A) 2012–13
    (B) 1982–83
    (C) 2001–02
    (D) 1992–93

12. Which statement is true based on the evidence provided in the graph?

    (A) Four-year private institutions experienced the greatest single year increase in cost between 1982–83 and 2001–02.
    (B) On average in 2012–13, a private four-year institution cost just under twice as much as a public four-year institution.
    (C) The cost of public and private four-year institutions has increased since 1982–83.
    (D) The cost of four-year institutions will decrease in 2013–14.

13. Which of the following statements is not supported by the information in the graph?

   (A) The cost of four-year public institutions was lower than the cost of four-year private institutions in every year from 1982–2013.
   (B) Accounting for inflation, the cost of four-year public institutions was more in 1982–83 than in 2001–02.
   (C) The cost of private four-year institutions increased the least between 2008–09 and 2009–10.
   (D) The cost of public four-year institutions remained under $10,000 until 2003–04.

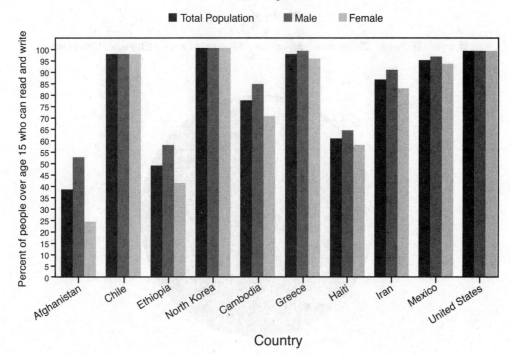

Literacy Rates

Source: CIA World Factbook

14. Which country has a female literacy rate under 50%?

   (A) Ethiopia
   (B) Haiti
   (C) North Korea
   (D) Cambodia

15. In Afghanistan, the female literacy rate is

   (A) more than the male literacy rate.
   (B) roughly half the male literacy rate.
   (C) approximately two-thirds the male literacy rate.
   (D) the same as the overall literacy rate.

16. According to the graph, which of the following is true?

    (A) In Greece, more women can read than men.

    (B) The male literacy rate in North Korea is more than the female literacy rate.

    (C) Iran has a greater overall literacy rate than Mexico.

    (D) 70% of the countries presented have a male literacy rate greater than the overall literacy rate.

200 students were surveyed about their pie preferences, and the percentages of pies that were considered the "favorite" by respondents are graphed below:

Pie Preference

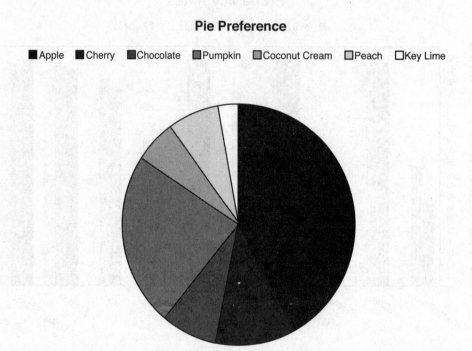

■ Apple ■ Cherry ■ Chocolate ■ Pumpkin ■ Coconut Cream ■ Peach □ Key Lime

17. The favorite pie of approximately 25% of people is

    (A) cherry.

    (B) pumpkin.

    (C) apple.

    (D) peach.

18. More people prefer _____ pie than _____ pie.

    (A) chocolate, apple

    (B) key lime, peach

    (C) cherry, coconut cream

    (D) chocolate, cherry

Total Revenue for Khan Grocery

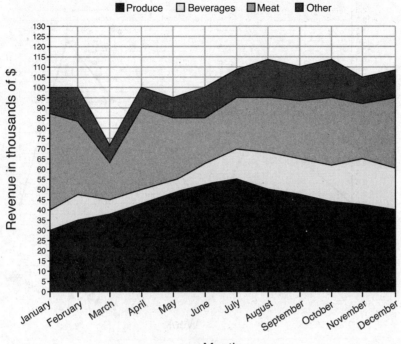

Produce □ Beverages ▨ Meat ■ Other

19. In February, what was the approximate total revenue for beverages?

    (A) $45,000
    (B) $50,000
    (C) $28,000
    (D) $12,000

20. In January, what percent of total revenue was made up of produce?

    (A) 50%
    (B) 30%
    (C) 25%
    (D) 20%

21. What month had the lowest total revenue?

    (A) March
    (B) October
    (C) May
    (D) August

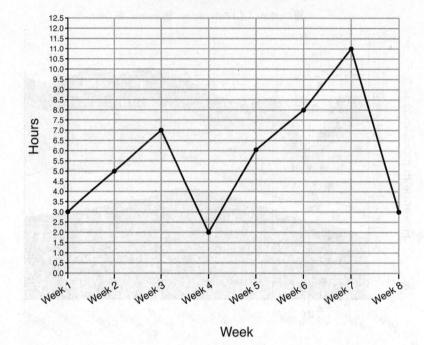

Hours Spent Watching TV

22. Between which weeks was the greatest total hour decrease in hours spent watching TV?

(A) Weeks 3 and 4
(B) Weeks 4 and 7
(C) Weeks 7 and 8
(D) Weeks 5 and 6

23. How many total hours were spent watching TV between Weeks 1 and 8?

(A) 45
(B) 8
(C) 46
(D) 15

24. Based on the evidence in the graph, which of the following is true?

(A) The fewest number of hours was spent watching TV in Week 4.
(B) Screen time is a health concern for American children.
(C) Week 4 was the busiest with other activities.
(D) A new TV contributed to the increase in hours watched in Week 7.

Ground Covering

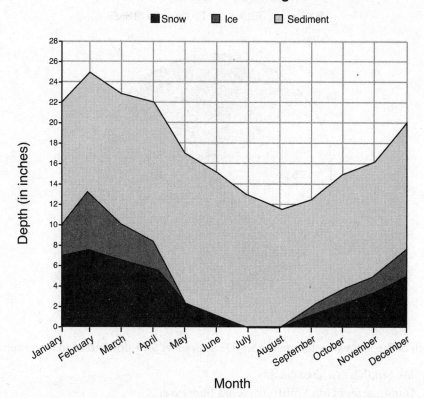

■ Snow ■ Ice □ Sediment

25. Between which months is the percentage of sediment covering the ground the greatest?

(A) January and February
(B) August and September
(C) July and August
(D) November and December

26. According to the graph, what can be said about sediment as a ground covering?

(A) It remains roughly the same depth throughout the year.
(B) It is thickest in February.
(C) It is thinnest in August.
(D) It increases in depth from August to December.

27. What is the depth in inches of ice in April?

(A) 8
(B) 2
(C) 10
(D) 5

Eye Colors in Ms. Smith's Class

■ Brown □ Blue ■ Green ■ Hazel

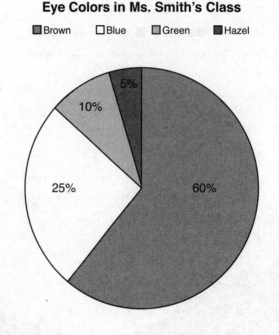

28. Which of the following statements is NOT supported by information in the graph?

    (A) Ms. Smith has a large class.
    (B) One-quarter of Ms. Smith's class has blue eyes.
    (C) Twice as many students have green eyes as have hazel eyes.
    (D) Most of the students have brown eyes.

29. Using the graph, what is true about the relationship between the number of students with green eyes and the number of students with brown eyes?

    (A) The number of students with green eyes equals one-sixth of the number of students with brown eyes.
    (B) Green eyes are a recessive trait and more uncommon than brown eyes.
    (C) Hazel eyes are a variant of green and should be included in the green eyes total.
    (D) For every 10 students with green eyes there are six students with brown eyes.

Population Structure

■ 0–14　■ 15–24　■ 25–54　■ 55–65　□ 65 and older

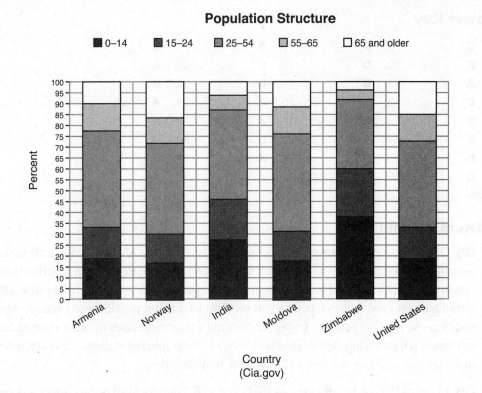

Country
(Cia.gov)

30. Which country has the highest percentage of people age 0–14?

(A) India
(B) Moldova
(C) Armenia
(D) Zimbabwe

31. In Armenia, people age 15–24 make up approximately what percentage of the total population?

(A) 10%
(B) 15%
(C) 35%
(D) 75%

32. Which of the following is true based on the information in the graph?

(A) Norway has the greatest percentage of people age 65 and older.
(B) Norway has the best healthcare for older adults.
(C) Most Norwegians choose not to have children.
(D) Norway will soon feel the economic effects of its low birth rate.

Answer Key

1.	**D**	9.	**D**	17.	**B**	25.	**C**
2.	**B**	10.	**D**	18.	**C**	26.	**A**
3.	**A**	11.	**B**	19.	**D**	27.	**B**
4.	**C**	12.	**C**	20.	**B**	28.	**A**
5.	**B**	13.	**B**	21.	**A**	29.	**A**
6.	**B**	14.	**A**	22.	**C**	30.	**D**
7.	**B**	15.	**B**	23.	**A**	31.	**B**
8.	**C**	16.	**D**	24.	**A**	32.	**A**

Answers Explained

1. **(D)** Be sure to read the answer choices carefully. Choices (A), (B), and (C) all make assumptions. While "falls" account for four times the amount of brain injuries than "assault," that does not necessarily mean they happen four times as often. Likewise, (B) introduces external factors like seat belt use that we cannot provide evidence for. And just because they are labeled "Other," it does not mean the causes of brain injuries are unknown. (D) is the only definite choice based on the graph; together the two categories make up 31% or about one-third of traumatic brain injuries.

2. **(B)** 15 out of 100 can be rewritten as 15/100 or 15%. Therefore, (B) is the correct answer because "unintentional blunt trauma" is 15% of the chart.

3. **(A)** The bars of the graph follow the key chronologically, so the fourth category, "umpire," is the highest likelihood with 98.3%.

4. **(C)** Again, only use the evidence given. We cannot make conclusions about any employment outlooks as in (A) and (B). Nor can we make assumptions about the number of people currently employed in these professions as in (D). However, we can use the graph to show that janitorial jobs are more likely to be completed by machinery than historian jobs, making (C) correct.

5. **(B)** 1.2 is three times 0.4, making (B) correct. You can move the decimals if it makes it easier to think about: $12 = 3 \times 4$.

6. **(B)** A line of best fit, or a trend line, is a straight line that best represents the data values given. Since this line would have a downward slope in the graph shown, (B) is the accurate answer.

7. **(B)** According to the graph, beef consumption was lowest in 2014.

8. **(C)** From 2006 to 2007, beef consumption remained steady at about 28 billion pounds, so (C).

9. **(D)** While (B) looks persuasive, be very careful to consider the units along the y-axis. The units start at 26,200 instead of 0, so all of these mountains are relatively close to one another in height, making "none of the above" correct.

10. **(D)** This graph shows the names and the heights of the world's tallest mountains, so (D) is the only answer for which we have direct evidence. (C) can be tempting, but height is not necessarily correlated with the danger of climbing. For instance, Lhotse could pos-

sibly have safer paths and be in a more temperate climate, while Nanga Parbat, though much smaller, could provide only risky climbing and exposure to dangerous weather and wildlife.

11. **(B)** To approach this question, find where the two lines are nearest each other. Thus, (B) is correct.

12. **(C)** Choice (C) is the only answer evidenced by the graph. Both types of institutions have increased dramatically in price since 1982. (A) does not name a single year, but a two-decade span, so we cannot know the annual increases per year during that range. In 2012–13, a private education was just over, not under, twice the cost of a public education, making (B) wrong. And we have no information for 2013–14, but could project that it would continue to rise rather than drop.

13. **(B)** There is no evidence to support (B) since the graph does not address inflation and we are not provided any other information. The remaining choices can all be proven by the graph.

14. **(A)** Afghanistan and Ethiopia have the lowest literacy rates, with female rates being about 24% and 41%, respectively. Since Afghanistan is not a choice, (A) is the correct answer.

15. **(B)** According to the graph, about 52% of men in Afghanistan are literate, compared to 24% of women, so this is roughly twice as much. Thus, (B) is accurate.

16. **(D)** The male literacy rate is slightly higher than the female literacy rate, ruling out (A). (B) doesn't work because the rates are even in North Korea. And overall, Mexico's numbers are slightly higher than Iran's as in (C). Since there are three countries listed where female literacy is equal to male literacy and the other seven options all have higher male literacy, we can say 7/10 or 70% of the countries have a greater male literacy rate.

17. **(B)** To approach this question, look for a chunk that makes up about one-fourth of the entire pie chart. (B) is the best answer. (C) is much bigger than a fourth and the other options are obviously less.

18. **(C)** The cherry section of the pie chart is larger than the coconut cream section. This is the only option for which the general relationship holds.

19. **(D)** To find this, draw lines from February over to the y-axis to see that the revenue for beverages covers from about 35 to 47, meaning $12,000.

20. **(B)** Produce had a revenue of $30,000 according to the graph, and the total revenue was right at $100,000. So, for January produce made up 30/100 or 30% of total revenue.

21. **(A)** The total revenue is measured by the top curve of the graph, and the top curve was the lowest in March, making (A) correct.

22. **(C)** The largest drop was between Weeks 7 and 8 where the graph went from 11 hours to 3 hours.

23. **(A)** To calculate total hours, find the hours for each week. You should find that $3 + 5 + 7 + 2 + 6 + 8 + 11 + 3 = 45$.

24. **(A)** According the graph, only 2 hours were spent watching TV in Week 4, making that the lowest of all the given data. There is no concrete evidence for or against choices (B), (C), and (D).

25. **(C)** This question is asking about percentage rather than depth. Between July and August, sediment made up 100% of ground covering, since the other elements were not present.

26. **(A)** The sediment curve fluctuates between 12 and 14 inches all year long, making (A) the correct choice. (D) may be appealing, but be careful; the overall ground covering increases, but the amount of sediment stays pretty steady.

27. **(B)** In April, the ice curve takes up the 6 to 8 inch part of the graph, so its depth is approximately 2 inches.

28. **(A)** Notice the *NOT* in the question. Since this graph is dealing in percentages, there is no evidence for the actual class size or what might constitute a large class.

29. **(A)** In this graph, "green" takes up 10% while "brown" takes up 60%. Therefore, the ratio is 1:6 or one-sixth.

30. **(D)** Ages 0–14 make up the category closest to the *x*-axis, which makes it easy to see that Zimbabwe has the highest percentage with about 38%.

31. **(B)** According to the graph, Armenia's percentage of population between the ages of 15 and 24 is about 15%, or 34 – 19.

32. **(A)** The graph does not provide evidence on healthcare or birth rates, ruling out choices (B), (C), and (D). Additionally, we can confirm (A) by seeing that about 17% of the population is made up of those 65 and older. The only country close to this percentage is the United States with about 15% of the population being in this category.

Practice Exercises of Increasing Difficulty

4

PRACTICE EXERCISE A

These passages and questions are representative of the easier passages you will find on the actual SAT. Use these to practice new strategies and to build your confidence. Take about 13 minutes for each passage (including reading and answering the questions). Detailed answer explanations follow.

Passage A1

Charles Dickens's Great Expectations *was first published in 1861. Pip, a poor orphan who is cared for by his sister and her husband, meets the young girl who will become the lifetime object of his affections while simultaneously becoming aware of his lowly position in the caste system.*

I must have been about ten years old when I went to Miss Havisham's, and first met Estella.

My uncle Pumblechook, who kept a cornchandler's shop in the high-street of the
Line town, took me to the large old, dismal house, which had all its windows barred. For
(5) miles round everybody had heard of Miss Havisham as an immensely rich and grim lady who led a life of seclusion; and everybody soon knew that Mr. Pumblechook had been commissioned to bring her a boy.

He left me at the courtyard, and a young lady, who was very pretty and seemed very proud, let me in, and I noticed that the passages were all dark, and that there was a
(10) candle burning. My guide, who called me "boy," but was really about my own age, was as scornful of me as if she had been one-and-twenty, and a queen. She led me to Miss Havisham's room, and there, in an armchair, with her elbow resting on the table, sat the strangest lady I have ever seen, or shall ever see.

She was dressed in rich materials—satins and lace and silks—all of white—or rather,
(15) which had been white, but, like all else in the room, were now faded yellow. Her shoes were white, and she had a long white veil dependent from her hair, and bridal flow-ers in her hair; but her hair was white. I saw that the bride within the bridal dress had withered like the dress.

"Who is it?" said the lady at the table.

(20)   "Pip, ma'am. Mr. Pumblechook's boy."

"Come nearer; let me look at you; come close. You are not afraid of a woman who has never seen the sun since you were born?"

"No, ma'am."

"Do you know what I touch here?" she said, laying her hands, one upon the other, (25) on her left side.

"Yes, ma'am; your heart."

"Broken!" She was silent for a little while, and then added, "I am tired; I want diversion. Play, play, play!"

What was an unfortunate boy to do? I didn't know how to play.

(30)   "Call Estella," said the lady. "Call Estella, at the door."

It was a dreadful thing to be bawling "Estella" to a scornful young lady in a mysterious passage in an unknown house, but I had to do it. And Estella came, and I heard her say, in answer to Miss Havisham, "Play with this boy! Why, he is a common labouring boy!"

(35)   I thought I overheard Miss Havisham answer, "Well? You can break his heart."

We played at beggar my neighbour, and before the game was out Estella said disdainfully, "He calls the knaves Jacks, this boy! And what coarse hands he has! And what thick boots!"

I was very glad to get away. My coarse hands and my common boots had never (40) troubled me before; but they troubled me now, and I determined to ask Joe why he had taught me to call those picture cards Jacks which ought to be called knaves.

For a long time I went once a week to this strange, gloomy house—it was called Satis House—and once Estella told me I might kiss her.

And then Miss Havisham decided I was to be apprenticed to Joe, and gave him £25 (45) for the purpose; and I left off going to see her, and helped Joe in the forge. But I didn't like Joe's trade, and I was afflicted by that most miserable thing—to feel ashamed of home.

I couldn't resist paying Miss Havisham a visit; and, not seeing Estella, stammered that I hoped she was well.

(50)   "Abroad," said Miss Havisham; "educating for a lady; far out of reach; prettier than ever; admired by all who see her. Do you feel that you have lost her?"

I was spared the trouble of answering by being dismissed, and went home dissatisfied and uncomfortable, thinking myself coarse and common, and wanting to be a gentleman.

1. The passage can best be summarized as which one of the following statements?

   (A) A boy has interesting interactions at an old woman's house and reflects on these experiences.
   (B) A boy seduces a girl into falling in love with him for the years to come.
   (C) A woman teaches a young boy about the merits of apprenticeship.
   (D) A girl travels abroad for her education, leaving her companion behind to fend for himself.

2. The passage is generally organized

   (A) from most to least important details.
   (B) chronologically.
   (C) spatially.
   (D) through a sequence of flashbacks and present-day reflection.

3. The second paragraph (lines 3–7) serves to explain

   (A) why Pip wanted to be a gentleman.
   (B) why Miss Havisham desired companionship.
   (C) how Pip came to be at Miss Havisham's.
   (D) how Pip came to fall in love with Estella.

4. As used in line 12, the word "resting" most closely means

   (A) suppressing.
   (B) dreaming.
   (C) sleeping.
   (D) laying.

5. What best describes Miss Havisham's appearance?

   (A) Typical
   (B) Unusual
   (C) Colorful
   (D) Vivacious

6. Which option gives the best evidence for the answer to the previous question?

(A) Lines 3–4 ("My . . . barred")
(B) Lines 11–13 ("She . . . see")
(C) Lines 27–28 ("Broken . . . Play")
(D) Lines 31–32 ("It was . . . do it")

7. How does Pip feel about his current social and economic circumstances?

(A) Dissatisfied
(B) Content
(C) Serene
(D) Entertained

8. Which option gives the best evidence for the answer to the previous question?

(A) Lines 8–10 ("He left . . . burning")
(B) Lines 23–26 ("No . . . heart")
(C) Line 35 ("I thought . . . heart")
(D) Lines 52–54 ("I was . . . gentleman")

9. The paragraph in lines 39–41 highlights Pip's feeling

(A) a sense of belonging.
(B) a need to show off.
(C) out of place.
(D) ready to argue.

10. As used in line 46, the word "afflicted" most closely means

(A) diseased.
(B) strengthened.
(C) emboldened.
(D) troubled.

Passage A2

PASSAGE 1

The first is a speech given by Sojourner Truth in 1851 at the Women's Convention in Akron, Ohio. (As a historical text, this uses antiquated language.) The second is part of Carrie Chapman Catt's "Address to the Congress on Women's Suffrage" in 1917.

Ain't I a Woman?

"Well, children, where there is so much racket there must be something out of kilter. I think that 'twixt the negroes of the South and the women of the North, all talking about rights, the white men will be in a fix pretty soon. But what's all this here talking about?

(5)   That man over there says that women need to be helped into carriages and lifted over ditches, and to have the best place everywhere. Nobody ever helps me into carriages, or over mud-puddles, or gives me any best place! And ain't I a woman? Look at me! Look at my arm! I could have ploughed and planted, and gathered into barns, and no man could head me! And ain't I a woman? I could work as much and eat as much

(10) as a man—when I could get it—and bear the lash as well! And ain't I a woman? I have borne thirteen children, and seen them most all sold off to slavery, and when I cried out with my mother's grief, none but Jesus heard me! And ain't I a woman?

Then they talk about this thing in the head; what's this they call it? [Intellect, somebody whispers] That's it, honey. What's that got to do with women's rights or negroes'

(15) rights? If my cup won't hold but a pint, and yours holds a quart, wouldn't you be mean not to let me have my little half measure-full?

Then that little man in black there, he says women can't have as much rights as men, 'cause Christ wasn't a woman! Where did your Christ come from? Where did your Christ come from? From God and a woman! Man had nothing to do with Him.

(20) If the first woman God ever made was strong enough to turn the world upside down all alone, these women together ought to be able to turn it back, and get it right side up again!

And now they is asking to do it, the men better let them.

Obliged to you for hearing me, and now old Sojourner ain't got nothing more to say."

PASSAGE 2

(25) Do you realize that in no other country in the world with democratic tendencies is suffrage so completely denied as in a considerable number of our own states? There are thirteen black states where no suffrage for women exists, and fourteen others where suffrage for women is more limited than in many foreign countries.

Line (with (5) marking as shown in original)

Do you realize that when you ask women to take their cause to state referendum
(30) you compel them to do this: that you drive women of education, refinement, achievement, to beg men who cannot read for their political freedom?

Do you realize that such anomalies as a college president asking her janitor to give
her a vote are overstraining the patience and driving women to desperation?

Do you realize that women in increasing numbers indignantly resent the long delay
(35) in their enfranchisement?

Your party platforms have pledged women suffrage. Then why not be honest, frank
friends of our cause, adopt it in reality as your own, make it a party program, and "fight
with us"? As a party measure—a measure of all parties—why not put the amendment
through Congress and the legislatures? We shall all be better friends, we shall have a
(40) happier nation, we women will be free to support loyally the party of our choice, and
we shall be far prouder of our history.

"There is one thing mightier than kings and armies"—aye, than Congresses and
political parties—"the power of an idea when its time has come to move." The time for
woman suffrage has come. The woman's hour has struck. If parties prefer to postpone
(45) action longer and thus do battle with this idea, they challenge the inevitable. The idea
will not perish; the party which opposes it may. Every delay, every trick, every political
dishonesty from now on will antagonize the women of the land more and more, and
when the party or parties which have so delayed woman suffrage finally let it come,
their sincerity will be doubted and their appeal to the new voters will be met with sus-
(50) picion. This is the psychology of the situation. Can you afford the risk? Think it over.

1. Passage 1 as a whole emphasizes what qualities of women?

   (A) Their strength and independence
   (B) Their significant dependence on men
   (C) Their desire to be homemakers
   (D) Their willingness to fight in wars

2. As used in line 3, the word "fix" most closely means

   (A) repair.
   (B) predicament.
   (C) securing.
   (D) settling.

3. Lines 15–16 ("If my . . . full?") most directly suggest that

   (A) it would be wrong to deny her the opportunity to be all she can be.
   (B) men have no business involving themselves in culinary activities.
   (C) careful measurements are needed when investigating these issues.
   (D) barriers to female advancement had been largely removed.

4. How does Sojourner Truth primarily use religious teachings to make her argument?

   (A) She uses them to demonstrate the strength of females.
   (B) She emphasizes the need for women to quietly pray.
   (C) She contradicts them with her personal experiences.
   (D) She believes that she speaks on behalf of divine forces.

5. Which option gives the best evidence for the answer to the previous question?

   (A) Lines 6–7 ("Nobody . . . woman")
   (B) Lines 13–14 ("Then . . . honey")
   (C) Lines 20–22 ("If the . . . again")
   (D) Lines 23–24 ("And . . . say")

6. As used in line 30, the word "compel" most closely means

   (A) suggest.
   (B) force.
   (C) demonstrate.
   (D) list.

7. Passage 2 argues that women's suffrage should happen

   (A) after a long delay.
   (B) when all foreign countries have done so.
   (C) after political parties have considered the issue thoroughly.
   (D) immediately.

8. Which option gives the best evidence for the answer to the previous question?

   (A) Lines 26–28 ("There . . . countries")
   (B) Lines 34–35 ("Do . . . enfranchisement")
   (C) Lines 36–38 ("Your . . . us")
   (D) Lines 42–44 ("There . . . come")

9. Lines 45–46 ("The idea . . may") can best be paraphrased as which one of the following statements?

(A) Women who do not have the right to vote are finally starting to come around to the idea.
(B) Those politicians who oppose women's suffrage will likely face major political consequences.
(C) A complete overthrow of the U.S. government is about to occur.
(D) Policy makers need to have a better grasp of the true threats to internal security.

10. The authors of both passages seek social

(A) hierarchy.
(B) repression.
(C) equality.
(D) isolation.

11. The aims of Passage 1 and Passage 2 are, respectively,

(A) more general and more focused.
(B) more casual and less goal-oriented.
(C) less opinionated and more detailed.
(D) less intense and more historical

Passage A3

Earthquakes

In 2010, a devastating earthquake in Haiti left over 100,000 people dead and thousands more injured. Hundreds of thousands of homes and businesses were destroyed in a matter of minutes. Several factors contributed to the loss of life and property in Haiti, including socioeconomics and the magnitude of the quake.

Line

(5)   But what even causes an earthquake and what makes it so severe? Think about sitting still at your desk. Even if you aren't actively moving, your body is still technically in motion. This is due to plate tectonics and the constant shift of those plates on the surface of the earth. When tension builds up between these plates, they sometimes fracture and fault. This fracturing and faulting is what causes an earthquake.

(10)   Specifically, the rocks have a tremendous amount of potential energy built up between them as they press on each other. When these rocks break or "fault," it causes a seismic wave that makes the "ground shake" characteristic of an earthquake. People can sometimes feel earthquakes, but other times they're so small that only specialized machines detect them. These machines are called "seismographs."

(15)   Earthquakes are measured on the Richter scale, which is named for its inventor, Charles Francis Richter. The Richter scale goes from 0 to 10 plus, with lower numbers representing smaller quakes, and higher numbers representing larger quakes. People rarely feel an earthquake with a magnitude of 2 or lower. These are the types that need to be picked up by a seismograph or they will go largely unnoticed.

(20)   An earthquake with a magnitude of 3.0–3.9 is called a "minor earthquake." These can usually be felt by most people, but very rarely cause any damage. Often times, people end up attributing these small quakes to other causes like large trucks passing or large public transit vehicles. Earthquakes on the higher end of this range may cause slight shaking of household objects.

(25)   Once an earthquake reaches the range of 4.0–4.9, it is almost always felt by the majority of people. These "light earthquakes" will cause marginally more severe shaking, and may knock objects off shelves. These quakes are still highly unlikely to cause any damage, other than to knocked over tchotchkes.

An earthquake with a magnitude of 5.0 or higher will definitely be felt by people,
(30) and at this level, there will start to be damage to buildings. "Moderate earthquakes," those with a magnitude of 5.0–5.9, rarely cause damage to well-constructed buildings, but sometimes older ones will experience cracked foundations, electrical trouble, and sinking.

In a "strong earthquake," a quake with a magnitude of 6.0–6.9, damage will be seen
(35) in most buildings unless they are built to be "earthquake resistant." The damage seen

in these buildings will be similar to those done by moderate quakes except it will be more severe and happen to more buildings.

Typically, there will not be complete collapse of buildings until the level of a "major earthquake." These earthquakes with a magnitude of 7.0–7.9 can be felt many miles (40) from the epicenter of the earthquake and can cause thousands of dollars' worth of damage.

"Great earthquakes" are those with a Richter level of 8.0 or higher. Major damage will occur even to earthquake resistant buildings. At 9.0 or higher, there will be perma- nent changes to the ground geography. There will also be near to total destruction of (45) most buildings in the area.

The earthquake in Haiti had a magnitude of 7.0. However, the damage was more severe than one would expect due to the types of buildings common in Haiti. To make buildings "earthquake resistant," as mentioned above, is much more expensive than building typical structures. This is an unimaginable luxury to many Haitians who live (50) on less than $2 a day. Additionally, the lack of infrastructure led many buildings to be in violation of "codes" meant to keep people safe in times of disaster.

Dates and Locations of Major Earthquakes

Year	Location	Magnitude
1138	Aleppo, Syria	8.5
1556	Shaanxi, China	8.0
1908	Messina, Italy	7.1*
1927	Xining, China	7.9
1960	Valdivia, Chile	9.5
1976	Tangshan, China	8.2
2004	Sumatra, Indonesia	9.2
2008	Sichuan, China	8.0
2010	Port-au-Prince, Haiti	7.0
2011	Tohoku, Japan	9.0
2015	Kathmandu and Pokhara, Nepal	7.8

1. What is the point of the passage?

    (A) To educate the reader about Haiti's economy and culture
    (B) To discuss in detail the major earthquakes throughout history
    (C) To inform about earthquake science and a specific earthquake
    (D) To review plate tectonics and the science of seismographs

2. Assume that a moderate earthquake damaged 30% of the buildings built before 1960 in Town A. If the earthquake had been a strong earthquake instead, the passage most strongly suggests that what would be the resulting damage?

    (A) More than half of the buildings would fall down.
    (B) Fifty percent of the buildings would be damaged.
    (C) The town would experience no damage.
    (D) There would be permanent changes to the geography.

3. According to the passage, what can be done to minimize earthquake damage to buildings?

    (A) New buildings should replace old buildings.
    (B) Buildings should not be built on fault lines.
    (C) Buildings can be built to be earthquake resistant.
    (D) Early repairs after earthquakes are essential.

4. Which option gives the best evidence for the answer to the previous question?

    (A) Lines 25–28 ("Once an . . . tchotchkes")
    (B) Lines 29–33 ("An earthquake . . . sinking")
    (C) Lines 34–37 ("In a . . . buildings")
    (D) Lines 38–41 ("Typically . . . damage")

5. As used in line 24, "slight" most nearly means

    (A) mild.
    (B) quick.
    (C) luminous.
    (D) irrelevant.

6. According to the passage, why did the 2010 earthquake in Haiti result in more damage than would typically be expected for earthquakes of similar magnitude?

    (A) Earthquakes on islands tend to be more severe than on the mainland.
    (B) Many buildings in Haiti were not built to code standards or earthquake resistant.
    (C) Haiti is located in an area that is susceptible to major earthquakes.
    (D) The seismograph in Haiti was faulty and incorrectly measured the magnitude.

7. Which option gives the best evidence for the answer to the previous question?

    (A) Lines 1–3 ("In 2010 . . . minutes")
    (B) Lines 25–27 ("Once . . . shelves")
    (C) Lines 42–44 ("Great . . . geography")
    (D) Lines 47–51 ("To make . . . disaster")

8. As used in line 42, "great" most nearly means

    (A) numerous.
    (B) high.
    (C) boundless.
    (D) big.

9. According to the chart, the greatest magnitude earthquake occurred in which country?

    (A) China
    (B) Chile
    (C) Japan
    (D) Haiti

10. Using the information in the passage and chart, which countries have experienced permanent geographical changes due to earthquakes?

    (A) Chile, China, Italy
    (B) Indonesia, Japan, China
    (C) Haiti, Chile, Italy
    (D) Japan, Chile, Indonesia

11. The Richter scale is a base-10 logarithmic scale in which a 3.0 magnitude earthquake has a shaking amplitude 10 times greater than a 2.0 magnitude earthquake, and a 5.0 magnitude earthquake would have a shaking amplitude 1,000 times greater than a 2.0 magnitude earthquake. Given this information and the information in the chart, how much greater in shaking amplitude was the 2011 Japanese earthquake than the 2010 Haitian earthquake?

    (A) 10 times
    (B) 100 times
    (C) 1,000 times
    (D) 10,000 times

Passage A4

Buyer's Remorse: the European Union and the *Grexit*

Ernest Hemingway once boasted that he could tell a story in six words: "For sale: baby shoes, never worn." Nonetheless, I'm not impressed; ask me to summarize something as vast as the global whole of the 20th Century, and I think I can do him four bet-
Line ter: *Europe fought.* 100 years, eight Popes, and two world wars all boiled down to just
(5) those words. *Europe. Fought.*

Such a volatile connected history makes it all the more fascinating that the entirety of the combative continent was able to redress its respective grievances, apply the salve to decades-old festering wounds, shuck off fervent nationalism, and join together in marital bliss as a veritable European Union.

(10) But the honeymoon—as honeymoons are wont to do—has ended. The initial endorphin rush of uniting toward a greater purpose has long passed, and all of Europe now finds itself in something very much like international relationship counseling. "*He can't manage our finances,*" Germany bemoans as the reluctant breadwinner. "*She refuses to help now that I need her most,*" Greece exclaims. "*Listen to you two! You have no idea of*
(15) *the sordid sort of things that we've seen!*" the rest of the continent marvels, obliged to play a role somewhere between character witness and neutral arbiter in this geopolitical lovers' quarrel. Yet, as the saying goes, "breaking up is *hard to do.*" Now that all lowhanging fruit romantic metaphors have been exhausted, at that crossroads is where we now find ourselves.

(20) Tomorrow, Greece will go before its creditors to learn its fate: either the rest of Europe (read: Germany and Chancellor Angela Merkel) will extend a £1.5 billion loan to the Greeks so that they might pay off a previous International Monetary Fund float, or this idyllic Mediterranean Titan of yore will finally meet its end, defaulting on its debt and hopping the next train toward the ghost town called European Banishment.
(25) Such an exit (dubbed *Grexit* by the media, in their eminent wit) might well be the first domino to fall in a series of developments that could destabilize the region and threaten the validity and vitality of the E.U. henceforth.

Consequential possibilities abound. For one, should Greece receive said funding and be permitted to remain, at what point does Germany tire of paying child support?
(30) The natural conclusion to that fatigue in Berlin would be a harried rummaging through the attic in search of leftover Deutsche marks, desperate to replace the Euro and nostalgic for the autonomy of yesteryear when currency was their own and not some perverted fiscal tragedy of the commons. Moreover, the precedent is set for further disqualification with a *Grexit*; perhaps Spain, Portugal, Ireland, or Italy might be the
(35) next one left without a chair when the music stops, resigned to their fate as wallflowers on the outside looking in.

Yet, perhaps the most troublesome possibility is that an isolated Greece would be an impressionable Greece—desperate both for allies and access to their coffers. Current

Greek optimistic sentiment is that Russia might don its shining armor and rescue the
(40) fledgling castaways with a godsend of a loan. But, given Putin's recent sleight of hand in Crimea, any such lending may not be so much an act of charity as a Trojan Horse; Vladimir's Kremlin friends are a crafty bunch, and their endgame is opaque. Alas, such is the problem with deciphering ulterior motives: they often aren't clear until the history books go to print. The trillion dollar question is, when the ink dries, will the
(45) E.U. be listed in the chapters of current events? Or, will it be relegated to the annals of academia, its skeleton but a diplomatic case study of oil and water, its ashes little more than a *Kennedy School* lecture on the perils of collaboration between square pegs and round holes?

1. What is the overall point of the passage?

    (A) To explain the current challenges of the European Union and ponder its future
    (B) To make the case that Greece should have never been admitted to the European Union
    (C) To convince the reader that a continent-wide currency is a rejection of sound economic theory
    (D) To demonstrate how Russia is often helpful to floundering countries

2. What is the purpose of paragraph 1 with respect to the passage as a whole?

    (A) To give the reader a brief overview of European history
    (B) To demonstrate that the author is a superior writer to Hemingway
    (C) To show that even long stories can be concisely summarized
    (D) To draw the reader's interest by placing the topic of the passage in a global and historical context

3. Which option gives the best evidence for the answer to the previous question?

    (A) Lines 6–9 ("Such . . . Union")
    (B) Lines 10–12 ("But the . . . counseling")
    (C) Lines 20–24 ("Tomorrow . . . Banishment")
    (D) Lines 40–42 ("But . . . opaque")

4. In paragraph 3 (lines 10–19), what primary purpose does the personification of the countries serve?

    (A) To give the reader further insight into the thoughts of the countries' leaders
    (B) To demonstrate how the countries might discuss extending a loan to Greece
    (C) To use a metaphor to further explain the conflict between the countries
    (D) To further predict the consequences of military conflict

5. As used in line 16, "arbiter" most nearly means

    (A) pundit.
    (B) legate.
    (C) helper.
    (D) referee.

6. With which of these statements would the author most likely agree?

   (A) The European Union is innovative and serves as a sound model for other
       continents.
   (B) Without the European Union, Greece may make desperate diplomatic decisions.
   (C) Germany and Chancellor Merkel want to exit the European Union and return to
       Deutsch marks.
   (D) If the *Grexit* occurs, Greece will certainly exploit Russia's finances and natural
       resources.

7. Which option gives the best evidence for the answer to the previous question?

   (A) Lines 6–9 ("Such . . . Union")
   (B) Lines 17–19 ("Now that . . . ourselves")
   (C) Lines 30–33 ("The natural . . . commons")
   (D) Lines 37–38 ("Yet . . . coffers")

8. Lines 25–27 ("Such . . . henceforth.") primarily suggest that the author believes that a
   Greek exit from the European Union

   (A) is all but certain, so must be embraced.
   (B) could have unforeseen and negative consequences.
   (C) will cause the downfall of European civilization.
   (D) should be avoided at all costs.

9. As used in line 33, "perverted" most nearly means

   (A) deviant.
   (B) foreign.
   (C) unfortunate.
   (D) premeditated.

10. Which of the following would most accurately paraphrase lines 44–48 ("The
    trillion . . . holes")?

   (A) Will the countries of the European Union end their conflicts peacefully or by
       resorting to an expensive arms race?
   (B) Will the European Union become obsolete and only read about in textbooks as a
       lesson in things that are dysfunctional?
   (C) Will the *Kennedy School* give frequent lectures about the European Union and its
       success?
   (D) Will the European Union extend a loan to Greece to ensure future success and
       prosperity for all countries?

Passage A5

The Value of Engineering

One of the greatest vocations one could pursue is engineering. Engineers play a central role in transforming our world into a safer, more enjoyable place to live. Consider just one area, which is very close to each of us: our own health. Biomedical engineers
Line have designed incubators that sustain the lives of premature babies, devices and
(5) procedures to diagnose conditions and fight diseases, and equipment to restore bodily functions such as being able to walk or to see. Agricultural and biological engineers develop medicines, create better ways of growing and protecting our food supply, and, along with environmental engineers, help to create a cleaner, safer environment in which to breathe, grow food, and have safe drinking water. Even if you have not met
(10) such an engineer before, they have set an example of how to be good stewards of our resources, and we have all benefitted from what they have done for us.

What exactly is engineering? It is the practical application of scientific knowledge. There are many different areas of engineering. Dr. Seuss helped to open our minds to all the possibilities of what we can do in life in his book *Oh, The Places You'll Go!*
(15) Engineers make this a reality, both literally and figuratively. In the area of transportation, engineers design vehicles to help many people daily get from one place to another, as well as airplanes, space shuttles, and submarines that enable us to explore the far reaches of the planet and beyond. More broadly, there are four major branches of engineering, including chemical, civil, electrical, and mechanical engineering, each
(20) of which has a number of subdisciplines. Then there are different interdisciplinary areas of engineering. From the smallest scope, where nanoengineers and biomolecular engineers design at the level of atoms and molecules, to the largest scope, where civil engineers design bridges and buildings, the options are many.

Being an engineer is intellectually stimulating and provides continual challenges.
(25) You will learn not only how things work, but also why different materials such as woods, metals, or plastics have the properties that they do, depending on their atomic structure and how they were formed. You become trained to identify what problems may exist and how to use your knowledge, skills, and creativity to figure out innovative solutions to fix them. One interesting challenge outlined by the National Academy
(30) of Engineering is to figure out how to control a fusion reaction to provide us with energy in a more efficient, economic, and environmentally friendly way. Or how about discovering how to diagnose and treat conditions people have, based on individual differences? Quickly assessing someone's genetic profile and having a way to deliver patient-specific medications to precise locations using nanoparticles are important
(35) engineering challenges that could improve many people's lives.

It is hard to imagine what life would be like without the contributions engineers have already made. They have not just helped us to survive, be healthy, explore, and move around better, but they have also made life more enjoyable through advances in areas such as communications, computing, and sports. Computer engineers, for

(40) example, have helped develop devices and software that we can use to make and share documents and home videos, listen to our favorite music, and talk with co-workers, friends, and family members across the globe. In sports, different engineers have made systems and devices that provide us with better, safer equipment, communications that enable teams to interact better and games to be televised, and environments and
(45) infrastructure that improve the playing and watching of games.

It is true that everyone has unique desires, so you may prefer a vocation in some other area. But even our desires themselves can be changed and need to be developed, so why not try engineering on a smaller level with a project around the house or follow an engineer around for a while? It might just become the kind of thing you would enjoy
(50) doing even if you were not getting paid, and perhaps you could become the next Orville or Wilbur Wright, coming up with a whole new design that takes us to new heights. Consider also the fruits of engineers' labors: if they have benefitted you so much, why not do something that could benefit others in kind? At the very least, we need to be aware that without the contributions of engineers, our lives would be more impover-
(55) ished, so we have a lot for which to be thankful.

1. What is the overall theme of the passage?

   (A) To convince the reader to pursue engineering and abandon other career goals
   (B) To demonstrate the value of engineering and highlight the field's contributions to society
   (C) To give in-depth examples of how biomedical engineering has improved life for everyone
   (D) To provide context for how even small do-it-yourself home projects should be approached with an engineer's mindset

2. As used in line 10, "stewards" most nearly means

   (A) attendants.
   (B) curators.
   (C) assistants.
   (D) guardians.

3. With which statement would the author most likely agree?

   (A) Everyone can incorporate engineering into his or her life as a hobby or personal interest.
   (B) Biomedical engineering is the most useful branch of engineering and most worthy of academic pursuit.
   (C) Dayton, Ohio, is home to the world's greatest engineering minds, including Orville and Wilbur Wright.
   (D) Colleges should increase their scholarships for students studying engineering.

4. Which option gives the best evidence for the previous question?

    (A) Lines 21–23 ("From the . . . many")

    (B) Lines 29–31 ("One interesting . . . way")

    (C) Lines 47–50 ("But even . . . paid")

    (D) Lines 50–53 ("you could . . . like kind")

5. Why does the author reference Dr. Seuss and his book "Oh The Places You'll Go!" in Paragraph 2 (lines 12–23)?

    (A) To reminiscence with the reader about a beloved childhood book

    (B) To set up a transition to discuss the numerous engineering subspecialties

    (C) To signal to the reader that the author is switching to discussion of a new topic

    (D) To use hyperbole while outlining the various types of engineering

6. What is the purpose of lines 21–23?

    (A) To convince students that engineering is applicable to any field

    (B) To inform the reader of the range of engineering careers

    (C) To make the case that engineering is an intellectually stimulating career

    (D) To review the four main branches of engineering

7. Which paragraph gives the most specific evidence in support of the author's statement in line 4 that engineering has made the world a "more enjoyable place to live?"

    (A) Paragraph 2 (lines 12–23)

    (B) Paragraph 3 (lines 24–35)

    (C) Paragraph 4 (lines 36–45)

    (D) Paragraph 5 (lines 46–55)

8. Why does the author mention the National Academy of Engineering challenge in lines 29–31?

    (A) To inform the reader about the difficulty of controlling a fusion reaction

    (B) To lament about the lack of clean, renewable energy sources

    (C) To encourage the reader to enter the contest

    (D) To cite an authority to add credibility to his case

9. What is the point of paragraph 4 (lines 36–45)?

    (A) To make the reader feel that engineering is an accessible career

    (B) To show how life would be different without engineers

    (C) To highlight the contributions of computer and sport engineers

    (D) To give examples of how engineers' contributions are used in daily life

10. As used in lines 54–55, the phrase "more impoverished" most nearly means

    (A) emptier.

    (B) insolvent.

    (C) unproductive.

    (D) indigent.

ANSWER KEY

Passage A1

1.	**A**	3.	**C**	5.	**B**	7.	**A**	9.	**C**
2.	**B**	4.	**D**	6.	**B**	8.	**D**	10.	**D**

Passage A2

1.	**A**	4.	**A**	7.	**D**	10.	**C**
2.	**B**	5.	**C**	8.	**D**	11.	**A**
3.	**A**	6.	**B**	9.	**B**		

Passage A3

1.	**C**	4.	**C**	7.	**D**	10.	**D**
2.	**B**	5.	**A**	8.	**D**	11.	**B**
3.	**C**	6.	**B**	9.	**B**		

Passage A4

1.	**A**	3.	**A**	5.	**D**	7.	**D**	9.	**C**
2.	**D**	4.	**C**	6.	**B**	8.	**B**	10.	**B**

Passage A5

1.	**B**	3.	**A**	5.	**B**	7.	**C**	9.	**D**
2.	**B**	4.	**C**	6.	**B**	8.	**B**	10.	**A**

ANSWERS EXPLAINED

Passage A1

1. **(A)** The passage as a whole describes the unusual experiences of a boy in the "Satis House" and how those experiences come to change his life. The passage does not give evidence that the boy seduces the girl. (C) and (D) are related to details within the passage, but not accurate summaries of the main idea.

2. **(B)** The passage progresses chronologically, beginning with Pip's first time meeting Miss Havisham and Estella, and moving to sequential meetings. It is not structured around spaces or the significance of details. (D) is tempting, but incorrect because the passage is told in past tense rather than "flashbacks," and there is no evidence that the narrator's reflections have been altered by time.

3. **(C)** Lines 3–7 provide the backstory for how Pip came to the house of Miss Havisham. (A), (B), and (D) all come later.

4. **(D)** *Laying* is the best choice here since it refers to Miss Havisham's elbow "resting" on the table.

5. **(B)** Miss Havisham is described by the narrator as strange, so *unusual* is correct. (A) is the opposite of strange. (C) and (D) don't work because the room and the bride are dull

and colorless. Similarly, words like *grim, seclusion,* and *withered* give evidence that Miss Havisham is anything but lively.

6. **(B)** gives direct evidence that the narrator believes Miss Havisham is strange looking. (A) gives detail of the appearance of the house rather than the inhabitant. (C) describes Miss Havisham's emotional state rather than her appearance. (D) doesn't refer to Miss Havisham at all.

7. **(A)** This can be seen best in lines 39–41 and 52–54. Pip becomes aware of his lowliness and becomes dissatisfied with himself, even "ashamed of home." (B) and (C) are opposite of his feelings. Finally, (D) has a positive connotation that does not make sense here.

8. **(D)** Lines 52–54 refer to Pip's feelings upon leaving Miss Havisham's after inquiring about Estella. He "went home dissatisfied and uncomfortable." (A), (B), and (C) don't discuss Pip's feelings about his social and/or economic situation.

9. **(C)** These lines refer to Pip's first time leaving the gloomy house of Miss Havisham. Here, he feels ill at ease and disquieted, becoming insecure with himself for the first time in his life. The other options don't fit this mood accurately.

10. **(D)** *Troubled* is the best choice. (A) is too strong of a word. (B) and (C) inaccurately portray the narrator's shame as a power or strong point.

Passage A2

1. **(A)** Sojourner Truth, the speaker of Passage 1, is adamant that women can do the things men can do, and do them without a man's help. Thus, it is accurate to say she is emphatic about (A). She does not believe women are dependent on men or confined to the home as in (B) and (C). (D) is not discussed.

2. **(B)** *Predicament* fits here because line 3 refers to white men being in a *fix*, or a difficult situation. Choices (A), (C), and (D) refer to synonyms of *fix*, but don't precisely fit this meaning.

3. **(A)** Lines 15–16 indicate that measure of intellect is irrelevant on the basis that one should be allowed to pursue whatever it is they are capable of pursuing. For the speaker, even if she is not as intellectual as some, she should be afforded the little she is qualified for. Thus, (A) is the accurate choice.

4. **(A)** Truth's first reference to religion involves the reversal of an objection that women are inferior because Jesus Christ was a man. In reply, she states that Christ came from "God and a woman," attesting to women's significance. Next, she uses the story of Eve to contend that women are strong enough to upset and repair the world. Choice (A) is the only answer that accurately interprets her use of religion to exhibit womanly import.

5. **(C)** Lines 20–22 state that the first woman "was strong enough to turn the world upside down all alone," and that the united female population is certainly strong enough "to turn it back." Thus, these lines provide evidence of women's strength and give the answer for the previous question. Choices (A), (B), and (D) are incorrect because they do not refer to the speaker's use of religious teachings.

6. **(B)** In lines 29–31, Catt argues that Congress's approach to suffrage compels, or forces, women to beg their intellectual inferiors for freedom. It is not precise to say women are *suggested*, *demonstrated*, or *listed* to beg their inferiors.

7. **(D)** According to the second passage, "The time for woman suffrage has come." Hence, *immediately* is the correct answer. None of the other choices refer to instantaneous action.

8. **(D)** Lines 42–44 state that ideas are more powerful than Congress, and that the time for women's suffrage "has come." Hence, these are the lines that provide direct evidence for the previous question. (A) refers to the limitations on women's freedoms. (B) indicates the current attitude of women. And (C) urges Congress to act on their promises, but doesn't specify a time.

9. **(B)** To paraphrase, Catt proposes that the idea of suffrage will only get stronger, while the political party that refuses to acknowledge it will fade. So, (B) is the right choice. (A) is too lukewarm. (C) is too extreme. And while Catt is acknowledging the dying out of a party who refuses to adopt women's freedoms, she is not discussing internal security as in (D).

10. **(C)** Both speakers are advocating for women's right to vote, so *equality* is correct. *Hierarchy* refers to an uneven ranking system. *Repression* is "to control or hold back by force." And *isolation* means "a state of solitude or separation."

11. **(A)** Truth advocates for general suffrage, and she includes all women in her speech. Catt specifies a type of woman and calls for immediate action. Both women are passionate and earnest. So, (A) is accurate. It is wrong to characterize Truth as casual or Catt as without firm goals. And while Catt's goals are specified and detailed, Truth is not less opinionated. And finally, (D) is incorrect because in no way is Truth less intense.

Passage A3

1. **(C)** The purpose of this passage is twofold. The author is informative about earthquakes generally, and also focuses more specifically on one earthquake which devastated the nation of Haiti in 2010. The passage doesn't focus on Haiti's economy or culture, doesn't discuss several major earthquakes, and doesn't get into the science of seismographs.

2. **(B)** According to the passage, a moderate earthquake will cause damage to only older buildings, while a strong earthquake will cause damage in most buildings. However, collapse is not common until the level of a major earthquake. So, (B) is the only plausible answer.

3. **(C)** The author points out that buildings can avoid damage in a strong earthquake if they are "built to be 'earthquake resistant.'" Thus, (C) is correct. While choices (A), (B), and (D) could all be true, they are not evidenced in the passage.

4. **(C)** Lines 34–37 specifically state that buildings which are "earthquake resistant" will remain intact while most other buildings suffer real damage in a strong earthquake. (A) discusses light earthquakes that do not cause infrastructural damage. (B) indicates that moderate level quakes will only damage unsound buildings. And (D) refers to the severe level of earthquakes that will collapse buildings despite their structure.

5. **(A)** *Mild* is an appropriate word, since this line refers to "slight earthquakes." The other choices do not accurately depict a level of severity or magnitude.

6. **(B)** According to the author, lack of sound infrastructure within Haiti resulted in a major earthquake in 2010 causing aberrant (unusual or abnormal) damage. The passage provides no support for (A) or (D). And while (C) explains why Haiti would be more likely to experience earthquakes, the question is focused on why an earthquake of a given magnitude caused more severe damage than would have been the case with an earthquake of the same intensity in another location.

7. **(D)** Lines 46–50 return to the topic of Haiti, stating that "the damage was more severe than one would expect due to the types of buildings common in Haiti." So, these lines testify to the previous question. (A) underscores the widespread death and destruction caused by the earthquake in 2010, but doesn't address why the damage might be unexpected for the quake's magnitude. Finally, choices (B) and (C) merely address the classifications for different levels of earthquakes.

8. **(D)** Line 42 refers to "great earthquakes" which cause major damage. *Big* is the only word choice to depict an immense size and strength. And unlike the previous Words in Context question, there is not a higher level that could be confused with *big*. *Boundless* could refer to an immense size or space, but inaccurately suggests that the earthquake is unlimited.

9. **(B)** A 9.5 earthquake—the highest on the graph—occurred in Chile in 1960, making (B) the correct option.

10. **(D)** Permanent changes to the ground geography only occur in earthquakes at a level of 9.0 or higher according to lines 43–44. The graph only shows three instances of such magnitude, in Chile, Indonesia, and Japan.

11. **(B)** According to the question, the Richter scale operates on a scale that multiplies a shaking amplitude by 10 for every increment. So, if the Haitian earthquake was a 7.0 and the Japanese earthquake was a 9.0, there is a two-increment difference—or 10 × 10. Thus, (B) is the correct answer.

Passage A4

1. **(A)** The author considers the fate of the European Union, specifically deliberating on the current conflict regarding Greece. So (A) is correct. The author does not argue (B) or take up economic theory as in (C). Last, Russia is but a detail within the passage.

2. **(D)** Paragraph one emphasizes the unpredictable violence of an entire century in Europe which makes its subsequent solidarity more unlikely. Since the author only covers one century, (A) is not accurate. Choices (B) and (C) misunderstand the literary reference to be the author's point, when really it is a device to initiate the topic.

3. **(A)** Lines 6–9 are the lines that directly follow the first paragraph and suggest fascination that such a violent interaction could result in the European Union. Thus, they support the previous question. (B) introduces the current conflict within the E.U. (C) details the decision that must be made to address the current conflict. And (D) describes Russia's unreliability as an ally. So the remaining choices do not address how the first paragraph works with respect to the rest of the passage.

4. **(C)** Lines 10–19 give details of the current conflict in Europe using personification to generally outline what's going on, so (C). The dialogue is not representative of actual conversations, ruling out (A) and (B). And finally, the passage doesn't refer to military conflict as in (D).

5. **(D)** *Arbiter* can be defined as a person or party who has authority over or settles a dispute. In line 16, the author posits the majority of European countries as "somewhere between character witness and neutral arbiter." *Pundit* means expert. *Legate* refers to "an emissary" or "representative of the pope." And (C) doesn't suggest any authority.

6. **(B)** The author suggests that the most alarming possibility of the current conflict is "an impressionable Greece" that would take bold measures to gain friends and resources. There is obvious uncertainty around the EU model, so (A) is nonsensical. And (C) and (D) are not evidenced by the passage.

7. **(D)** Lines 37–38 directly state that the biggest worry involves a Greece "desperate both for allies and access to their coffers," thereby providing evidence for the previous question. (A) simply states the discrepancy of a volatile continent unifying. (B) references the crossroads where the E.U. is now. And (C) is a mere speculation of how Germany could respond if things continue the way they are.

8. **(B)** Lines 25–27 compare Greece's exit to "the first domino to fall in a series of developments that could destabilize the region." Hence, we might say that the Greek exit could provoke other adverse circumstances. The matter is unresolved at the writing of this passage, so (A) wouldn't work. (C) is much too extreme. And finally, the passage doesn't take sides so (D) is incorrect as well.

9. **(C)** *Unfortunate* works here because "perverted" is used to describe the common currency that Germany could imaginably neglect in favor of their own independent currency. Choice (C) is the only word choice that suggests undesirability.

10. **(B)** Lines 44–48 pose the question of whether the E.U. will survive. An appropriate paraphrasing can be found in choice (B). The passage does not indicate an arms race as in (A). The concern is not actually whether lectures will be given about the E.U., but instead if it will become something purely historical. And finally, the question of whether Greece is afforded a loan was risen earlier, and is a sub-question to this larger question.

Passage A5

1. **(B)** The passage is very interested in conveying the extensive impacts of the vast field of engineering, and is supremely appreciative of engineering contributions thus far. So, (B) is right. While the author does bring up engineering as a career field and offers examples of biomedical contributions, they are details rather than themes of the passage. (D) is not supported by the passage.

2. **(D)** Lines 10–11 states that engineers have exemplified "how to be good stewards of our resources." Before this statement, the author discusses how agricultural, biological, and environmental engineers have helped to create a cleaner, safer, and all-around higher quality environment for us. Hence, *guardian*, or "protector" is the closest meaning. *Curators* are keepers of museums. Finally, both *attendants* and *assistants* indicate helpers, so they are too tepid for this context.

3. **(A)** The author would surely agree that engineering can be incorporated into everyone's life since he or she sees it as an expansive field with unlimited affiliations. He or she does not advocate for one branch over another, ruling out (B). While the passage does reference the Wright brothers, the author doesn't compare intellect as in (C). And the author doesn't address college scholarships, making (D) irrelevant.

4. **(C)** Lines 46–49 indicate that despite one's interests or desires, there is some applicability within the field of engineering for everybody, even just for fun. This provides evidence for the previous question. (A) suggests the expansiveness of engineering careers. (B) delivers an intriguing challenge that specific engineers face. And (D) discusses rewards of engineering. Although all three of these other choices advocate for engineering, none address engineering as a hobby.

5. **(B)** Look directly before this sentence and directly after it. Dr. Seuss is used as a set-up for the infinite areas and interests of the engineering profession. Hence, (B) is the accurate choice. The author does not become reminiscent as in (A). Although the book is used as a transition, the change of topic was signaled in the previous sentence. And since *hyperbole* means "exaggeration," we can rule this out on the grounds that the author is not exaggerating the various fields of engineering.

6. **(B)** Lines 21–23 state that "the options are many" for professional engineers. Hence, (B) is correct. While the other choices are addressed within the passage, they are not engaged within these lines.

7. **(C)** The question is asking which lines prove that engineering has made daily life enjoyable. Lines 36–45 consider the implications of engineers on "communications, computing, and sports," focusing on the entertainment industry. Paragraph 2 defines engineering more broadly. Paragraph 3 expresses the enticement of the career itself. And Paragraph 5 describes how engineering can be part of everyone's life even if it isn't one's career choice.

8. **(D)** In this paragraph, the author is explaining the intellectual stimulation of life as an engineer. When he or she references the National Academy of Engineering, it is to provide an authentic example of this stimulation. So, (D) is correct because he or she is making a case and adding credibility.

9. **(D)** Paragraph 4 discusses the contributions engineers have made to making life more enjoyable, specifically in the daily areas of "communications, computing, and sports." Hence, (D) is right. The author has moved away from discussing engineering specifically as a career, ruling out (A). And (C) is incorrect because the author is considering how engineers from varying fields have impacted communications and sports, rather than focusing on two types of engineers. Choice (B) is tempting, but the author's purpose is to show how entirely engineers have impacted certain aspects of our daily life, not to illustrate how our lives would be different without them.

10. **(A)** Lines 54–55 states that without engineers, "our lives would be more impoverished." The best word meaning is (A), *emptier. Insolvent* means "bankrupt." *Unproductive* indicates "barrenness or unprofitability." *Indigent* is "poor and needy." So, all the remaining choices imprecisely imply that our economic situations would be different without engineers, which is not the point the passage is making.

PRACTICE EXERCISE B

These passages and questions are generally representative of average-difficulty passages and questions you could face on the SAT. Take about 13 minutes for each passage (including reading and answering the questions). Detailed answer explanations follow.

Passage B1

This is an excerpt from Charlotte Bronte's Jane Eyre, *written in 1847. Jane, previously a governess at Thornfield Hall, is engaged to marry the wealthy homeowner Mr. Rochester. She fretfully relays unexpected events to him that have recently occurred in his absence.*

"I dreamt another dream, sir: that Thornfield Hall was a dreary ruin, the retreat of bats and owls. I thought that of all the stately front nothing remained but a shell-like wall, very high and very fragile-looking. I wandered, on a moonlight night, through
Line the grass-grown enclosure within: here I stumbled over a marble hearth, and there
(5) over a fallen fragment of cornice. Wrapped up in a shawl, I still carried the unknown little child: I might not lay it down anywhere, however tired were my arms—however much its weight impeded my progress, I must retain it. I heard the gallop of a horse at a distance on the road; I was sure it was you; and you were departing for many years and for a distant country. I climbed the thin wall with frantic perilous haste, eager
(10) to catch one glimpse of you from the top: the stones rolled from under my feet, the ivy branches I grasped gave way, the child clung round my neck in terror, and almost strangled me; at last I gained the summit. I saw you like a speck on a white track, lessening every moment. The blast blew so strong I could not stand. I sat down on the narrow ledge; I hushed the scared infant in my lap: you turned an angle of the road: I
(15) bent forward to take a last look; the wall crumbled; I was shaken; the child rolled from my knee, I lost my balance, fell, and woke."

"Now, Jane, that is all."

"All the preface, sir; the tale is yet to come. On waking, a gleam dazzled my eyes; I thought—Oh, it is daylight! But I was mistaken; it was only candlelight. Sophie, I
(20) supposed, had come in. There was a light in the dressing-table, and the door of the closet, where, before going to bed, I had hung my wedding-dress and veil, stood open; I heard a rustling there. I asked, 'Sophie, what are you doing?' No one answered; but a form emerged from the closet; it took the light, held it aloft, and surveyed the garments pendent from the portmanteau. 'Sophie! Sophie!' I again cried: and still it was silent. I
(25) had risen up in bed, I bent forward: first surprise, then bewilderment, came over me; and then my blood crept cold through my veins. Mr. Rochester, this was not Sophie, it was not Leah, it was not Mrs. Fairfax: it was not—no, I was sure of it, and am still—it was not even that strange woman, Grace Poole."

"It must have been one of them," interrupted my master.

(30)   "No, sir, I solemnly assure you to the contrary. The shape standing before me had never crossed my eyes within the precincts of Thornfield Hall before; the height, the contour were new to me."

"Describe it, Jane."

"It seemed, sir, a woman, tall and large, with thick and dark hair hanging long down
(35) her back. I know not what dress she had on: it was white and straight; but whether gown, sheet, or shroud, I cannot tell."

"Did you see her face?"

"Not at first. But presently she took my veil from its place; she held it up, gazed at it long, and then she threw it over her own head, and turned to the mirror. At that
(40) moment I saw the reflection of the visage and features quite distinctly in the dark oblong glass."

"And how were they?"

"Fearful and ghastly to me—oh, sir, I never saw a face like it! It was a discoloured face—it was a savage face. I wish I could forget the roll of the red eyes and the fearful
(45) blackened inflation of the lineaments!"

"Ghosts are usually pale, Jane."

"This, sir, was purple: the lips were swelled and dark; the brow furrowed: the black eyebrows widely raised over the bloodshot eyes. Shall I tell you of what it reminded me?"

(50)   "You may."

"Of the foul German spectre—the Vampyre."

"Ah!—what did it do?"

"Sir, it removed my veil from its gaunt head, rent it in two parts, and flinging both on the floor, trampled on them."

1. What option best summarizes the passage?

   (A) A character shares troubling portents for the future.
   (B) A character seeks counsel for her terrifying dreams.
   (C) Two characters determine how to overcome supernatural forces.
   (D) Two characters recount their respective travels.

2. Mr. Rochester's overall attitude towards Jane is best described as

   (A) dismissive impatience.
   (B) skeptical depression.
   (C) anxious trepidation.
   (D) respectful curiosity.

3. As used in line 7, the word "retain" most closely means

   (A) remember.
   (B) collect.
   (C) hold onto.
   (D) sacrifice.

4. In her dream, how did Jane first perceive the presence of Mr. Rochester?

   (A) Through sight
   (B) Through hearing
   (C) Through smell
   (D) Through touch

5. Which option gives the best evidence for the answer to the previous question?

   (A) Lines 7–9 ("I heard . . . country")
   (B) Lines 9–12 ("I climbed . . . summit")
   (C) Lines 14–16 ("I bent . . . woke")
   (D) Lines 43–45 ("Fearful . . . lineaments")

6. The most likely purpose of Jane's statement in line 18 ("All . . . come") is to

   (A) give a description.
   (B) demonstrate her respect.
   (C) describe a character.
   (D) provide a transition.

7. As used in line 23, the word "form" most closely means

   (A) entity.
   (B) creation.
   (C) system.
   (D) clothing.

8. Lines 26–28 ("Mr. . . . Poole") mainly serve to

   (A) vividly describe an apparition.
   (B) describe residents of Thornfield Hall.
   (C) anticipate and address a likely objection.
   (D) recount troubling memories from a dream.

9. The frightening intruder as described by Jane

   (A) strongly resembles a household servant.
   (B) is quite unique in its terrible attributes.
   (C) is weak and about to suffer collapse.
   (D) is rather likely to transform into a bat.

10. Which option gives the best evidence for the answer to the previous question?

    (A) Line 3 ("Very high . . . looking")
    (B) Lines 22–23 ("I asked . . . closet")
    (C) Lines 43–44 ("Fearful . . . face")
    (D) Line 51 ("Of . . . Vampyre")

Passage B2

Chemistry of Cooking

We tend to think of cooking as an art, but much of its basis actually comes from chemistry. Let's take, for instance, the example of cooking meat. Why do we bother with cooking meat? For one, it kills the bacteria that can live in meat and be harmful to us. But additionally, it makes the meat much more tender—easier to eat and easier to digest.

Line

(5)   Typically, protein is the second-highest component of meat behind water. Proteins have several levels of organization. A protein's primary structure is the order in which the amino acids are joined by their peptide bonds. A protein's secondary structure is made up of local interactions of the primary structure. Secondary structure includes alpha helices, beta sheets, turns, and loops. Tertiary structure is formed when various

(10)   secondary structures interact, typically over long distances. Finally, quaternary structure is the interaction of different protein subunits. Proteins fold tightly in complex ways that are energetically and sterically favorable. So what happens to this complex organization when meat is heated? These interactions become weaker. Proteins denature, meaning their interactions weaken and their quaternary, tertiary, and second-

(15)   ary structures break down. Instead of tightly folded proteins, they become loose and stretched out. This denaturation is what makes meat more tender. However, continuing to cook meat after this initial denaturation serves only to remove water, making the meat tougher and drier. In particular, the denaturation of collagen makes meat more tender. Collagen is the most abundant protein in animal connective tissue. Tougher

(20)   cuts of meat tend to have more connective tissue, and thus more collagen.

But heating proteins isn't the only way to denature them: they can also be denatured by adding certain denaturing substances. Many of these substances, like strong acids and bases, you wouldn't want to add to your food; however, one common denaturing agent is salt. This is why you may want to brine a tougher cut of meat in

(25)   addition to cooking it. Brining involves soaking something in a solution of salt water. Another benefit of brining is that when the meat absorbs the salt, this draws water into the meat to dilute the salt. Thus, brining also serves to keep meat moist. Some chefs will advise searing the outside of a cut of meat before cooking it through to lock in the moisture. However, chemistry doesn't support this approach: steam is equally capable

(30)   of escaping through a seared crust as it is through non-seared meat.

If you've ever cooked red meat, you know that as it cooks, it turns brown. Red meat is red because of its high myoglobin content. Myoglobin is an oxygen-storing protein found in muscle cells. It is associated with an iron atom. Before the meat is cooked, the iron atom is in the +2 oxidation state. Cooking it removes an electron, thus changing it to the

(35)   +3 oxidation state. This transforms the color to brown. On the other hand, white meat doesn't turn brown because it doesn't have nearly as much myoglobin to be oxidized.

We rarely pause mid-recipe to consider the chemistry of cooking, but understanding the chemical reactions occurring in our food will help us to become better cooks. Isn't that some food for thought?

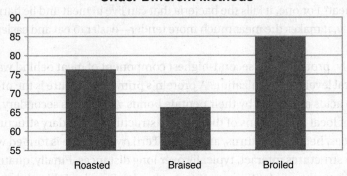

Mean Percent Yield of Meat Cooked Under Different Methods

1. It can be reasonably inferred from the passage that which of these protein structures is LEAST impacted by heating?

   (A) Primary
   (B) Secondary
   (C) Tertiary
   (D) Quaternary

2. Which option gives the best evidence for the answer to the previous question?

   (A) Lines 7–9 ("A protein's . . . loops")
   (B) Lines 9–10 ("Tertiary . . . distances")
   (C) Lines 10–12 ("Finally . . . favorable")
   (D) Lines 13–15 ("Proteins . . . down")

3. The sentence in lines 12–13 ("So what . . . heated") serves to

   (A) define a term.
   (B) explain an effect.
   (C) provide a transition.
   (D) analyze an observation.

4. As used in line 13, the word "weaker" most closely means

   (A) defeated.
   (B) loosened.
   (C) pathetic.
   (D) fatigued.

5. According to the passage, which of these cooking approaches would have the most negligible effect on the tenderness of meat?

   (A) Cooking past protein denaturation
   (B) Brining it in salt water
   (C) Searing it before further cooking
   (D) Using an acid or base to denature

6. Which option gives the best evidence for the answer to the previous question?

   (A) Lines 16–18 ("However . . . drier")
   (B) Lines 22–24 ("Many . . . salt")
   (C) Lines 26–27 ("Another . . . salt")
   (D) Lines 29–30 ("However . . . meat")

7. As used in line 39, the phrase "some food for thought" most closely means

   (A) an appetizing situation.
   (B) a next step for researchers.
   (C) a plan for actionable change.
   (D) something worth considering.

8. The passage explicitly states that the substance most directly responsible for the browning of meat is

   (A) collagen.
   (B) myoglobin.
   (C) quaternary structure.
   (D) zirconium.

9. Based on the information in the graph and on lines 19–20 ("Collagen . . . collagen"), what type of cooking method would most likely be most appropriate for a tough cut of meat?

   (A) Roasting, given its moderate yield.
   (B) Braising, given its potential to eliminate a greater proportion of the undesirable parts of the meat.
   (C) Broiling, since virtually all of the meat tissue would be preserved.
   (D) All three methods would be equivalent as far as their appropriateness.

10. According to the graph, broiled meat's yield is about how much greater than braised meat's yield?

    (A) Three times
    (B) Two times
    (C) Fifty percent more
    (D) A third more

Passage B3

Two passages from 2015 written about the Philosophy of Education

PASSAGE 1

Teachers have one true job: to inspire. *Educate* comes from the Latin word *educare* meaning "bring out and lead forth;" therefore, it is the duty of the teacher to open the minds of students and to guide them into new places. It is not nearly as important
Line to divulge knowledge as it is to stimulate a desire and love for the thing itself. Teaching,
(5) when done properly, allows a second chance for students to contemplate those values and beliefs that have been imparted to them. In venturing to these new places, teachers have the opportunity to unleash active and independent-thinking humans.

Consider the average student, constantly told what to believe and how to act—a
(10) robotic imitator of cultural values and societal standards. Yet, the teacher has the power to make all the difference. The teacher is the opener of the dormant mind, the bringer of the epiphany, the supplier of the moment of change. A classroom that fails to challenge a student's fundamental principles and create a hunger for lifetime learning fails altogether. Whether teaching the humanities or the sciences, the educa-
(15) tor is the one who lays out a puzzle and pilots instances of profound, sublime enlight-enment. A student lucky enough to study under a true teacher is never satisfied, but instead is relentlessly looking for answers.

It is through inspiration that a teacher teaches a student to think. Educating is not the business of memorization but the business of inquiry. The student-teacher
(20) dichotomy is one of reciprocated wonderment with each party undergoing continu-ous improvement. And an effective instructor is merely the one responsible for that curiosity in the minds of his or her students. It was Robert Frost who said, "I am not a teacher, but an awakener."

PASSAGE 2

I became a teacher because it was the noblest profession I could think of. Get this:
(25) I impart knowledge. I am responsible for instilling the foundation in the next genera-tion of professionals and leaders. It all sounds very romantic, but the job comes down to an ability to simplify and explain those concepts that make up the core curriculum. If I cannot communicate clearly with my students, if I cannot come to their level and make the instruction relevant and accessible, then I fail.

(30)   In the words of Ralph Waldo Emerson: "The man who can make hard things easy is the educator." And that is my job. My philosophy relies on giving your children the best possible start. I am the opener of doors. I believe in providing an optimal learning environment to attack the core subjects rigorously, allowing each student to walk out feeling confident and prepared, whether it be for graduation tests, college-entrance

(35) exams, or the job market. So my skill is just this: I bridge the gap between student and textbook.

As a compassionate *and* passionate educator, I know the competition your child faces. I am interested in breaking down the barriers that intimidate students and providing the path that will get them better college offers, better careers, and most sig-
(40) nificantly, a better quality of life. To do this, I adopt a perspective of peak preparation at all costs. My classroom is responsible for instilling the concepts and skills that will be tested and evaluated, and it is a responsibility that I do not take lightly. It is these standards and basics—which every student of mine will come to know and under-stand—that often determine a student's future success. Because I take my position as
(45) educator so seriously, you can trust me to have your child ready for the next step.

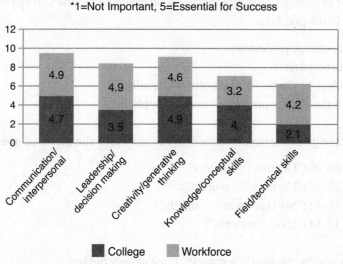

Survey of 100 randomly selected college professors and 100 randomly selected employers.

1. As used in lines 6–7, the phrase "venturing to these new places" most closely means

   (A) traveling to a new location.
   (B) investing in a new business.
   (C) introducing new ideas.
   (D) questioning one's past choices.

2. Based on lines 16–17 ("A student . . . answers"), a teacher is most responsible for imparting which virtue to his or her students?

   (A) Knowledge
   (B) Truth
   (C) Diligence
   (D) Curiosity

3. The author of passage 2 would most likely be interested in the survey responses, as portrayed in the graph, of

   (A) just the college professors.
   (B) just the employers.
   (C) the college professors and employers equally.
   (D) neither the college professors nor the employers.

4. Which option gives the best evidence for the answer to the previous question?

   (A) Lines 24–26 ("Get this . . . leaders")
   (B) Lines 32–35 ("I believe . . . market")
   (C) Lines 41–42 ("My classroom . . . lightly")
   (D) Lines 42–44 ("It is . . . success")

5. As used in line 26, the word "romantic" most closely means

   (A) idealistic.
   (B) passionate.
   (C) loving.
   (D) emotional.

6. Lines 37–41 most strongly imply that the author of Passage 2 places a premium on

   (A) physical exertion.
   (B) intellectual contemplation.
   (C) rigorous expectations.
   (D) logical reasoning.

7. Based on the information in the graph, which skill sets are considered to be more important to success in college than in the workforce?

(A) Communication/interpersonal and field/technical
(B) Leadership/decision making and knowledge/technical
(C) Field/technical and leadership/decision making
(D) Creativity/generative and knowledge/conceptual

8. The relationship between the two passages is best described as

(A) Passage 1 is more reasonable and Passage 2 is more emotional.
(B) Passage 1 is more humble and Passage 2 is more arrogant.
(C) Passage 1 is more dreamy and Passage 2 is more contemplative.
(D) Passage 1 is more lofty and Passage 2 is more practical.

9. The intended audiences of Passage 1 and Passage 2, respectively, are most likely

(A) global and cosmopolitan.
(B) broad and focused.
(C) specialized and scholarly.
(D) narrow and wide.

10. How would the author of Passage 1 most likely respond to the statement in lines 42–44 ("It is . . . success")?

(A) With disgust
(B) With concern
(C) With ambivalence
(D) With appreciation

11. Which option gives the best evidence for the answer to the previous question?

(A) Lines 1–2 ("*Educate* . . . forth")
(B) Lines 6–8 ("In venturing . . . humans")
(C) Lines 12–14 ("A classroom . . . altogether")
(D) Lines 16–17 ("A student . . . answers")

Passage B4

Is It the Heart or the Brain?

*I saw you from across the room, and I knew immediately. My pulse began to race; I
started to sweat; I could barely breathe. From the first moment that I laid eyes on you, I
was convinced that you were the one. On our first date, the chemistry was obvious. We*
Line *laughed and smiled and held hands and talked for hours. I couldn't sleep or eat or even*
(5) *pay attention at work. I just had to be with you.*

*Within one-fifth of a second, your physical appearance and body language caused an
excessive release of dopamine in my brain creating feelings of excitement and happiness.
We made eye contact for 8.2 seconds; your pheromones were indistinguishable from
my mother's. Then, your voice triggered my brain mechanism for generating long-term*
(10) *attachment; and, for the next several days, my neurotransmitters sent obsessive message
after message, accompanying thoughts of you with feelings of euphoria. Once vasopressin and oxytocin reached my receptors, I knew that I could never be without you.*

Although the former description of "falling in love" is far more prevalent, it is the
latter that has scientists speculating that love is more biological than cultural. Helen
(15) Fisher, American anthropologist and professor at Rutgers University, studies romantic
interpersonal attraction and states that love begins with a focus on one person that
results in obsessive thinking. In her essay, "The Realities of Love at First Sight," Fisher
explains how we evaluate an individual within three minutes of meeting them based
on their physical attributes, voice, and words. First, we decide if they are attractive,
(20) then we evaluate their clothing and stature, before moving on to the sound and tone of
their voice. Lastly, we consider what they actually say. She concludes that we choose
partners whose biological chemicals complement our own.

Fisher's research has even gone further to explain the science behind falling in
love. She theorizes that humans have three brain systems for loving: lust, which is
(25) associated with testosterone; attraction, which is linked to dopamine; and attachment,
which is brought on by increased levels of oxytocin and vasopressin. While these three
systems can surely overlap, they also exist separately from one another which, for
Fisher, explains why loving more than one person at a time is quite possible. However,
Fisher isn't convinced that love is entirely biological. *The Economist* describes the
(30) phenomenon like this: "a chemical state with genetic roots and environmental
influences."

Yet, the connection between love and brain chemicals is far too certain to ignore.
Psychology Today renders love a three-step scientific process. First, a release of the
(35) hormone dopamine causes "feel good" emotions. In this stage, we feel attracted to an
individual and associate them with feelings of intense joy. Next, our neurotransmitters—norepinephrine and phenylethylamine—lead to focused attention on the object
of our attraction and feelings of giddiness that make it hard to sleep and decrease our
appetite. Lastly, our brain reward system is activated, sending chemical messages to

(40) various parts of the body that elevate mood and make an addiction-like urge to be with that person. Biologically, that is the extent of love.

Comparing love to a chemical addiction is actually a quite common metaphor, within poetry and music, but it also happens within the sciences. Deepak Chopra, physician and public speaker, postulates that love stems from an impulse and behaves
(45) within our brain very similarly to a drug addiction. Stephanie Ortigue is a professor at Syracuse University and describes the addiction-like qualities as a result of twelve different areas of the brain working in tandem to release euphoria-inducing chemicals such as adrenaline, dopamine, oxytocin, and vasopressin. Oxytocin, known as "the love hormone," is why we feel calm and cuddly with our significant others.

(50) When it comes to "love at first sight," biologists are asserting that it actually does happen—in about 11% of love encounters, the attachment mechanism within the brain can be triggered within the first few minutes of meeting someone. *The Huffington Post* contends that the optimal environment for love at first sight takes place in encounters with about 8 seconds of continuous eye contact; in cases where
(55) individuals stared into one another's eyes for 4.5 seconds or less, the chances for love were dismal. It would appear that new research has love down to a science.

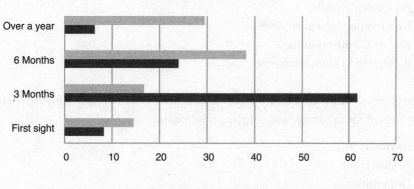

Percentage of polled individuals in relationships for 20+ years

1. What is the overall point of the passage?

    (A) To argue in favor of a scientific basis for matchmaking
    (B) To present the latest findings on the science of love
    (C) To present two sides on a major philosophical question
    (D) To give evidence in support of societal reform

2. The different perspectives represented by the first and second paragraphs are generally described as what, respectively?

    (A) ethical, scientific
    (B) trivial, important
    (C) authentic, misguided
    (D) subjective, objective

3. As used in line 3, the word "chemistry" most closely means

    (A) attraction.
    (B) emotion.
    (C) collegiality.
    (D) biology.

4. The author makes the most broad use of which of the following to build her case?

    (A) Personal anecdote
    (B) Dismantling logical fallacies
    (C) Rhetorical questioning
    (D) Reference to authoritative sources

5. It can be reasonably inferred from the passage that which of the following chemicals is most important to a long-lasting loving relationship?

    (A) Oxytocin
    (B) Testosterone
    (C) Dopamine
    (D) Norepinephrine

6. Which option gives the best evidence for the answer to the previous question?

    (A) Lines 6–10 ("Within . . . attachment")
    (B) Lines 23–26 ("Fisher's . . . vasopressin")
    (C) Lines 36–39 ("Next . . . appetite")
    (D) Lines 45–48 ("Stephanie . . . vasopressin")

7. As used in line 22, the word "complement" most closely means

   (A) praise.
   (B) supplement.
   (C) reveal.
   (D) interact with.

8. Lines 42–43 ("Comparing . . . sciences") most strongly serve to

   (A) express the wide use of a comparison.
   (B) highlight the contributions of the arts to the sciences.
   (C) underscore a flawed assumption.
   (D) use literary techniques for added stylistic variety.

9. Based on the information in the graph, it is most likely that the sample of people researchers referred to in lines 50–52 ("When it . . . someone") was a

   (A) group of only men.
   (B) group of only women.
   (C) group of both men and women.
   (D) group of scholars in the subject.

10. After approximately how many months into their current relationship would the majority of men surveyed in the graph state that they were in love with their partner?

    (A) First sight
    (B) 1 month
    (C) 3 months
    (D) 6 months

11. The information in the graph most directly contradicts what evidence from the passage?

    (A) Fisher's point of view in lines 13–22
    (B) Fisher's theories in lines 23–31
    (C) The findings presented in *Psychology Today* outlined in lines 32–41
    (D) The authoritative views presented in lines 42–49

Sages and Fools

The entirety of human interaction fits under just three umbrellas. In the first, both parties emerge from the rubble worse than before; the perpetrator of a murder gets life in prison and the victim's day is ruined, so to speak. In the second, everybody wins;
Line   I'm terrible at cooking and you're abysmal at housework, so you make us pizza while I
(5)   attack the fungus under your couch. And as for the third, well, a cynic will say that this is by far the largest umbrella—if it were a pie chart, we're talking everything but the *à la mode*. We call this interaction category the *zerosum*, because anything gained must come at the loss of another. Put another way, your tragedy is my windfall.

Welcome to the New Wall Street.

(10)   Poker players are fond of saying that if you look around the table and can't spot the fool, run away as fast as you can; you're it. The same goes for the world of finance, which has quickly become as adversarial as a duel at high noon. Such is the nature of equities, futures, bonds, and derivatives (to name a few): any transaction has both a winner and a loser. Either the buyer has purchased an instrument that is undervalued
(15)   and will be worth more tomorrow, or the seller has unloaded a bloated instrument that will fall back closer to its "true" market valuation in the near future. Either way, dollars (both unrealized and actual) will flow from one pocket to another.

Thus, within such a contentious system, it is to the advantage of all participants to trade with the *fool*. And, if the fool can't be readily found, trust that one will be
(20)   enticed. Leading up to the Crash of 2008, fools were aplenty as wild speculation was the flavor *du jour* and sound financial theory was disregarded. Nowhere was this act of *leapingbeforeyoulook* as flagrant as in the mortgage industry, where loans were repeatedly and systematically extended to Americans with little to no chance of repaying the *interest,* let alone the initial capital. Known as "subprime," high-risk
(25)   borrowers with poor credit scores were extended money at interest rates far above par. The banks' deluded thought process behind this was that the interest rates were so high that, even if an inordinately large percentage of the borrowers defaulted, huge profits were still guaranteed. Besides, worse comes to worst, the bank still owns the house. It was a foolproof plan.

(30)   Until it wasn't. The housing bubble had finally burst. It wasn't just that a few people defaulted; rather, foreclosures were everywhere you looked. And, even worse, when the banks came by to collect the keys, the houses were now worth only fractions of what the banks lent for them. Consequently, they lost billions.

Here's the kicker: while the American financial system nearly collapsed, some had
(35)   seen the fool coming from miles away, secretly cheering with each misstep by the savings and loan industry. So, while the guardians of the money boxes continued specu-

lating on what they thought to be diamonds, a small handful on the fringes knew that it was nothing but coal. And they profited spectacularly.

(40) Through a convoluted, abstruse instrument known as a "credit default swap," these sages were able to make fortunes off of the mortgage implosions, laughing all the way to the bank (where nobody else most certainly was laughing). It was an adroit play by the sages, recognizing an obscure opportunity and capitalizing on the perfect storm. But, such were the just deserts of each party, and such is the black and white duality of the system. One is destined to lose his shirt, and another expands his wardrobe.

1. Which choice best summarizes the passage?

   (A) An explanation of how structural flaws in the financial system led to a near economic collapse
   (B) An analysis of dishonesty in banking and what measures consumers should have taken to protect themselves when the housing bubble burst
   (C) A presentation of how foolish consumers fall prey to predatory "sage" investors
   (D) An account of how universal profitability would have prevented the 2008 stock market crash

2. The narrator indicates that banks and lenders thought subprime loans would end up profitable because

   (A) most borrowers pay back their loans.
   (B) high interest rates would offset defaults.
   (C) housing prices remain steady through economic cycles.
   (D) "credit default swap" was a safety net.

3. Which choice provides the best evidence for the answer to the previous question?

   (A) Lines 5–8 ("And as . . . windfall")
   (B) Lines 14–17 ("Either . . . another")
   (C) Lines 26–29 ("The banks' . . . plan")
   (D) Lines 39–41 ("Through . . . laughing")

4. As used in line 15, the word "bloated" most closely means

   (A) overvalued.
   (B) distended.
   (C) full.
   (D) waterlogged.

5. According to the paragraph in lines 18–29, what factors contributed to the Crash of 2008?

(A) Greedy banks attempted to profit off unsuspecting homeowners.
(B) There were too many speculators and sound financial theory was rejected.
(C) "Zerosum" interactions do not work in economic theory.
(D) Stocks were undervalued and Wall Street was adversarial.

6. In line 30 "The housing bubble had finally burst" means what happened?

(A) Homes were worth less than when they were mortgaged.
(B) Homes were destroyed across the country.
(C) No new homes were being built.
(D) Home prices remained steady for several years.

7. In line 36, "guardians of the money boxes" most nearly refers to

(A) fringe investors.
(B) the American consumer.
(C) mainstream banks.
(D) the Federal government.

8. As used in line 39, the word "abstruse" most closely means

(A) sinister.
(B) perplexing.
(C) sub rosa.
(D) weighty.

9. The narrator would agree that all of the following are examples of "zerosum" EXCEPT

(A) selling an overvalued stock and making a profit.
(B) using "credit default swap" to capitalize on defaulted mortgages.
(C) ordering a pizza dinner while another person completes housework.
(D) defaulting on a loan and discharging the balance in bankruptcy court.

10. Which choice provides the best evidence for the answer to the previous question?

(A) Lines 3–5 ("In the . . . couch")
(B) Lines 26–29 ("The banks' . . . plan")
(C) Lines 34–36 ("Here's . . . industry")
(D) Lines 39–41 ("Through . . . laughing")

Passage B1

1.	**A**	3.	**C**	5.	**A**	7.	**A**	9.	**B**
2.	**A**	4.	**B**	6.	**D**	8.	**C**	10.	**C**

Passage B2

1.	**A**	3.	**C**	5.	**C**	7.	**D**	9.	**B**
2.	**D**	4.	**B**	6.	**D**	8.	**B**	10.	**D**

Passage B3

1.	**C**	4.	**B**	7.	**D**	10.	**A**
2.	**D**	5.	**A**	8.	**D**	11.	**C**
3.	**C**	6.	**C**	9.	**B**		

Passage B4

1.	**B**	4.	**D**	7.	**B**	10.	**D**
2.	**D**	5.	**A**	8.	**A**	11.	**A**
3.	**A**	6.	**B**	9.	**C**		

Passage B5

1.	**A**	3.	**C**	5.	**B**	7.	**C**	9.	**C**
2.	**B**	4.	**A**	6.	**A**	8.	**B**	10.	**A**

ANSWERS EXPLAINED

Passage B1

1. **(A)** The passage as a whole is Jane Eyre's recount of a dream and a seemingly super-natural event that occurred upon her awakening, both terrifying omens that suggest an unhappy and uncertain future. (C) and (D) don't discuss this main idea. (B), although tempting, is incorrect because Jane is sharing her experience rather than asking for advice, and because only one of her forewarning stories is said to be a dream.

2. **(A)** Mr. Rochester's attitude toward Jane can be inferred through his lack of partici-pation and interest, and by his assumption that the intruder is a ghost or figment of Jane's imagination. He interrupts her, contradicts her descriptions, and never says more than one sentence at a time. Although he is skeptical, he is not depressed as in (B). He shows neither panic nor fear as in (C). And though he listens to her telling, Mr. Rochester doesn't display any genuine curiosity in what Jane says as in (D); instead, he seems determined to dismiss her worries.

3. **(C)** In this case, Jane is referring to the fact that she must "hold onto" the "unknown little child." The other choices fail to capture the point that she cannot lay down the child.

4. **(B)** Lines 7–8 state that Jane is first made aware of Mr. Rochester's presence when she hears "the gallop of a horse."

5. **(A)** These lines give direct evidence that within her dream Jane first perceives Mr. Rochester through a sense of hearing. (B) describes her attempt to see him after hearing his horse. (C) tells how her dream ends. (D) describes the appearance of the mysterious and frightening intruder who tears up her veil.

6. **(D)** Line 18 is used to transition from her dream to the ghastly and inexplicable occurrence afterwards. It is not a description as in (A) and (C). Nor is it a demonstration of respect since "sir" is common throughout the passage, and this line is more about moving from one idea to the next.

7. **(A)** *Entity* refers to an object that exists in itself, like a body, being, creature, or organization. This is the only choice that fits *form* in this context. *Creation* refers to a formation rather than a form, and (C) and (D) are incorrect choices because they do not refer to beings that can emerge from a closet.

8. **(C)** Lines 26–28 list the most likely individuals to be in Jane's room. Considering Mr. Rochester's dismissal and indifference to Jane's narration, these lines serve to rule out his anticipated response and attempt to reveal the severity of the incident. It is a list rather than a description, so (A) and (B) don't work. And (D) isn't correct because this occurrence is after, not during, Jane's dream, and can be accounted for by the torn veil.

9. **(B)** The figure is described as "tall and large," "fearful and ghastly," with a "savage face" and "red eyes." So, choice (B) is most fitting. (A) is incorrect because the form is distinctive from all the individuals in the house. (C) can be eliminated because the woman is portrayed as abominable and imposing rather than weak. And although Jane compares the woman to "the Vampyre," there is no evidence that she actually thinks the woman is a bat.

10. **(C)** Lines 43–44 give Jane's description of the intruder's features, and so serve as the best evidence for the previous question. (A) is a description of Thornfield Hall within Jane's dream. (B) is where the form first emerges, but is not yet described. (D) is a metaphor used to depict the horror of the ghost-like intruder, but is not very useful in depicting the woman's features.

Passage B2

1. **(A)** According to the passage, when meat is heated the proteins denature and "their quaternary, tertiary, and secondary structures break down." So, we can assume (A), the primary structure, is least affected.

2. **(D)** Lines 13–15 specifically address which structures are impacted by cooking in order to make the meat tender. As such, they provide direct evidence to the previous question. Answer choices (A), (B), and (C) afford details of each structure, but do not address which are broken down during cooking.

3. **(C)** Lines 12–13 can be said to transition from the description of the protein organization in meat to the effects of cooking on those structures. Thus, (C) is correct. As a question that moves from one idea to the next, it would be inaccurate to say this sentence is a definition, explanation, or analysis.

4. **(B)** "Loosened" is the closest meaning, since line 13 refers to the interactions becoming "weaker." In the following sentences, the author describes this as a breaking down

where proteins become "loose and stretched out." (A) and (D) inaccurately express an exhausting loss. And (C) would indicate that the breaking down of proteins arouses pity.

5. **(C)** *Negligible* means inconsequential, so this question is asking which approach would not change the end result. (A) removes moisture, so it is consequential even if it is an undesirable effect. (B) locks in moisture. And (D) would still denature the protein, impacting tenderness and moistness. According to the author, searing meat doesn't influence tenderness, and so, (C) is the correct answer.

6. **(D)** Lines 29–30 underscore the author's assertion that seared meat behaves the same as non-seared meat, which is evidence that searing is an inconsequential practice in cooking meat. Choice (A) implies that overcooking reduces moisture. Choice (B) addresses the fact that acids and bases can denature meat, despite being undesirable in foods. And finally choice (C) proves that brining increases moisture. Hence, all three choices are consequential and are not appropriate answers for the previous question.

7. **(D)** In line 39, the author uses an idiom in an ironic way, stating that despite the dissension, chemistry is extremely applicable to cooking, inferring that this is something to think about. (A) incorrectly understands it as stimulating one's appetite. (B) and (C) inaccurately assume action rather than contemplation.

8. **(B)** The author discusses the color of meat in lines 31–36, attributing redness to myoglobin content. Accordingly, cooking alters the composition of myoglobin to transform the color to brown. (A) is associated with tenderness, not color. (C) refers to the organization of the protein structure that breaks down for tenderness, but again is not associated with color. Finally, choice (D) is not mentioned.

9. **(B)** Lines 19–20 state that high amounts of collagen in connective tissues are associated with tougher cuts of meat. The graph considers how much meat is produced via different cooking methods. Therefore, we are looking for which method would eliminate the most connective tissue since this is what makes the meat especially tough. So, (B) is correct.

10. **(D)** Broiling meat yields about 85%, while braising meat yields about 66%. So, choice (D) is the only plausible option.

Passage B3

1. **(C)** The best approach to this question is to look at the context. The author is discussing the teacher as a guide who arouses curiosity, so we can infer that this phrase does not actually mean a change in location or a novel undertaking as in (A) and (B). Instead, the author most nearly means that a teacher can encourage new ideas as in (C). Choice (D) is appealing, but the author is referring to questioning one's preconceived values more than one's choices.

2. **(D)** Lines 16–17 refer to the first author's opinion that a quality education creates a lifelong persistent questioner. Thus, the author would think *curiosity* is the most important thing for a teacher to inspire in students. The author of Passage 2 might say (A), but not the author of Passage 1. Furthermore, the author would want students to search for *truth* with a certain *diligence*, but only as a result of their *curiosity*.

3. **(C)** According to lines 32–35, the author of Passage 2 hopes to prepare students for college and the job market, so choice (C), both professors and employers, makes sense here.

4. **(B)** These lines give direct evidence, advocating for an end result where students "walk out feeling confident and prepared whether it be for graduation tests, college-entrance exams, or the job market." This statement supports the idea that the teacher writing Passage 2 would value the skill sets desired by both college professors and workforce employers.

5. **(A)** *Idealistic* means "relating to noble principles" or "conceived as a standard of perfection." It is correct here since the author is indicating that her job description seems very romantic, but is in fact very pragmatic. While it could make sense to say her job sounds *passionate*, *loving*, or *emotional* in other contexts, none of these choices makes the contrast between how it sounds and how it is put into practice.

6. **(C)** Lines 36–41 convey the author's priority to prepare students for the challenges ahead "at all costs." So, we can assume that the author places an emphasis on (C), *rigorous expectations*. There is no evidence that the author values *physical exertion* as in (A). Choice (B) more closely resembles what the author of Passage 1 might stress. Finally, (D) usually refers to a process by which one supports and gives logical evidence for an argument or position.

7. **(D)** This question is just asking for the instances in the graph where a skill set is labeled at a higher importance by college professors than it is by employers. Both the third and fourth columns have a higher value for the college than workforce, so choice (D) is correct. The other choices all include a skill set that is more valued in the workforce.

8. **(D)** Passage 1 can be generally characterized as high-minded and visionary since it renders a philosophy of education based on inspiration. Passage 2 is a realistic approach to a defined, but limited curriculum. Since *lofty* means "exalted" and *practical* means "hands-on or sensible," choice (D) is accurate.

9. **(B)** Be sure to notice the "respectively" in the question, meaning that the answers must follow in the order already mentioned. The first author could be addressing anyone interested in education, while the second author seems to be speaking specifically to parents of potential or current students. Thus, (B) is an appropriate choice. *Cosmopolitan* means "worldly" or "cultured." Choices (C) and (D) have possible characteristics flipped.

10. **(A)** To approach a question like this, break it into two parts. Lines 42–44 indicate that the author of Passage 2 prioritizes test preparation and attributes standardized prowess for future success. Now, consider how the author of Passage 1 might respond. In lines 3–4, we learn that the author thinks a desire to learn is far more important than the knowledge itself, and in lines 12–14, that a classroom that fails to inspire, fails altogether. So, (A) *with disgust*, depicts how he or she might respond. *Concern* and *ambivalence* are both too indifferent, while *appreciation* is an opposite response from what we might expect.

11. **(C)** Choices (A), (B), and (D) all state and support the author's position, but do not address how he or she might view an opposing philosophy of education. (C) is the only option that addresses how the author feels toward adverse classroom environments.

Passage B4

1. **(B)** The purpose of this passage is to explore research regarding the science behind love, so (B) is correct. The author does not address matchmaking as in (A). Nor does he or she spend time addressing both sides as in (C). Finally, the passage isn't arguing for social reform or improvement.

2. **(D)** The first paragraph is very personal and emotional in its approach to describing love. The second takes a very scientific and factual approach to love. Since the first is not based on principles of morality, *ethical* is an inaccurate description. (B) takes an opinion on which basis is more significant, assuming an emotional, heartfelt description of love is *trivial* or foolish. And (C) indicates that the technical approach is *misguided*. Thus, (D) is the only accurate choice. *Subjective* means based on personal experience, while *objective* means based on a representation of facts.

3. **(A)** Line 3 is within the traditional thought process surrounding what happens when one falls in love, and states that the couple had "chemistry." Here, the word does not refer to a branch of science, but to an affinity or *attraction* between people.

4. **(D)** The question is asking what device the author generally uses to build a case. The author doesn't use personal stories of falling in love as in (A). Nor does the passage concern itself with finding errors in logic or presenting rhetorical questions. However, (D) is widely used throughout the passage.

5. **(A)** Oxytocin, according to the passage, is known as the "love hormone" and is associated with attachment. Thus, it is crucial for long-lasting romantic love. (B) is connected with feelings of lust or desire. And (C) and (D) are connected with attraction and "feelings of giddiness."

6. **(B)** In lines 23–26, the author explains an expert's research on the three brain systems for loving, connecting long-lasting love, or attachment, with "oxytocin and vasopressin." Hence, these lines give evidence for the previous question. (A) and (C) refer to chemicals that induce excitement and attraction. (D) names all the chemicals in the brain directly associated with love, but does not discuss which chemicals are connected to longer, serious relationships.

7. **(B)** *Supplement* is the closest word choice. Lines 21–22 indicates research that affirms that "we choose partners whose biological chemicals complement our own." So, "complement" within the context means "go well together" rather than *praise*, *reveal*, or merely *interact with*.

8. **(A)** In lines 42–43, the author suggests that love is often compared to chemical addiction—in poetry, music, and science. As such, (A) correctly depicts the purpose of the lines. The other choices don't consider the variety of uses for the metaphor. (B) incorrectly infers that the metaphor within the arts is contributing to science. (C) is inaccurate because the author is not calling the metaphor flawed. Finally, (D) is wrong in that it attributes the metaphor to stylistic aspirations.

9. **(C)** The graph shows men citing "first sight" at about 15% and women citing "first sight" at about 8%. So, the 11% figure in lines 50–52 most likely accounts for both men and women, since it would average these numbers out.

10. **(D)** According to the graph, the majority of men fall in love by the 6 month mark, making (D) correct. Approximately 14% of men said "first sight," 17% said after "three months," and 38% said after "6 months." 14 + 17 + 38 = 69, which is clearly a majority. The numbers are such that you can easily estimate that it would be a majority, since you won't have a calculator available on the Reading Test.

11. **(A)** The question is asking if there is conflict between the graph and the passage. (A) is the only choice which presents a timeframe for evaluating a partner, namely 3 minutes. So, since the majority of persons surveyed don't fall in love within 3 minutes, the graph could possibly conflict with Fisher's perspective. Choices (B), (C), and (D) do not specify a timeframe for the science behind love, so they do not oppose the graph's findings in any way.

Passage B5

1. **(A)** To summarize, the author uses the recent financial crisis to explore the system's unjust nature, making (A) the correct choice. According to the author, the system is more at fault than the consumers, ruling out (B) and (C). Choice (D) is incorrect because the passage makes no mention of how "universal profitability" could have occurred.

2. **(B)** Subprime loans are those extended with "little to no chance" of repayment. Yet, the author states in lines 26–29 that the banks overlooked default, thinking that the extreme interests would still ensure "huge profits." He suggests that the banks knew many wouldn't be able to pay back their loans, making (A) wrong. (C) and (D) are not supported by the passage.

3. **(C)** Lines 26–29 depict the "banks' deluded thought process" in regard to subprime loans, and so, give direct evidence for the previous question. (A) introduces the third type of human interaction in which one party advances at another's expense. (B) gives an example of that type of interaction. And finally, choice (D) presents the method by which a very insightful few were able to benefit from the crisis.

4. **(A)** In line 15, the author refers to a seller ridding himself of a "bloated instrument" which will certainly devalue. Hence, *overvalued* is a precise word choice. While the other choices are synonyms of *bloated*, they do not capture the author's meaning as related to inflated value.

5. **(B)** In lines 20–21, the author attributes the Crash of 2008 to "wild speculation" and a disregard for "sound financial theory." (C) and (D) can be ruled out because they are not discussed in these lines and diverge from the author's argument. Choice (A) is appealing, but notice that the author claims the mortgage industry was the best and biggest example of these failures, so (B) is the definite choice. Likewise, "homeowners" is inaccurate, because the banks owned the homes until the borrowers could pay back the loans.

6. **(A)** The author explains this line in the following sentences, stating that a majority of borrowers defaulted and the houses' values plummeted, so (A) is the correct choice.

The line doesn't refer to actual physical destruction or construction as in (B) and (C). Similarly, we know values greatly fell, making (D) incorrect.

7. **(C)** In this paragraph, the author indicates that a few "sages" were able to reverse the consequences of the financial crash, while "the guardians of the money boxes" mistook coal for diamonds. Since the sages profited and the guardians did not, we can assume the guardians are those banks who were supplying subprime loans and "lost billions."

8. **(B)** *Abstruse* means difficult to understand, so *perplexing* is the correct choice. This word is coupled with a synonym that might help: "convoluted," or "complicated," suggests the meaning of *abstruse*. *Sinister* means "menacing" and is too negative. *Sub rosa* refers to something being done in secret. And *weighty* means "heavy or impactful."

9. **(C)** The author defines *zerosum* as an interaction where "anything gained must come at the loss of another." (C) is the only option where one party does not suffer at the hands of another; it is an example of his second interaction type in which everybody wins.

10. **(A)** Lines 3–5 provide a very similar example of an "everybody wins" situation, and so give evidence for the previous question. Choices (B) and (D) provide instances of "zero-sum" since one party flourishes while another loses. Choice (C) is irrelevant.

PRACTICE EXERCISE C

These passages and questions are generally representative of the toughest passages and questions you could face on the SAT. They are designed to help you push your limits and to make the actual SAT seem easier. Take about 13 minutes for each passage (including reading and answering the questions). Detailed answer explanations follow.

Passage C1

The following passage is from A Portrait of the Artist as a Young Man *by James Joyce, 1916. Stephen Dedalus, Joyce's protagonist, yearns to be an artist but was raised and educated to join the clergy. Below he contemplates the diverging paths before him after a priest warns him of the permanence of his intended holy position.*

As he descended the steps the impression which effaced his troubled self-communion was that of a mirthless mask reflecting a sunken day from the threshold of the college. The shadow, then, of the life of the college passed gravely over his consciousness.
Line It was a grave and ordered and passionless life that awaited him, a life without material
(5) cares. He wondered how he would pass the first night in the novitiate and with what dismay he would wake the first morning in the dormitory. The troubling odour of the long corridors of Clongowes came back to him and he heard the discreet murmur of the burning gasflames. At once from every part of his being unrest began to irradiate. A feverish quickening of his pulses followed, and a din of meaningless words drove his
(10) reasoned thoughts hither and thither confusedly. His lungs dilated and sank as if he were inhaling a warm moist unsustaining air and he smelt again the moist warm air which hung in the bath in Clongowes above the sluggish turf-coloured water.

Some instinct, waking at these memories, stronger than education or piety, quickened within him at every near approach to that life, an instinct subtle and hostile, and
(15) armed him against acquiescence. The chill and order of the life repelled him. He saw himself rising in the cold of the morning and filing down with the others to early mass and trying vainly to struggle with his prayers against the fainting sickness of his stomach. He saw himself sitting at dinner with the community of a college. What, then, had become of that deep-rooted shyness of his which had made him loth to eat or drink
(20) under a strange roof? What had come of the pride of his spirit which had always made him conceive himself as a being apart in every order?

The Reverend Stephen Dedalus, S.J.

His name in that new life leaped into characters before his eyes and to it there followed a mental sensation of an undefined face or colour of a face. The colour faded
(25) and became strong like a changing glow of pallid brick red. Was it the raw reddish glow he had so often seen on wintry mornings on the shaven gills of the priests? The face was eyeless and sour-favoured and devout, shot with pink tinges of suffocated anger. Was it not a mental spectre of the face of one of the Jesuits whom some of the boys called Lantern Jaws and others Foxy Campbell?

(30)   He was passing at that moment before the Jesuit house in Gardiner Street and wondered vaguely which window would be his if he ever joined the order. Then he wondered at the vagueness of his wonder, at the remoteness of his own soul from what he had hitherto imagined her sanctuary, at the frail hold which so many years of order and obedience had of him when once a definite and irrevocable act of his threatened
(35)   to end for ever, in time and in eternity, his freedom. The voice of the director urging upon him the proud claims of the church and the mystery and power of the priestly office repeated itself idly in his memory. His soul was not there to hear and greet it and he knew now that the exhortation he had listened to had already fallen into an idle formal tale. He would never swing the thurible before the tabernacle as priest. His destiny
(40)   was to be elusive of social or religious orders. The wisdom of the priest's appeal did not touch him to the quick. He was destined to learn his own wisdom apart from others or to learn the wisdom of others himself wandering among the snares of the world.

The snares of the world were its ways of sin. He would fall. He had not yet fallen but he would fall silently, in an instant. Not to fall was too hard, too hard; and he felt the
(45)   silent lapse of his soul, as it would be at some instant to come, falling, falling, but not yet fallen, still unfallen, but about to fall.

1. The dilemma faced by the narrator in the passage as a whole is best characterized as a choice between

    (A) embracing a life of priestly holiness or a life of criminal depravity.
    (B) following an orderly prescribed path or an intuitively authentic one.
    (C) listening to his sensory passions or the demands of logical consistency.
    (D) attending to memories of religious rituals or memories of worldly decadence.

2. The overall organization of the passage is best described as

    (A) logically argumentative.
    (B) spatially progressive.
    (C) gradually convergent.
    (D) strictly chronological.

3. The principal manifestations of the narrator's anxieties are what thought processes in the first and second paragraphs respectively?

    (A) Conscious perception and unconscious sensation
    (B) Extroverted discussion and introverted analysis
    (C) Analytical reasoning and intuitive reflection
    (D) Sensory memory and imaginative prediction

4. How would the narrator most likely characterize how most priests handle their emotions?

   (A) By repressing them
   (B) By embracing them
   (C) By eliminating them
   (D) By expressing them

5. Which option gives the best evidence for the answer to the previous question?

   (A) Lines 8–10 ("At once . . . confusedly")
   (B) Lines 18–20 ("What . . . roof")
   (C) Lines 23–24 ("His name . . . face")
   (D) Lines 26–27 ("The face . . . anger")

6. As used in line 21, the phrase "apart in every order" most nearly expresses the narrator's feelings of

   (A) acceptance by his peers.
   (B) emotional isolation.
   (C) apathetic indifference.
   (D) optimistic decisiveness.

7. The type of education that best fits the narrator is most likely

   (A) religiously formal.
   (B) self-directed.
   (C) literary.
   (D) scholarly lecture.

8. Which option gives the best evidence for the answer to the previous question?

   (A) Lines 13–15 ("Some . . . acquiescence")
   (B) Line 18 ("He saw . . . college")
   (C) Lines 28–29 ("Was it . . . Campbell")
   (D) Lines 41–42 ("He was . . . world")

9. As used in line 41, the phrase "to the quick" most closely means

   (A) with speed.
   (B) very deeply.
   (C) intelligently.
   (D) in isolation.

10. The tone of the final paragraph is one of

   (A) resignation.
   (B) terror.
   (C) corruption.
   (D) decreasing.

Passage C2

Surfactants

While significant structural and functional differences exist between the various classes, a surfactant, simply put, describes any compound capable of reducing the surface tension between a liquid and one other substance. Surface tension, one will recall,
Line refers to the tendency of liquid molecules to coalesce with one another, thus minimiz-
(5) ing their collective surface area. This phenomenon is the physical principle underlying a familiar adage, "oil and water do not mix." Phrased more precisely, oils, which contain primarily nonpolar hydrocarbon bonds, are immiscible with aqueous solutions, meaning they will not spontaneously dissolve in water, which consists of highly polar hydrogen-oxygen bonds. Instead, oils will tend to form a film over polar solvents, while
(10) surface tension serves to stabilize this film at the oil-water interface.

Because they are amphiphilic—meaning they possess both polar and nonpolar domains—surfactants may interact with both components of this interface, and interfere with the electrochemical forces that maintain its integrity. Due to this unique property, surface tension lowering agents have found a host of applications in diverse
(15) commercial products, and are used in particular as emulsifiers, foaming agents, and detergents.

An emulsion is merely a mixture of two normally immiscible liquids. The word *emulsion* derives from a Latin root meaning "to milk," and, as an easily homogenized mixture of fats within an aqueous solution of sugars, proteins, and minerals, milk itself
(20) is a quintessential example of an emulsion. Moreover, without the surfactant activity of the complex lipids it contains, the fat globules dispersed throughout a given volume of milk would coalesce into a film on its surface. Similarly, the surfactants found in foaming agents decrease the tendency of soap bubbles to coalesce, and are responsible for the lathering effect found in many hygiene products such as toothpaste and
(25) shampoo.

Soap itself, interestingly enough, can also be considered a surfactant. Principally, soap is a salt consisting of a positively charged sodium ion and a negatively charged fatty acid. Importantly, the structure of an ionized fatty acid includes a nonpolar hydrocarbon "tail," and a polar, carboxyl "head." The polar head allows the fatty acid
(30) to partially dissolve in water, while the nonpolar tail facilitates its interaction with other nonpolar compounds, such as oils. Thus, by interrupting surface tension, soap allows oil to be washed away with water.

At the risk of oversimplifying, soaps are created by exposing triglycerides gathered from either plant or animal sources to a strong base in a process called *saponification*.
(35) The base hydrolyzes triglycerides to form glycerol and amphipathic free fatty acids. The glycerol, in turn, is removed, and the fatty acids are complexed with sodium. While the words *soap* and *detergent* are sometimes used interchangeably in common parlance, one should note that detergents are not synthesized by saponification.

Structurally, detergents differ from soaps only in the composition of their polar
(40) heads. That is, whereas soaps contain an ionized carboxyl group, detergents contain
an ionized sulfonate. The significance of this alteration is twofold. First, detergent
compounds are far less prone to precipitate and become ineffective in hard water.
Hard water, of course, refers to water that is rich in dissolved calcium and magnesium
as a result of exposure to limestone, and it is present in an estimated 80% of American
(45) households. Second, the sulfonate component of detergents makes their degradation products far more toxic to the environment than those of soaps. Owing both to
their low cost of production and to their impressive utility, detergents are produced
and sold on a scale that dwarfs all other commercially synthesized surfactants. Not
surprisingly, this has become a cause of growing concern with regard to the potential
(50) impacts on aquatic ecosystems, as well as on human health, as exposure to detergent
derivatives has been convincingly implicated in several endocrine and reproductive
disorders.

Though this controversy is heated, complex, and unlikely to be settled in the fore-
seeable future, it has also sparked significant support for a fascinating field of biotech-
(55) nology that deals with the surfactants produced endogenously by living organisms,
and particularly those produced by microbes. With regard to their structure, these
so-called "biosurfactants" are highly distinct from both soaps and detergents, and
yet several promising preliminary studies have shown them to be functionally viable
alternatives to more conventional cleaning products. The advantage lies in the high
(60) biodegradability and biologically benign character of biosurfactants. The obstacle, of
course, lies in the nightmarish logistics of isolating them on a large, industrial scale.

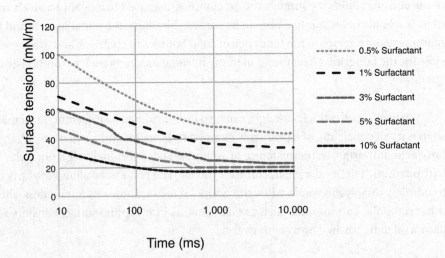

Surface Tension of Soap Bubbles

*The graph illustrates changes in surface tension over time in milliseconds (ms) for soap
bubbles made with varying concentrations of surfactant. The time label on the x-axis is
exponential and is compressed as the values increased.*

1. The author most likely uses the phrase "oil and water do not mix" in line 6 to

    (A) explain the process in which two immiscible substances are emulsified.
    (B) imply that most laypeople cannot understand the topic of this article.
    (C) show that substances that do not have triglycerides cannot undergo saponification.
    (D) connect the esoteric analysis to a commonly understood phenomenon.

2. As used in line 13, the word "integrity" most closely means

    (A) rectitude.
    (B) solidarity
    (C) cohesion.
    (D) decadence.

3. According to the passage, what property of surfactants is most responsible for their widespread human applications?

    (A) They are produced by microbes.
    (B) They are amphiphilic.
    (C) They are an emulsion.
    (D) Their saponification

4. Which option gives the best evidence for the answer to the previous question?

    (A) Lines 13–16 ("Due to . . . detergents")
    (B) Lines 17–20 ("An emulsion . . . emulsion")
    (C) Lines 33–35 ("At the . . . acids")
    (D) Lines 53–56 ("Though . . . microbes")

5. It can most reasonably be inferred from the passage that the relative amounts of these man-made surfactants are currently what, from least to greatest?

    (A) Biosurfactants, detergents, soaps
    (B) Biosurfactants, soaps, detergents
    (C) Soaps, detergents, biosurfactants
    (D) Detergents, soaps, biosurfactants

6. The author's overall description of soaps and detergents is that they are

    (A) commonly thought of as interchangeable, but having important differences.
    (B) one and the same insofar as their chemical properties, such as molecular structure.
    (C) different with respect to their capacity to mix in emulsions.
    (D) major obstacles to the widespread acceptance of biosurfactants.

7. Which option gives the best evidence for the answer to the previous question?

(A) Lines 16–20 ("The word . . . emulsion")
(B) Lines 28–31 ("Importantly . . . oils")
(C) Lines 37–38 ("While . . . saponification")
(D) Lines 56–59 ("With regard . . . products")

8. As used in line 53, the word "settled" most closely means

(A) firm.
(B) resolved.
(C) disturbed.
(D) mobilized.

9. Based on the information in the graph, if soap bubbles (like the ones measured in the graph) with a concentration of 8.5% surfactant were measured 10 ms after their creation, the surface tension in mN/m would be closest to

(A) 30.
(B) 40.
(C) 50.
(D) 60.

10. According to the information in the graph, an increase in surfactant percentage from what to what would most likely result in the largest relative increase in surface tension?

(A) From 0.5% to 1.5%
(B) From 4.5% to 5.5%
(C) From 8% to 9%
(D) All of these would result in equivalent surface tension increases.

11. What is the most logical reason why the author used a logarithmic scale on the *x*-axis of the graph?

(A) It helps give a more accurate compilation of the data than would a typical linear scale.
(B) It enables readers to more easily see the directly proportional relationship between the variables.
(C) It impresses the reader because of the author's obvious mastery of advanced mathematical reasoning.
(D) It makes it easier to visualize the changes in surface tension over the ever-increasing orders of magnitude of time.

Passage C3

Below is the beginning excerpt from Meditations on First Philosophy, *by René Descartes, 1641, in which he muses about the nature of knowledge.*

MEDITATION I.
Of the Things of Which We May Now Doubt

1. SEVERAL years have now elapsed since I first became aware that I had accepted,
Line even from my youth, many false opinions for true, and that consequently what I
(5) afterward based on such principles was highly doubtful; and from that time I was convinced of the necessity of undertaking once in my life to rid myself of all the opinions I
had adopted, and of commencing anew the work of building from the foundation, if I
desired to establish a firm and abiding superstructure in the sciences. But as this enter-
prise appeared to me to be one of great magnitude, I waited until I had attained an age
(10) so mature as to leave me no hope that at any stage of life more advanced I should be
better able to execute my design. On this account, I have delayed so long that I should
henceforth consider I was doing wrong were I still to consume in deliberation any of
the time that now remains for action. Today, then, since I have opportunely freed my
mind from all cares [and am happily disturbed by no passions], and since I am in the
(15) secure possession of leisure in a peaceable retirement, I will at length apply myself
earnestly and freely to the general overthrow of all my former opinions.

2. But, to this end, it will not be necessary for me to show that the whole of these
are false—a point, perhaps, which I shall never reach; but as even now my reason con-
vinces me that I ought not the less carefully to withhold belief from what is not entirely
(20) certain and indubitable, than from what is manifestly false, it will be sufficient to jus-
tify the rejection of the whole if I shall find in each some ground for doubt. Nor for this
purpose will it be necessary even to deal with each belief individually, which would be
truly an endless labor; but, as the removal from below of the foundation necessarily
involves the downfall of the whole edifice, I will at once approach the criticism of the
(25) principles on which all my former beliefs rested.

3. All that I have, up to this moment, accepted as possessed of the highest truth and
certainty, I received either from or through the senses. I observed, however, that these
sometimes misled us; and it is the part of prudence not to place absolute confidence in
that by which we have even once been deceived.

(30) 4. But it may be said, perhaps, that, although the senses occasionally mislead us
respecting minute objects, and such as are so far removed from us as to be beyond the
reach of close observation, there are yet many other of their informations (presenta-
tions), of the truth of which it is manifestly impossible to doubt; as for example, that I
am in this place, seated by the fire, clothed in a winter dressing gown, that I hold in my
(35) hands this piece of paper, with other intimations of the same nature. But how could
I deny that I possess these hands and this body, and withal escape being classed with
persons in a state of insanity, whose brains are so disordered and clouded by dark

bilious vapors as to cause them pertinaciously to assert that they are monarchs when they are in the greatest poverty; or clothed [in gold] and purple when destitute of any
(40) covering; or that their head is made of clay, their body of glass, or that they are gourds? I should certainly be not less insane than they, were I to regulate my procedure according to examples so extravagant.

1. Descartes' overall attitude towards knowledge as presented in the passage is best described as

   (A) dogmatic.
   (B) credulous.
   (C) skeptical.
   (D) popular.

2. Descartes uses lines 8–13 to express why

   (A) he believes that the foundations for knowledge are error ridden.
   (B) the intellectual project he is tackling is so important.
   (C) his mental and physical health have begun to decline.
   (D) he has chosen this point in time to write this work.

3. As used in line 10, the word "advanced" most closely means

   (A) increasingly complex.
   (B) far along in time.
   (C) with great skill.
   (D) significantly improved.

4. Descartes' minimal threshold for dismissing a knowledge claim is if it is

   (A) completely in error.
   (B) moderately wrong.
   (C) even slightly flawed.
   (D) any claim to knowledge.

5. Which option gives the best evidence for the answer to the previous question?

   (A) Lines 7–8 ("if I . . . sciences")
   (B) Lines 15–16 ("I will . . . opinions")
   (C) Lines 20–21 ("it will . . . doubt")
   (D) Lines 39–40 ("or clothed . . . gourds")

6. Lines 30–35 primarily illustrate Descartes' thinking about

   (A) the pitfalls of human perception.
   (B) the superiority of logical reasoning.
   (C) the importance of proper observational tools.
   (D) the spectrum of sensory certainty.

7. The passage strongly implies that Descartes believes that the structure of knowledge is best described as

   (A) hierarchical.
   (B) disconnected.
   (C) indubitable.
   (D) nonexistent.

8. Which option gives the best evidence for the answer to the previous question?
   (A) Lines 7–8 ("commencing . . . sciences")
   (B) Lines 11–13 ("On this . . . action")
   (C) Lines 21–23 ("Nor for . . . labor")
   (D) Lines 34–35 ("I hold . . . nature")

9. Descartes uses the phrase in lines 37–38, "so disordered and clouded by dark bilious vapors," to illustrate what he believes to be

   (A) the religious source of demonic possession.
   (B) the physical source of hallucinogenic visions.
   (C) the psychological source of chronic depression.
   (D) the environmental source of mathematical logic.

10. As used in line 42, the word "extravagant" most closely means
    (A) luxurious.
    (B) conservative.
    (C) psychological.
    (D) excessive.

Passage C4

Alternative Splicing

   With James Watson and Francis Crick's landmark article on the double helical structure of DNA now more than a half-century old, the sheer volume of knowledge we have since amassed regarding the regulation and expression of genetic material is staggering, and continues to expand daily. Yet for all that has been accomplished in the study of genetics, there comes now and again a discovery to underscore just how many mysteries we have yet to unravel.

   Historically, we have defined a gene as a region of DNA responsible for encoding and regulating the expression of a discrete, heritable trait. The use of *regulating* here is of no small importance, as the protein-coding sequence itself represents only a fraction of the DNA contained within a given gene. A "promoter" region, for instance, does not directly contribute to the mRNA transcript, but instead provides binding sites for transcription factor proteins, and functions as sort of an "on" or "off" switch for the expression of the gene's corresponding trait. Similarly, "silencer" and "enhancer" regions can also bind regulatory proteins, and help to fine-tune the precise degree to which a gene will be expressed under various circumstances and in response to varying stimuli. However, perhaps the most implicitly fascinating non-coding regions of DNA are those embedded within the protein-coding region itself.

   During transcription, nucleotides are polymerized into a strand of mRNA whose sequence is complementary to that of the template DNA. This "pre-mRNA" typically contains several regions of non-coding material, or "introns," that must be excised prior to translation of the protein-coding regions, which are referred to as "exons." In a complex process known as *splicing*, the introns are removed and degraded, while the adjacent ends of exons are adjoined, and trafficked out of the nucleus to the endoplasmic reticulum, where protein synthesis can at last begin.

   Predictably, mutations that affect a gene's splicing pattern may precipitate severe functional impairments to its encoded protein, and some studies have estimated that as many as half of all disease-causing mutations in humans—including those responsible for Alzheimer's disease, Parkinson's disease, and certain forms of cystic fibrosis—are ultimately a result of altered splicing. Furthermore, an increasing body of research has also reported patterns of altered splicing in a wide variety of cancer cells, though it remains to be seen as to whether these changes contribute to oncogenesis, or are simply symptomatic of dysregulated growth.

   With such grim potential for genetic misstep, one might wonder how evolution could have ever favored the development of such a precarious and seemingly superfluous system of gene expression in the first place. The answer to this lies in the fact that alternative splicing patterns are not exclusively pathological, but can and do occur under physiological circumstances as well. That is to say, through tightly controlled changes to the differential removal of introns and retention of exons, two identi-

cal strands of pre-mRNA can, ultimately, code for two entirely different proteins.
(40) Calcitonin gene-related peptide, or CGRP, was among the first proteins identified as a product of physiological alternative splicing. Whereas calcitonin is a well-known hormone produced by the medullary cells of the thyroid gland, and is involved in the regulation of calcium levels in the blood, CGRP is believed to mediate pain sensations within central and peripheral neurons. Despite their unique structures and vastly dif-
(45) fering functions, both proteins are nonetheless encoded by the same gene.

The discovery of physiological alternative splicing came as a challenge to our traditional understanding of genes, which held that each coding region was responsible
for the expression of a single protein. Today, of course, we know this line of thought
to be an elegant but erroneous oversimplification. Scientists have demonstrated that
(50) the vast majority of animal genes participate in alternative splicing to one extent
or another; far from a mere biochemical curiosity, it is a vital biological strategy to
maximize the economy of genetic material, which must be laboriously reproduced
with each cell division, while maintaining an immense diversity in the protein-encod-
ing capacity of a genome. In an extreme example, the genome of the insect species
(55) *Drosophila melanogaster* contains about 15,000 genes. Yet, through alternative splicing, one single D *melanogaster* gene—known as DSCAM—has been shown to encode
about 38,000 different proteins.

The table illustrates the corresponding exons for the pre-mRNA transcipt and nine alternative splicing isoforms of the the α-tropomyosin gene.

mRNA Splicing Isoforms of α-tropomyosin

Isoform	Exons contained within mRNA Transcript														
Pre-mRNA	1a	2a	2b	1b	3	4	5	6a	6b	7	8	9a	9b	9c	9d
Tm1	1a	2b	3	4	5	6b	7	8	9a	9b	9c				
Tm6	1a	2a	3	4	5	6b	7	8	9d						
Tm2	1a	2a	3	4	5	6b	7	8	9d						
Tm3	1a	2b	3	4	5	6a	7	8	9d						
Tm5a	1b	3	4	5	6b	7	8	9d							
Tm5b	1b	3	4	5	6a	7	8	9d							
TmBr1	1a	2b	3	4	5	6b	7	8	9c						
TmBr2	1b	3	4	5	6b	7	8	9b							
TmBr3	1b	3	4	5	6b	7	8	9d							

1. What is the overall purpose of this passage?

   (A) To make an argument
   (B) To introduce a topic
   (C) To present opposing views
   (D) To give medical advice

2. The first paragraph of the essay (lines 1–6) primarily serves to

   (A) pay homage to the great scientists who made the discoveries highlighted in the passage.
   (B) put the subject of the passage in a wider context.
   (C) illustrate how little is known about a particular topic.
   (D) express the optimism the author has toward scientific advancement.

3. As used in line 3, the word "amassed" most closely means

   (A) inquired.
   (B) fused.
   (C) accumulated.
   (D) weighed.

4. As used in line 20, the word "excised" most closely means

   (A) removed.
   (B) translated.
   (C) coded.
   (D) mutated.

5. Lines 29–32 ("Furthermore . . . growth.") most strongly suggest that the author of the passage believes that scientific thinking regarding the contribution of altered splicing to cancer is

   (A) malignant.
   (B) skeptical.
   (C) assured.
   (D) unsettled.

6. Based on lines 54–57, which expression gives the most likely range of values for the total number of proteins in a *Drosophila melanogaster* genome?

   (A) Number of total proteins = 15,000 + 38,000
   (B) Number of total proteins = 38,000 − 15,000
   (C) Number of total proteins ≤ 38,000 × 15,000
   (D) Number of total proteins > 38,000 / 15,000

7. Which of the following statements accurately describes the relationship between the pre-mRNA and all the other isoforms portrayed in the table?

   (A) The pre-mRNA is spliced into the different isoforms in the sequence provided from top to bottom.
   (B) The other isoforms represent alternative splicing patterns derived from the original pre-mRNA.
   (C) The pre-mRNA represents a combination of the other isoforms' exons when they mutate during cellular reproduction.
   (D) The other isoforms use alternative splicing to create the given sequence of pre-mRNA.

8. Which option gives the best evidence for the answer to the previous question?

   (A) Lines 10–13 ("A 'promoter' . . . trait")
   (B) Lines 13–16 ("Similarly . . . stimuli")
   (C) Lines 18–19 ("During . . . DNA")
   (D) Lines 37–39 ("That is . . . proteins")

9. Scientists who thought along the lines outlined in lines 49–54 ("Scientists . . . genome") would most likely have what opinion about the information in the given table?

   (A) Supportive, because it demonstrates how alternative splicing can help maximize the economy of genetic material.
   (B) Supportive, because it shows the process whereby mRNA transforms into a potential variety of isoforms.
   (C) Unsupportive, because this data illustrates the potential pitfalls, such as cancerous mutations, associated with alternative splicing.
   (D) Unsupportive, because it mentions exons but ignores introns and their deletion during the alternative splicing process.

10. Based on the passage, what would someone who believed in the first historical theory of DNA most likely think would be the number of unique protein transcripts that would result from the replication of the α-tropomyosin gene outlined in the table?

   (A) 1
   (B) 3
   (C) 9
   (D) 12 or more

11. Which option gives the best evidence for the answer to the previous question?
   (A) Lines 1–4 ("With . . . daily")
   (B) Lines 4–6 ("Yet for . . . unravel")
   (C) Lines 29–32 ("Furthermore . . . growth")
   (D) Lines 46–48 ("The discovery . . . protein")

Passage C5

An English professor and a Master of Fine Arts candidate share their thoughts on literary standards.

PASSAGE 1

There is and must remain a standard by which good writing is measured and acknowledged. Take a moment to consider the alternative, and you'll surely come to agree with me. Without standard, anything and everything could be considered "litera-
Line ture." More so, it would change from person to person and place to place based solely
(5) on the rudimentary preference of varied individuals. Without a clear idea of what is meant by "literary," all writing is a chaotic mess of opinion and idiosyncratic inter-est with genre romance being just as viable as those rare works of art that embody the human experience, raise significant social and political questions, and remain in the readers' minds long after the book is finished. Without measure, the *Twilight* series sits
(10) right next to the works of Toni Morrison.

Let us think about what makes important writing. Writing, like all great forms of art, has the power to make us see the world more clearly. It is, when done effectively, a carrier of history and truth, a script of humanity that can be felt. It is lasting, or as Ezra Pound once remarked, "news that stays news." And it moves us. What I mean
(15) is that literature plays with the big questions, searches for the big things. It pursues beauty, purpose, and meaning in an aesthetic way that arouses emotion. The canon is acknowledged as superior and of artistic merit not because everyone likes reading the stuff, but because it heightens our understanding of life and rattles our comfort levels.

In essence, reading literature makes us better humans, and certainly, not all writing
(20) can do that. To say that writing cannot be measured or that there is not a clear stan-dard is absurd. While you may not like everything deemed "literary," it surely has the power to make you think and feel and wonder. It is this exploration of universal truths that intensifies our understanding of humanity and stirs something deep within us that makes literature. While you may laugh or cry or shout while reading *Harry Potter*,
(25) that in itself cannot classify it as one of the greats.

PASSAGE 2

I used to revel at my anxiety after turning in an assignment in my first years of my Creative Writing degree. One moment, I was quite sure that my work was genius. And another, I was the most dim-witted simpleton to ever put pen to paper. I had abso-lutely no idea whether my fiction would come back with an "A" or an "F" stamped on
(30) it—no clue how the professor might decide between the two. Often, I'd pull decent grades, but moan aloud when the instructor picked out my very favorite sentence—the one that was going to mark me the next Vonnegut or Kerouac—and crossed it out in red ink. *Rethink this* she'd scribble underneath. It took me two years and the onset of carpal tunnel to realize that there is no real way to know what's good, and that what's
(35) good is entirely subjective.

To test my theory, I submitted a few poems from previous semesters (highly frowned upon by the university, but necessary for my experiment) in hopes of getting a second opinion. I found that my grades varied only imperceptibly, but more inter-estingly, instructor feedback bordered on polarity. And so, I realized there is no true
(40) standard of measurement for writing, not creative writing at least. Once you venture past the "thesis statement" and "logical reasoning" and "coherent organization" of the purely academic writing, the concession on what is good is really nonexistent.

Sure, we might be able to agree that something particularly terrible is just that, and we might be able to nod our heads to a piece that is particularly brilliant and say
(45) that, at the very least, it isn't terrible. But overall, many will adore language that others detest, and some will gasp appreciatively at a metaphor that makes the masses vomit. I find enchanting what you find dull, and so it goes. And Mary Wright (fall semester) will find the same image "ineffective," which Tobias Dalton (spring semester) calls "delightful and provocative." And so I say, to each their own. What is thoughtful, good,
(50) and stirring is without impartiality, contingent not only on the reader, but the reader's mood, location, and even on what the reader has recently read. Therefore, write what you will and read what you wish, and if you like it, then declare with authority that it is indeed exceptional.

1. How would the author of Passage 1 most likely respond to someone who contended that the quality of literature is directly related to the intensity of the reader's emotional response?

   (A) Agree with it wholeheartedly.
   (B) Argue that a more precise standard is needed.
   (C) Dismiss the statement outright.
   (D) Argue that emotions are irrelevant to literary analysis.

2. Which option gives the best evidence for the answer to the previous question?

   (A) Lines 4–5 ("More so . . . individuals")
   (B) Lines 11–12 ("Let us . . . clearly")
   (C) Lines 20–21 ("To say . . . absurd")
   (D) Lines 24–25 ("While . . . greats")

3. To what idea does the word "alternative" (line 2) most likely refer?

   (A) Aesthetic beauty
   (B) Artistic interpretation
   (C) Literary relativism
   (D) Linguistic impartiality

4. As used in line 17, the word "merit" most closely means

   (A) quality.
   (B) literature.
   (C) artwork.
   (D) honesty.

5. Which of the following, if true, would present the greatest challenge to the argument of Passage 2?

   (A) Some people adore Shakespeare, while others do not care for his work.
   (B) Well-trained literary minds are able to use more sophisticated language to give their views on the quality of different texts.
   (C) American book readership has steadily declined in the past three decades.
   (D) The writer's academic evaluators graded in a hurried, haphazard way.

6. Lines 40–42 ("Once . . . nonexistent.") serve to acknowledge that the author of Passage 2 believes that

   (A) writing for scholarly journals is like other literary forms in the randomness of its quality.
   (B) there are at least some writing qualities that in certain contexts are more objective.
   (C) those who have confidence in scientific objectivity need only review literature to see the error of their ways.
   (D) there are three key components to a high-quality piece of writing.

7. The author of Passage 2 would contend that she would be more likely to receive a better grade from a certain instructor if he or she

   (A) happened to be in a pleasant mood and nice setting while grading.
   (B) had rigorous training by reviewing past student essays on the topic.
   (C) received positive feedback on the fairness of his or her grading from past students.
   (D) was well-versed in the different types of rubrics that could be used for evaluation.

8. Which option gives the best evidence for the answer to the previous question?

   (A) Lines 27–28 ("One . . . paper")
   (B) Lines 30–33 ("Often . . . underneath")
   (C) Lines 43–45 ("Sure . . . terrible")
   (D) Lines 49–51 ("What . . . read")

9. As used in line 50, the word "contingent" most closely means

   (A) grouped.
   (B) dependent.
   (C) random.
   (D) disappointed.

10. The authors of both passages would most likely agree with which of the following statements?

(A) The root of literary quality is whether it can express timeless truths.
(B) We should agree to disagree on whether literary quality is a fact or opinion.
(C) We can certainly agree that there are some literary works that are horrible.
(D) Interest in high-quality literature has made significant progress in recent years.

11. Which option best expresses the overall relationship between the two passages?

(A) Passage 1 argues for the existence of literary objectivity, while Passage 2 argues for the opposite.
(B) Passage 1 asserts the primacy of reading literature, while Passage 2 asserts that writing is the only gateway to understanding.
(C) Passage 1 contends that good literature makes readers uncomfortable, while Passage 2 contends that good literature is what is most popular.
(D) Passage 1 focuses on the "great books," whereas Passage 2 focuses on excellence in poetic expression.

ANSWER KEY

Passage C1

1. **B**	3. **D**	5. **D**	7. **B**	9. **B**
2. **C**	4. **A**	6. **B**	8. **D**	10. **A**

Passage C2

1. **D**	4. **A**	7. **C**	10. **A**
2. **C**	5. **B**	8. **B**	11. **D**
3. **B**	6. **A**	9. **B**	

Passage C3

1. **C**	3. **B**	5. **C**	7. **A**	9. **B**
2. **D**	4. **C**	6. **D**	8. **A**	10. **D**

Passage C4

1. **B**	4. **A**	7. **B**	10. **A**
2. **B**	5. **D**	8. **D**	11. **D**
3. **C**	6. **C**	9. **A**	

Passage C5

1. **B**	4. **A**	7. **A**	10. **C**
2. **D**	5. **D**	8. **D**	11. **A**
3. **C**	6. **B**	9. **B**	

ANSWERS EXPLAINED

Passage C1

1. **(B)** Based on the context of the excerpt, the narrator is deliberating on the "mirthless" ceremonial life of a priest—the path that has been designated for him—and an unpremeditated destiny "elusive of social or religious orders." His choice is not between holiness and criminality, as in (A). Nor does it consist of memories of degeneracy as in (D). Finally, (C) is incorrect because his decision is about more than simple logical consistency—he wants his choice to be consistent with his authentic desires.

2. **(C)** The narrator's contemplation is a buildup of thoughts and emotions that eventually leads to his realization in lines 39–42. It is not as though his thoughts progress spatially, since he is not having observations based on what he is gradually seeing in space. The passage is not structured with regard to the passage of time, since it has flashbacks. It is also not an argument as much as an internal reflection.

3. **(D)** In the first paragraph, the narrator attributes his "unrest" to the smells, sounds, and gloomy images of his time at Clonglowes. In the second, he imagines what life will be like if he continues to pursue priesthood and finds his prognosis repulsive. None of the other choices reflects these thought processes accurately.

4. **(A)** Lines 26–29 give the most direct evidence to how the narrator understands priests: "eyeless" and "sour-favoured" individuals with "suffocated anger." So, he would describe them as *repressing* emotions, not *celebrating* or *expressing* them. (C) doesn't work because the narrator thinks the anger is still present, just suffocated.

5. **(D)** Lines 26–27 best depict the narrator's conception of repressed emotions within the clergy. (A) shows anxiety and discontent, but only in remembering a pious education. (B) is a reflection of the narrator's that shows divergence between his innate characteristics and the manifestations of priesthood. (C) is a hypothetical imagining of his own self in priesthood, but does not give evidence of how priests handle emotion.

6. **(B)** In considering the communal necessities of continuing his pious education, the narrator questions the value he places first on his shyness and then his prideful seclusion. This is not a phrase that expresses approval, disinterest, or optimism.

7. **(B)** This is best seen in lines 41–42 when the narrator says he will learn "apart from others" or "himself wandering." (A) describes his previous education, with which he is unhappy. There is no evidence for (C) or (D).

8. **(D)** gives the best evidence for the educational style that the narrator wants to pursue, and that he thinks will work best for him. (A) describes his hostility toward a formal religious education. (B) is a negative image the narrator conceives when he imagines pursuing a religious education. (C) doesn't give evidence about a type of education.

9. **(B)** The surrounding context supports the idea that the priestly life does not appeal to the narrator. It makes sense to say the efforts of the priest to persuade him did not affect him "deeply."

10. **(A)** At the conclusion of the passage, the narrator yields to his fate. He is "still unfallen, but about to fall," so the best description of this tone would be *resignation*. *Terror* is too strong. *Corruption*, although related to sin, is not depictive of the narrator's tone. And *decreasing* would be used improperly here since the tone is not lessening in size or strength.

Passage C2

1. **(D)** The phrase is provided as a relevant and recognizable example in a sea of very technical analysis. *Esoteric* means likely to be understood by only a specialized audience. (A) and (C) involve concepts introduced later in the passage. Choice (B) is incorrect because the example is used to extend understanding to laypeople rather than imply they cannot understand it.

2. **(C)** From the context, we understand that surfactants reduce surface tension and can interfere with the stability of an oil-water film. Therefore, if its properties allow a surfactant to interfere with forces that maintain *integrity*, we can assume the proper word choice is *cohesion*, or "the act of sticking together." *Rectitude* refers to another meaning of *integrity*, like "virtue." *Decadence* is, then, the opposite of *rectitude*. And *solidarity*, while a tempting choice, usually refers to unity among a group of individuals.

3. **(B)** Lines 11–16 attribute surfactants' many applications to their unique property of being amphiphilic. While they are used often as emulsifiers, "emulsion" is not the dis-

tinction that leads to their popularity but a manifestation of that distinction. (A) refers specifically to biosurfactants, and (D) applies to soap but not all other surfactants.

4. **(A)** Lines 13–16 state that "surface tension lowering agents have found a host of applications in diverse commercial products" as a result of a unique property. The unique property here is that they are amphiphilic, so these lines provide direct evidence for the previous question.

5. **(B)** The question is asking how much of each surfactant exists, and since the main obstacle to biosurfactants is isolating them for industrial production, we can assume they are not yet used on a large scale and would likely be less common. Then, according to lines 46–48, detergents are the most produced and distributed of all commercially synthesized surfactants. So, choice (B) is correct.

6. **(A)** is the correct choice since the author makes sure to differentiate soaps and detergents despite the fact that they "are sometimes used interchangeably." (B) and (C) give misleading information that doesn't account for the passage's explanation that they are neither identical in structure nor in creation. (D) is wrong because lines 61–62 attribute the obstacle to isolating biosurfactants on a large enough scale.

7. **(C)** Lines 37–38 state that the two surfactants are erroneously used interchangeably, but that unlike soaps, "detergents are not synthesized by saponification." Then, the author devotes a paragraph to the differences of detergents. So, these lines give direct evidence for the previous question. (A) is where the passage gives the origin of the word *emulsion*. (B) references those lines which explain the structure of soap, while (D) references lines that state that biosurfactants are structurally distinct; however, neither choice differentiates soaps from detergents.

8. **(B)** Line 53 states that the controversy around detergents is "unlikely to be settled," so *resolved* is the best answer choice. It is not accurate to say the controversy is unlikely to be *firm, disturbed,* or *mobilized.*

9. **(B)** Soap bubbles with a concentration of 8.5% surfactant would make up a line between the 5% and 10% lines on the given graph. So, at 10 milliseconds, that line would be somewhere between 30 and 45, making (B) the accurate choice.

10. **(A)** The question is simply asking for the lines on the graph which show the greatest difference in surface tension. As we see in the graph, when the percentage is lower, the changes in surface tension are greater. So, since (A) has the smallest percentages, it is the correct answer.

11. **(D)** Don't be intimidated by this question. To approach it, look at the x-axis of the graph and notice that the increments follow an exponential scale, i.e., the units are multiplied by ten rather than following a standard linear pattern. We can infer that this logarithmic scale would be used to express a large range of quantities—in this instance, to see the changes over a wide range of time. So, (D) is correct. A linear scale could still be accurate, ruling out (A). A proportional relationship would not require a scale to cover such wide expanse, so (B) is inaccurate. And we can assume the scale was chosen for utility rather than to impress readership as in (C).

Passage C3

1. **(C)** As seen in lines 3–8, Descartes believes that he has accepted false knowledge and built his own principles on untruths, so he is *skeptical*. *Dogmatic* refers to an inclination to lay down principles as truth—this is the type of knowledge he wants to get rid of. His ability to acknowledge his own preconceived notions shows that he is not naïve, or *credulous*. And while fallacy may be widespread or *popular*, that does not illustrate his attitude toward knowledge.

2. **(D)** Lines 8–13 refer to the fact that Descartes has waited until an optimal age to try to break down his false principles, making (D) accurate. (A) and (B) are done in other lines, and (C) is not supported by the passage.

3. **(B)** Here, the author is indicating that he has waited until this age purposely to ensure that he is ready. So, (B) correctly designates *advanced* as related to time. The other choices don't refer to the author's age.

4. **(C)** Lines 20–21 state that, at minimum, Descartes can reject a concept if he finds "some ground for doubt." Hence, (C) is his threshold for dismissal. (A) and (B) suggest that Descartes would have to find a more considerable flaw. Finally, dismissing all knowledge as in (D) isn't his goal.

5. **(C)** These lines give direct evidence of how Descartes plans to approach any and all knowledge claims. He states that he doesn't have to prove them wholly false, but instead can reject any with a precarious existence. Choices (A) and (B) are related to the actual objective of ridding himself of adopted beliefs, but do not consider his requirement to what is false. And (D) is where he explains the absurdity of rebuking the most fundamental knowledge.

6. **(D)** These lines refer to Descartes' acknowledgement that there are some truths that are "manifestly impossible to doubt." As examples, Descartes presents sensory observations like his location, clothing, and current activities as occurrences of knowledge that he cannot refute. So, (D) is right. He is emphasizing the certainties of human perception, rather than the pitfalls. Additionally, he is not referring to "logical reasoning" or "tools," but merely to fundamental senses.

7. **(A)** *Hierarchal* accurately depicts Descartes' belief that knowledge is based on an order of rank. To him, certain forms of knowledge are superior to others; those of particular subservience are based wholly on false, predetermined opinions. (B) is incorrect because Descartes states that we form principles based on those opinions, so they are connected. *Indubitable* means "unquestionable." And *nonexistent* would imply that Descartes doesn't believe in knowledge whatsoever.

8. **(A)** In lines 7–8, Descartes realizes that he must purge any peremptory knowledge in order to succeed in the sciences, so we can safely infer that he believes knowledge of the sciences—founded on proven truths—to be of higher quality. (B) can be ruled out because it specifies that it is time to act, but doesn't address any structure of knowledge. (D) refers only to Descartes' examples of sensory truths. Choice (C) is appealing because it signifies Descartes' intention to disprove foundational beliefs, rather than go through each opinion. However, it doesn't hint at how he might go about ordering claims of knowledge.

9. **(B)** Lines 37–38 are a depiction of whatever it is that clouds the brain of the insane to make them think they are rich when they are poor, or they are clothed when naked, etc. So, it is related to *hallucinogenic visions*, not *demonic possession*, *chronic depression*, or *mathematical logic*.

10. **(D)** *Excessive* works here since it is referring to Descartes' acknowledgement that it would be irrational to question some forms of knowledge, such as those basic sensory perceptions, especially if he did so to the extent that the people who have delusions mentioned previously in this paragraph did. (A) is another definition of *extravagant*, but refers to expensive elegance. (B) is the opposite of this word meaning. And (C) does not reflect an extreme example as intended.

Passage C4

1. **(B)** This passage is explanatory and informative, but fails to argue or give medical advice. The author does compare historical scientific paradigms to more recent discoveries, but these are not opposing so much as replacing the outdated beliefs.

2. **(B)** The first paragraph introduces the topic of genetic material, states that the research up until now is "staggering," and indicates that there is still a lot more to discover, so (B), provides a wider context, is the appropriate choice. (A) is a detail but not the objective of these lines. The opening paragraph may state that there are "many mysteries," but it does not *illustrate* our limited knowledge in any way as in (C). It is not (D) because there is not a discussion of the author's feelings toward advancement.

3. **(C)** *Accumulated* makes the most sense here because we are discussing the volume of knowledge that has been compiled in the last fifty years. No one is *inquiring*, *fusing*, or *weighing* the knowledge.

4. **(A)** In lines 21–24, the author describes the process, stating that the introns are "removed and degraded" so (A) is the correct answer. The exons are *translated*, but the word *excised* is specifically referring to the introns.

5. **(D)** According to the author, "it remains to be seen," so *unsettled* is the best description for the connection between altered splicing and cancer. *Skeptical* means doubtful and is too negative here. *Assured* is much too confident. And *malignant* means diseased or uncontrollable and is usually associated with the severe effects of cancer.

6. **(C)** We can find the number of proteins by multiplying how many genes there are by how many proteins they code for. Line 54 tells us that this particular gene—that codes for 38,000 proteins—is "an extreme example." Therefore, if the genome has about 15,000 genes, it is highly unlikely that they all encode for that many proteins. Hence, we can assume that the total number of proteins is less than $15{,}000 \times 38{,}000$. In fact, even if the genes were all similarly extreme, (C) would still be correct because the total proteins would be equal to $15{,}000 \times 38{,}000$.

7. **(B)** From the context, we know that pre-mRNA develops after the template DNA and can code for a variety of proteins through alternative splicing. So, looking at the table, we can assume that the isoforms are different codes that occurred during splicing, making (B) the correct answer. It isn't (A) because there is no evidence that the codes always

occur in the same pattern. And (C) and (D) incorrectly have the pre-mRNA developing from the isoforms rather than vice versa.

8. **(D)** Lines 37–39 explain the phenomenon of alternative splicing in accessible language. Since this gives direct evidence that strands of pre-mRNA undergo splicing to code for different proteins, it is supportive of the previous question. Choices (A) and (B) are not helpful because they simply define the different regions of a gene. (C) isn't correct because, although it introduces pre-mRNA, it doesn't discuss the splicing that accounts for the different isoforms in the previous question.

9. **(A)** Lines 49–54 introduce the scientific idea that alternative spicing is essential to maximizing the economy of genetic material and maintaining diversity. Since the table exhibits several isoforms that arise from splicing in one gene, it can reasonably be inferred that these same scientists would support the data. It isn't (B) because the table doesn't *show the process* and because the scientists are more interested in its implications for the economy of genetic material and diversity.

10. **(A)** According to lines 46–48, the traditional understanding of genes "held that each coding region was responsible for the expression of a single protein," so a believer in this theory would assume that the one α-tropomyosin gene would code for one protein. There is no evidence to support the other answer choices. Likewise, the nine alternative forms in the table might be anticipated by an up-to-date scientist, but not someone who supported the historical theory of DNA.

11. **(D)** These lines serve to define the traditional theory of DNA that is most useful in answering the previous question. The author tells us that we previously entertained a simplified understanding that genes coded for a single, distinct protein; this reasoning supports the idea that someone under that impression would expect only one transcript in the table. (A) and (B) provide the background and framework for the topic, but do not address the historical theory specifically. (C) is not correct because these lines merely discuss the unresolved patterns found within splicing and cancer.

Passage C5

1. **(B)** In lines 14–16, the author of Passage 1 makes it clear that what qualifies as literature "arouses emotion," but also states in lines 22–25 that emotion in and of itself is not enough. Therefore, answer (B) is correct because although a reader's emotional response is critical, it is not the sole standard.

2. **(D)** Lines 24–25 state that reader response alone cannot classify a work "as one of the greats." These lines directly contend that the author of Passage 1 would argue for a more precise standard than emotional response. (A) and (C) restate the author's argument that literature demands objectivity. Choice (B), though tempting, expresses the author's opinion that literature should help the reader to understand the world better, but doesn't give evidence of his or her feelings toward emotional reaction.

3. **(C)** *Literary relativism* works here because line 2 is referring to an instance where writing is without measure and is, therefore, preferential. Relativism is the concept that knowledge and truth do not exist outside culture and society, so choice (C) would render an alternative where the quality of literature varies with perception. (A) is an element that should be considered in measuring literature, according to the first passage.

(B) is incorrect because the alternative would be subjective to all interpretation, not just *artistic interpretation*. Finally, *linguistic impartiality* would imply a neutrality toward language, so (D) is wrong.

4. **(A)** Artistic *merit* refers to excellence or worthiness of the arts, so *quality* is the correct choice. Choices (B) and (C) would be repetitive, and choice (D) would indicate artistic integrity rather than value.

5. **(D)** The author of Passage 2 believes that the quality of writing is "entirely subjective," and bases his or her argument on inconsistent grading. So, choice (D) would rule out the evidence and undermine the author's argument. (A) would support Passage 1. (B) and (C) don't affect the argument either way.

6. **(B)** To paraphrase lines 40–42, the author of Passage 2 understands that basic academic writing requires at least a loose organization, while anything beyond it is sans guideline. Only choice (B) considers the author's acknowledgment of certain contextual requirements despite his or her opinion that writing is generally without measure.

7. **(A)** According to lines 49–51, a reader's evaluation is "contingent not only on the reader, but the reader's mood, location, and even on what the reader has recently read." So, we can infer that he or she would believe a grade would depend on both mood and setting as in choice (A). An evaluator's training, past feedback, or familiarity with different rubrics would not influence a reader's response as much as disposition and/or atmosphere.

8. **(D)** These lines directly support the author's opinion that several factors influence reader response, so (D) is the proper option because it is the only one that considers an instructor's inconsistency. Choices (A) and (B) refer to the author's personal experiences with discrepancy in writing. Choice (C) indicates that only writing extremes can be agreed on.

9. **(B)** *Contingent* is defined as "subject to chance" or "dependent on," so (B) is the correct answer. It is not appropriate to say writing standards are *grouped*, *random*, or *disappointed* on multiple factors.

10. **(C)** Both authors acknowledge that some writing is particularly bad as in (C). Passage 1 contends that standards are precise and clearly measurable, while Passage 2 grants that "particularly terrible" and "particularly brilliant" writing are the only areas of concession. Only the first author would agree with (A). Since both authors show a strong opinion on the matter, neither would support (B). Finally, there is no evidence in either passage for (D).

11. **(A)** The first passage argues that literature is a term reserved for writing that is artistically superior and timeless, pursuing "beauty, purpose, and meaning." The second passage, on the other hand, postulates that standards of evaluation are illusory and biased. Therefore, (A) is the only option that captures the overall relationship between the two passages.

Reading
Practice Tests

Reading
Practice Tests

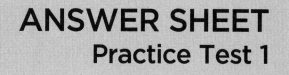

ANSWER SHEET
Practice Test 1

Reading

1. Ⓐ Ⓑ Ⓒ Ⓓ
2. Ⓐ Ⓑ Ⓒ Ⓓ
3. Ⓐ Ⓑ Ⓒ Ⓓ
4. Ⓐ Ⓑ Ⓒ Ⓓ
5. Ⓐ Ⓑ Ⓒ Ⓓ
6. Ⓐ Ⓑ Ⓒ Ⓓ
7. Ⓐ Ⓑ Ⓒ Ⓓ
8. Ⓐ Ⓑ Ⓒ Ⓓ
9. Ⓐ Ⓑ Ⓒ Ⓓ
10. Ⓐ Ⓑ Ⓒ Ⓓ
11. Ⓐ Ⓑ Ⓒ Ⓓ
12. Ⓐ Ⓑ Ⓒ Ⓓ
13. Ⓐ Ⓑ Ⓒ Ⓓ

14. Ⓐ Ⓑ Ⓒ Ⓓ
15. Ⓐ Ⓑ Ⓒ Ⓓ
16. Ⓐ Ⓑ Ⓒ Ⓓ
17. Ⓐ Ⓑ Ⓒ Ⓓ
18. Ⓐ Ⓑ Ⓒ Ⓓ
19. Ⓐ Ⓑ Ⓒ Ⓓ
20. Ⓐ Ⓑ Ⓒ Ⓓ
21. Ⓐ Ⓑ Ⓒ Ⓓ
22. Ⓐ Ⓑ Ⓒ Ⓓ
23. Ⓐ Ⓑ Ⓒ Ⓓ
24. Ⓐ Ⓑ Ⓒ Ⓓ
25. Ⓐ Ⓑ Ⓒ Ⓓ
26. Ⓐ Ⓑ Ⓒ Ⓓ

27. Ⓐ Ⓑ Ⓒ Ⓓ
28. Ⓐ Ⓑ Ⓒ Ⓓ
29. Ⓐ Ⓑ Ⓒ Ⓓ
30. Ⓐ Ⓑ Ⓒ Ⓓ
31. Ⓐ Ⓑ Ⓒ Ⓓ
32. Ⓐ Ⓑ Ⓒ Ⓓ
33. Ⓐ Ⓑ Ⓒ Ⓓ
34. Ⓐ Ⓑ Ⓒ Ⓓ
35. Ⓐ Ⓑ Ⓒ Ⓓ
36. Ⓐ Ⓑ Ⓒ Ⓓ
37. Ⓐ Ⓑ Ⓒ Ⓓ
38. Ⓐ Ⓑ Ⓒ Ⓓ
39. Ⓐ Ⓑ Ⓒ Ⓓ

40. Ⓐ Ⓑ Ⓒ Ⓓ
41. Ⓐ Ⓑ Ⓒ Ⓓ
42. Ⓐ Ⓑ Ⓒ Ⓓ
43. Ⓐ Ⓑ Ⓒ Ⓓ
44. Ⓐ Ⓑ Ⓒ Ⓓ
45. Ⓐ Ⓑ Ⓒ Ⓓ
46. Ⓐ Ⓑ Ⓒ Ⓓ
47. Ⓐ Ⓑ Ⓒ Ⓓ
48. Ⓐ Ⓑ Ⓒ Ⓓ
49. Ⓐ Ⓑ Ⓒ Ⓓ
50. Ⓐ Ⓑ Ⓒ Ⓓ
51. Ⓐ Ⓑ Ⓒ Ⓓ
52. Ⓐ Ⓑ Ⓒ Ⓓ

Practice Test 1

65 MINUTES, 52 QUESTIONS

> **Directions:** Each passage or pair of passages is accompanied by several questions. After reading the passage(s), choose the best answer to each question based on what is indicated explicitly or implicitly in the passage(s) or in the associated graphics.

Questions 1–10 are based on the following reading selection.

Below is the beginning of Harriet Beecher Stowe's 1852 novel, Uncle Tom's Cabin. *Her own remark on the chapter is as follows: "in which the reader is introduced to a man of humanity."*

Late in the afternoon of a chilly day in February two gentlemen were sitting over their wine, in a well-furnished parlour in the
Line town of P---- in Kentucky in the midst of an
(5) earnest conversation.

"That is the way I should arrange the matter," said Mr. Shelby, the owner of the place. "The fact is, Tom is an uncommon fellow; he is certainly worth that sum anywhere; steady,
(10) honest, capable, manages my farm like a clock. You ought to let him cover the whole of the debt; and you would, Haley, if you'd got any conscience."

"Well, I've got just as much conscience
(15) as any man in business can afford to keep," said Haley, "and I'm willing to do anything to 'blige friends; but this yer, ye see, is too hard on a feller, it really is. Haven't you a boy or gal you could thrown in with Tom?"
(20) "Hum!—none that I could well spare; to tell the truth, it's only hard necessity makes

me sell at all." Here the door opened, and a small quadroon boy, remarkably beautiful and engaging, entered with a comic air
(25) of assurance which showed he was used to being petted and noticed by his master. "Hulloa, Jim Crow," said Mr. Shelby, snapping a bunch of raisins towards him, "pick that up, now!" The child scampered, with all his
(30) little strength after the prize, while his master laughed. "Tell you what," said Haley, "fling in that chap, and I'll settle the business, I will."

At this moment a young woman, obviously the child's mother, came in search of him,
(35) and Haley, as soon as she had carried him away, turned to Mr. Shelby in admiration.

"By Jupiter!" said the trader, "there's an article now! You might make your fortune on that one gal in Orleans, any way. What shall I
(40) say for her? What'll you take?"

"Mr. Haley, she is not to be sold. I say no, and I mean no," said Mr. Shelby, decidedly.

"Well, you'll let me have the boy, though."

"I would rather not sell him," said Mr.
(45) Shelby; "the fact is, I'm a humane man, and I hate to take the boy from his mother, sir."

"Oh, you do? La, yes, I understand perfectly. It is mighty unpleasant getting on with women sometimes. I al'ays hates these
(50) yer screechin' times. As I manages busi-

GO ON TO THE NEXT PAGE

ness, I generally avoids 'em, sir. Now, what
if you get the gal off for a day or so? then the
thing's done quietly. It's always best to do the
humane thing, sir; that's been my experi-
(55) ence." "I'd like to have been able to kick the
fellow down the steps," said Mr. Shelby to
himself, when the trader had bowed himself
out. "And Eliza's child, too! I know I shall have
some fuss with the wife about that, and for
(60) that matter, about Tom, too! So much for
being in debt, heigho!"

The prayer-meeting at Uncle Tom's Cabin
had been protracted to a very late hour, and
Tom and his worthy helpmeet were not yet
(65) asleep, when between twelve and one there
was a light tap on the window pane.

"Good Lord! what's that?" said Aunt Chloe,
starting up. "My sakes alive, if it aint Lizzy!
Get on your clothes, old man, quick. I'm
(70) gwine to open the door." And suiting the
action to the word, the door flew open, and
the light of the candle which Tom had hastily
lighted, fell on the face of Eliza. "I'm running
away, Uncle Tom and Aunt Chloe—carrying
(75) off my child. Master sold him."

"Sold him?" echoed both, holding up their
hands in dismay.

"Yes, sold him!" said Eliza firmly. "I crept
into the closet by mistress's door to-night,
(80) and I heard master tell missus that he had
sold my Harry and you, Uncle Tom, both to a
trader, and that the man was to take possession to-day."

Slowly, as the meaning of this speech
(85) came over Tom, he collapsed on his old chair,
and sunk his head on his knees.

1. Which choice provides the best summary of
what happened in the passage?

(A) A deal is reluctantly made and the
reactions of those affected are given.
(B) A slave successfully plots an escape from
an oppressive society.
(C) A man struggles to choose between what
is humane and what is profitable.
(D) A philosophical discussion is held
between a slave-owner and a
slave-trader.

2. Haley is best characterized as a/an

(A) humane empathizer.
(B) financial amateur.
(C) aggressive negotiator.
(D) passive mediator.

3. As used in line 31, the phrase "fling in" most
closely means

(A) include.
(B) hurl.
(C) relate.
(D) involve.

4. Mr. Shelby's treatment of the child in lines
27–32 is best described as

(A) purposely deceitful.
(B) unintentionally inhumane.
(C) openly belligerent.
(D) tenderly impartial.

5. As used in line 38, the word "article" most
closely means

(A) agreement.
(B) report.
(C) word.
(D) item.

GO ON TO THE NEXT PAGE

6. The passage most strongly implies that Tom's reaction to hearing of Mr. Shelby's plans for him is one of

   (A) unanticipated peacefulness.
   (B) delighted relief.
   (C) surprised despondency.
   (D) playful mockery.

7. Which option gives the best evidence for the answer to the previous question?

   (A) Lines 58–61 ("I know . . . heigho")
   (B) Lines 62–66 ("The prayer . . . pane")
   (C) Lines 73–75 ("I'm . . . him")
   (D) Lines 84–86 ("Slowly . . . knees")

8. It can reasonably be inferred that Mr. Shelby places the highest value on which character?

   (A) Tom
   (B) Eliza
   (C) Eliza's son
   (D) Chloe

9. Which option gives the best evidence for the answer to the previous question?

   (A) Lines 8–13 ("The fact . . . conscience")
   (B) Lines 27–32 ("Hulloa . . . will")
   (C) Lines 37–42 ("By . . . decidedly")
   (D) Lines 67–70 ("Good . . . door")

10. The "light tap" made by Eliza in line 66 suggests that she

   (A) feared unwanted detection.
   (B) respected nightly rituals.
   (C) was hesitant to share bad news.
   (D) understood her misdeeds.

Questions 11-21 are based on the following reading selection and accompanying material.

The Woes of Consumerism

Ah, but you see my friend, I fail to be "hipster" without the checkered shirt, bow tie, and skinny jeans.

Line My free-spirited best friend is only "boho"
(5) with her headband and fringe bag. And my "preppy" sister is rarely seen without her bean boots and striped cardigans. One day, I will drive a Mercedes-Benz because, well why wouldn't I? And when all of my aspirations
(10) and the labels attached to them cause in me a great migraine, I will take Tylenol before stopping at the neighborhood Starbucks for my daily mocha latte. You see where this is going because you are so perceptive and
(15) undoubtedly a Millennial, known for your skepticism, feelings of self-importance, and immunity to the pathetic propaganda that so easily tricked the previous generations. *But, are you immune to being tricked?*
(20) You would do well to study the following list of definitions before continuing. They were all found via a simple Google search for the respective term.

- *capitalism*: an economic and political
(25) system in which a country's trade and industry are controlled by private owners for profit, rather than by the state
- *consumerism*: a social and economic order and ideology that encourages the
(30) acquisition of goods and services in ever-increasing amounts
- *propaganda*: information, especially of a biased or misleading nature, used to influence an audience and further an
(35) agenda
- *advertising*: the marketing communication used by companies to persuade an audience to purchase their products and/or services

GO ON TO THE NEXT PAGE

(40) ■ *mere exposure*: a psychological phenomenon in which people develop a preference for things through familiarity

■ *affective conditioning*: the transfer of feelings from one set of items to another (45) to encourage the public to associate a product with positivity

Certainly, you have ascended beyond the manipulation accompanying such ridiculous subculture labels as those mentioned above. (50) You have seen it and heard it all. Advertising is all around you; we live in a commercial world—a capitalist economy with an unparalleled attachment to consumerism. But those sly little devils are far from bringing (55) you to the dark side. *Or so you think.*

Nobody wants to feel easily influenced. Yet, I beg you to hear me out: advertising is everywhere because it works. U.S. companies spend an annual $70 billion in televi- (60) sion ads, and this is before we take a look at other mediums of advertising like radios, magazines, website cookies, and even those terrible social media "sponsored" ads. The truth is we don't like to feel manipulated, but (65) we are. Advertising is by its nature a form of propaganda in that it changes perceptions with limited information—it is neither objective nor complete.

Advertising is meant to do a few things. (70) First, it informs the public of a product's existence (no harm in that, right?). Next, it is meant to build brand recognition—as consumers, we want to trust and recognize the names behind our products. Third, advertis- (75) ing creates lifestyle identification. The product is somehow "like you"; it says something about you; you can relate to the product and its other consumers. The world of advertising spends a lot of money and time developing (80) strategies to accomplish these three goals.

We will first look at logical persuasion, or the exposition of facts about products. This technique in itself is quite harmless. We cannot be informed consumers without (85) information. Yet, I urge you to be skeptical of even the most straightforward advertising. Mere exposure is an effective tool in leaving lasting impressions on the public. With your only basis as recognition, you would be (90) surprised to see how quickly you choose one product over another, even at a higher cost.

Perhaps more dangerous is the strategy of nonrational influence, in which advertising schemes circumvent consumers' conscious (95) awareness by depicting a fun or pleasant scene quite unrelated to the product itself. Here, affective conditioning allows you to

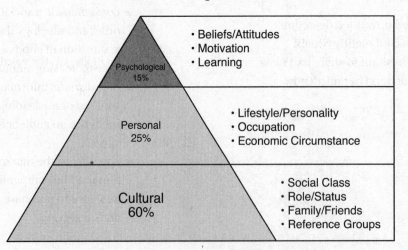

Factors Influencing Consumer Behavior

Psychological 15%
- Beliefs/Attitudes
- Motivation
- Learning

Personal 25%
- Lifestyle/Personality
- Occupation
- Economic Circumstance

Cultural 60%
- Social Class
- Role/Status
- Family/Friends
- Reference Groups

GO ON TO THE NEXT PAGE

associate positive feelings with specific products. For instance, a commercial might
(100) flash images of colorful flowers, sunshine, puppies, etc.; and even years later, your subconscious will recall these "feel good" images when you spot that product. *Psychology Today* found that this type of advertising
(105) lowers brain activity and causes less restraint in the consumer. According to the study, you are 70–80% more likely to buy an inferior product when you have paired it with positive feelings.
(110)   Just remember, my wary consumer, to use caution in a society of distortion and illusion. Advertising can be subtle, but powerful. And if you think you are unaffected, *think again.*

11. It is most reasonable to infer that the author believes the members of her readership think they are

(A) wealthier than their peers.
(B) above the influence of advertising.
(C) more politically astute than their elders.
(D) destined to leave a great legacy to their offspring.

12. What is the most likely reason that the author chose to begin the essay as she did rather than beginning with the second paragraph?

(A) To help her readers first understand the pitfalls of advertising before seeing its benefits
(B) To give examples of terms used in context prior to those same terms being defined
(C) To provide a modern case study before a discussion of historical precedents
(D) To build rapport with her readers before delving into a technical analysis

13. As used in lines 1–6, the words "hipster," "boho," and "preppy" most closely mean

(A) progressive youth.
(B) fashion subcultures.
(C) independent thinkers.
(D) unconventional labels.

14. The author most strongly suggests that the overall attitude that consumers should have towards advertising should be

(A) grateful.
(B) subconscious.
(C) distrustful.
(D) bellicose.

15. Which option gives the best evidence for the answer to the previous question?

(A) Lines 1–9 ("Ah . . . wouldn't I")
(B) Lines 50–55 ("Advertising . . . *think*")
(C) Lines 85–91 ("Yet . . . cost")
(D) Lines 97–103 ("Here . . . product")

16. What is most likely the purpose of lines 58–63 ("U.S. . . . ads")?

(A) To explain the process by which advertising is created
(B) To critique corporations for misleading, unethical practices
(C) To give concrete evidence to illustrate the impact of advertising
(D) To demonstrate instances when consumers feel consciously manipulated

17. As used in line 61, the word "mediums" most closely means

(A) middles.
(B) ranges.
(C) methods.
(D) medians.

GO ON TO THE NEXT PAGE

18. According to the graph, cultural factors are approximately what percentage greater in their influence than the combination of personal and psychological factors?

    (A) 30%
    (B) 40%
    (C) 50%
    (D) 60%

19. Based on the information in the graph and the passage, an advertiser wishing to effectively use affective conditioning would most likely show what sort of a scene to advertise a car?

    (A) The car being driven by a famous celebrity through a beautiful seaside landscape
    (B) The car driver shown listening to educational programs on the car's satellite radio
    (C) A car buyer looking at different car price tags and finding the one being advertised to be the cheapest
    (D) An engineer of the car carefully describing its unique design features

20. Which option gives the best evidence for the answer to the previous question?

    (A) Lines 99–103 ("For instance . . . product")
    (B) Lines 103–106 ("*Psychology* . . . consumer")
    (C) Lines 106–109 ("According . . . feelings")
    (D) Lines 110–113 ("Just . . . *again*")

21. Which of the following modifications to the graph would make it more helpful to a consulting firm advising clients from a wide range of industries as to how to best spend their advertising dollars?

    (A) Giving a greater degree of precision in the presented results by reporting the factor percentages to the nearest hundredth of a percent instead of a whole percent
    (B) Reporting the per capita income levels of the persons surveyed
    (C) Adding a breakdown of the relative influence of the three factors with respect to general categories of products, such as entertainment, finance, and consumer goods
    (D) Providing this same factor breakdown, but doing so with respect to different geographical regions

GO ON TO THE NEXT PAGE

Hemoglobin

This passage is adapted from A.F. Young, "Pathogenesis of Hemoglobinopathies."

There are few biochemical compounds as familiar to us as hemoglobin, and as the primary transporter of oxygen in our blood,
Line the celebrity of this curious little compound
(5) is not without just cause. Vital to almost every known vertebrate, hemoglobin appears within the very first week of embryogenesis, and while its role may not change throughout development, its molecular structure under-
(10) goes a series of significant transformations.

Within the red blood cell, hemoglobin exists as a four-subunit complex, or "tetramer," each subunit of which is made up of one "heme" metalloprotein, and one of sev-
(15) eral varieties of "globin." Comprised of iron and a carbon-nitrogen ring, heme is responsible for both the oxygen-binding capacity of hemoglobin, and for the red coloration of blood. Globin, meanwhile, refers to a folded
(20) chain of polypeptides, and it is the combination of these chains that imparts each type of hemoglobin with its unique characteristics.

In humans, six globin chains are expressed sequentially throughout development.
(25) Embryonic hemoglobin, or HbE, is composed of two ζ chains and two ε chains, both of which are expressed exclusively during the embryonic period. In the fetal period, another tetramer of two α chains and two
(30) γ chains emerges, and persists for the first six months of postnatal life. Due to its high affinity for binding gases, this fetal hemoglobin, or HbF, is able to extract oxygen from low-affinity maternal hemoglobin, and thus
(35) plays a crucial role in the oxygenation of fetal tissues. Like HbF, the final two physiologic hemoglobins, HbA and HbA_2, also require a pair of α chains, and differ only in being

coupled to two β chains, and two δ chains,
(40) respectively. Typically, both HbA and HbA_2 are synthesized at fairly stable concentrations, though HbA is produced in far greater abundance.

Given the tremendous import of these
(45) complexes, it should hardly be surprising that errors in their production can yield devastating results. What may be surprising, however, is that these errors—including sickle-cell disease and thalassemia—are
(50) among the most common of all inherited genetic disorders, with an estimated 7% of the world's population as carriers, two-thirds of whom reside in Africa.

Thalassemia describes a group of dis-
(55) orders in which either the α or β chain is quantitatively reduced. Depending on the mutation, these defects can present with a wide range of anemia-related symptoms, and are particularly prevalent throughout Africa,
(60) Southeast Asia, and the Mediterranean. This geographical distribution is anything but random. Many studies have demonstrated that the production of suboptimal hemoglobin confers a degree of protection against
(65) malaria, a potentially deadly infectious disease caused by members of the *Plasmodium* genus, which parasitize red blood cells. It follows, then, that whereas in many regions throughout the world thalassemia may
(70) merely constitute disease, in those where malaria is endemic, it represents a favorable evolutionary advantage.

Owing to a redundancy in the human genome, there are four copies of the α globin
(75) gene, with two α-coding regions on each copy of chromosome 16. For this reason, the spectrum of severity in α thalassemia is particularly broad. For instance, deletion of a single gene will result in a carrier state, and
(80) is unlikely to cause clinically acute symptoms. Deletion of all four, meanwhile, leads to a precipitation during the fetal period of nonfunctional γ tetramers, also called Hb Barts, and is universally lethal in utero.

GO ON TO THE NEXT PAGE

(85) Similarly, a deletion of three copies typically results in a serious but survivable anemia, and is characterized by the formation of Hb Barts in the fetal period, and nonfunctional β tetramers, termed HbH, through-
(90) out adulthood. Predictably, a deletion of two copies produces a still milder anemia, but can be subclassified based on whether the deletions occur on the same chromosome, termed "cis" deletion, or on opposite
(95) chromosomes, termed "trans" deletion. The trans subtype appears more commonly in the Mediterranean, while cis is more often found in Asia. Notably, it has been suggested

that the cis deletion may contribute to the
(100) relatively higher rates of failed pregnancies observed in this part of the world.

Like its α counterpart, β thalassemia also impairs the production of HbA. However, the symptoms of β thalassemia will not become
(105) evident until after the first six months of life, when the concentration of HbF wanes to a critical threshold. Often, a compensatory upregulation in the expression of HbA_2 occurs in affected individuals, the effects of
(110) which can be pharmaceutically augmented by a drug called hydroxyurea, which induces the expression of HbF in children and adults.

The graph shows varying concentrations of globin chains during human development.

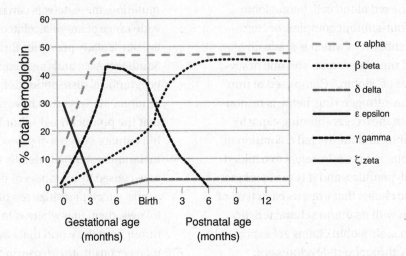

22. The general purpose of this passage is to

(A) make an argument.

(B) raise vital questions.

(C) introduce a concept.

(D) call for a course of action.

23. As used in line 4, the word "celebrity" most closely means

(A) notoriety.

(B) infamy.

(C) personage.

(D) festivity.

GO ON TO THE NEXT PAGE

24. Based on lines 11–22 and the information in the graph, what makes the hemoglobin varieties distinct?

(A) Whether there is a carbon-nitrogen ring
(B) Whether there is a red coloration of the blood
(C) Variation in the arrangement of metalloprotein chains
(D) Variation in the arrangement of polypeptide chains

25. Which option gives the best evidence for the answer to the previous question?

(A) Lines 11–15 ("Within . . . globin")
(B) Lines 15–16 ("Comprised . . . ring")
(C) Lines 16–19 ("heme . . . blood")
(D) Lines 19–22 ("Globin . . . characteristics")

26. The paragraph in lines 44–53 most strongly suggests that it is surprising that

(A) the vast majority of inherited genetic disorders occur due to malfunctions in hemoglobin production.
(B) biochemical compounds so important to human development can so frequently have errors in their production.
(C) such a critical part of human health is susceptible to widespread pandemic contagion.
(D) sickle-cell disease and thalassemia, despite being genetically inherited diseases, can be responsible for the majority of early deaths in Africa.

27. As used in line 50, the word "common" most closely means

(A) communal.
(B) lowly.
(C) widespread.
(D) famous.

28. The purpose of lines 60–72 is to connect

(A) hemoglobin development to migration patterns.
(B) cultural characteristics to evolutionary traits.
(C) geographic particularities to evolutionary adaptation.
(D) environmental forces to medical innovations.

29. Lines 73–78 ("Owing . . . broad") most directly imply that the intensity of thalassemia would be more uniform if there were

(A) fewer copies of the α globin gene in humans.
(B) the same number of copies of the α globin gene in humans.
(C) more copies of the α globin gene in humans.
(D) more information is needed than is given in the selected sentences.

30. The paragraph in lines 73–101 suggests that the relationship between the number of globin genes deleted and the severity of disease is

(A) inverse.
(B) proportional.
(C) equivalent.
(D) random.

GO ON TO THE NEXT PAGE

31. What evidence from the passage gives the best justification as to why the graph begins along the *x*-axis where it does?

    (A) Lines 5–7 ("Vital . . . embryogenesis")
    (B) Lines 19–22 ("Globin . . . characteristics")
    (C) Lines 47–53 ("What . . . Africa")
    (D) Lines 81–84 ("Deletion . . . utero")

32. Based on the graph, a rough measurement of which of the following globin chains would give the clearest indication that a child was born two months premature?

    (A) Alpha
    (B) Beta
    (C) Gamma
    (D) Zeta

Questions 33–42 are based on the following reading selection.

This excerpt from "The American Forests," was part of John Muir's 1897 campaign to save the American wilderness. He would later be called the godfather of the American environmental movement.

The forests of America, however slighted
by man, must have been a great delight to
God; for they were the best he ever planted.
Line The whole continent was a garden, and from
(5) the beginning it seemed to be favored above
all the other wild parks and gardens of the
globe. [...]
   So they appeared a few centuries ago
when they were rejoicing in wildness. The
(10) Indians with stone axes could do them no
more harm than could gnawing beavers and
browsing moose. Even the fires of the Indians
and the fierce shattering lightning seemed to
work together only for good in clearing spots
(15) here and there for smooth garden prairies,
and openings for sunflowers seeking the
light. But when the steel axe of the white man
rang out in the startled air their doom was
sealed. Every tree heard the bodeful sound,
(20) and pillars of smoke gave the sign in the sky.
   I suppose we need not go mourning the
buffaloes. In the nature of things they had to
give place to better cattle, though the change
might have been made without barbarous
(25) wickedness. Likewise many of nature's five
hundred kinds of wild trees had to make way
for orchards and cornfields. In the settlement
and civilization of the country, bread more
than timber or beauty was wanted; and in
(30) the blindness of hunger, the early settlers,
claiming Heaven as their guide, regarded
God's trees as only a larger kind of perni-
cious weeds, extremely hard to get rid of.
Accordingly, with no eye to the future, these
(35) pious destroyers waged interminable forest
wars; chips flew thick and fast; trees in their

GO ON TO THE NEXT PAGE

beauty fell crashing by millions, smashed to confusion, and the smoke of their burning has been rising to heaven more than two (40) hundred years. After the Atlantic coast from Maine to Georgia had been mostly cleared and scorched into melancholy ruins, the overflowing multitude of bread and money seekers poured over the Alleghenies into (45) the fertile middle West, spreading ruthless devastation ever wider and farther over the rich valley of the Mississippi and the vast shadowy pine region about the Great Lakes. Thence still westward the invading horde of (50) destroyers called settlers made its fiery way over the broad Rocky Mountains, felling and burning more fiercely than ever, until at last it has reached the wild side of the continent, and entered the last of the great aboriginal (55) forests on the shores of the Pacific.

Surely, then, it should not be wondered at that lovers of their country, bewailing its baldness, are now crying aloud, "Save what is left of the forests!" Clearing has surely now (60) gone far enough; soon timber will be scarce, and not a grove will be left to rest in or pray in. The remnant protected will yield plenty of timber, a perennial harvest for every right use, without further diminution of its area, (65) and will continue to cover the springs of the rivers that rise in the mountains and give irrigating waters to the dry valleys at their feet, prevent wasting floods and be a blessing to everybody forever.

(70) Every other civilized nation in the world has been compelled to care for its forests, and so must we if waste and destruction are not to go on to the bitter end, leaving America as barren as Palestine or Spain. In its (75) calmer moments in the midst of bewildering hunger and war and restless over-industry, Prussia has learned that the forest plays an important part in human progress, and that the advance in civilization only makes it (80) more indispensable. [...]

So far our government has done nothing effective with its forests, though the best in the world, but is like a rich and foolish spendthrift who has inherited a magnificent (85) estate in perfect order, and then has left his rich fields and meadows, forests and parks, to be sold and plundered and wasted at will, depending on their inexhaustible abundance. Now it is plain that the forests are not (90) inexhaustible, and that quick measures must be taken if ruin is to be avoided.

33. The overall point of the passage is to

(A) tell a story.
(B) survey current knowledge.
(C) make an argument.
(D) describe an environment.

34. Muir's tone in the passage is best described as

(A) urgent and earnest.
(B) arrogant and condescending.
(C) optimistic and cheerful.
(D) hopeless and depressed.

35. As used in line 19, the word "sealed" most closely means

(A) fastened.
(B) settled.
(C) authenticated.
(D) killed.

36. Based on the information in the passage, it is reasonable to infer that in the year 1897, which region of the United States had the greatest abundance of unharvested forests?

(A) The Atlantic Coast
(B) The Middle West
(C) The Mississippi Valley
(D) The Pacific Region

GO ON TO THE NEXT PAGE

37. Which option gives the best evidence for the answer to the previous question?

    (A) Lines 34–42 ("Accordingly . . . ruins")
    (B) Lines 43–45 ("Multitude . . . West")
    (C) Lines 47–48 ("rich . . . Lakes")
    (D) Lines 49–55 ("Thence . . . Pacific")

38. Muir uses lines 59–62 ("Clearing . . . pray in") to make appeals that focus on the themes of

    (A) nationalism, militarism, and expansionism.
    (B) environmentalism, scholarship, and piety.
    (C) economics, leisure, and religion.
    (D) justice, individualism, and truth.

39. Muir describes the overall approach to forest management by the U.S. Government at the time this passage was written as

    (A) hands-off.
    (B) legalistic.
    (C) progressive.
    (D) interventionist.

40. Which option gives the best evidence for the answer to the previous question?

    (A) Lines 1–3 ("The . . . planted")
    (B) Lines 40–42 ("After . . . ruins")
    (C) Lines 56–59 ("Surely . . . forests")
    (D) Lines 81–84 ("So far . . . spendthrift")

41. Muir suggests that the United States should emulate the philosophy of which country?

    (A) Palestine
    (B) Prussia
    (C) Spain
    (D) Georgia

42. As used in line 91, the word "ruin" most closely means

    (A) undoing.
    (B) hostility.
    (C) devastation.
    (D) ignorance.

Questions 43–52 are based on the following reading selections.

Alternative Energy—*two authors consider the state of alternative energy solutions.*

PASSAGE 1

No one is sure how much available oil is left, but considering our oil reserves took hundreds of millions of years to form, time to
Line depletion is little more than a blink of an eye.
(5) So we have two options—stop relying on oil or use it up and watch the ensuing chaos.

One promising alternative fuel source is ethanol. Our ancestors have been fermenting organic matter to make ethanol
(10) for thousands of years. Today ethanol is primarily consumed in alcoholic beverages, but why not also use it to power our cars? This alternative fuel is made by fermenting crops such as wheat, corn, and sugarcane.
(15) One glucose molecule is broken down to form two ethanol molecules and two carbon dioxide molecules. Because it is made from organic matter, it is renewable—a big pro compared to oil. Another benefit is that
(20) it's domestically made, so we don't have to rely on other countries for it. Unfortunately, it's slightly more expensive per mile than gasoline. Additionally, because its production uses crops, widespread implementation may
(25) cause an increase in some food prices.

Another promising alternative is biodiesel. Biodiesel is made out of animal fats, plant fats, and even used grease from restaurants. The glycerol backbone is removed from
(30) the fat, breaking the fat into three separate chains, which are then reacted with an alcohol to form the biodiesel. This type of chemical reaction is called a transesterification. Like ethanol, biodiesel is also renewable and
(35) domestically produced. It's also completely nontoxic and biodegradable. Unfortunately, like ethanol, it's also more expensive. While they may be more expensive, both of these

GO ON TO THE NEXT PAGE

fuel sources produce fewer greenhouse gases
(40) than regular gasoline. A couple extra dollars
is a small price to pay for the environmental
friendliness and self-sufficiency that these
alternatives would provide.

Our current alternatives may not be per-
(45) fect, but that's no reason to be discouraged.
The time for alternative fuel exploration is
now. Why wait for oil to run out when superior sources of energy are already available
and more are within reach?

PASSAGE 2

(50) There is a natural tendency to confuse
change with progress. This is perfectly under-
standable, especially considering that we
went from inventing electricity to perfecting
aviation to reaching the moon all in a time
(55) period analogous to just a blink in the grand
scheme of human history. Such prodigious
leaps have left us hungry for more leaps,
and there are benefits to restlessness, even
if entropic; throw enough aimless darts in
(60) every direction and you'll find a bull's eye,
even if by accident.

But, such leaps have also left us skeptical
against inaction, and now there is a proclivity
to mistake the status quo for the stagnation
(65) of standing still. Call it the *New Coke* effect,
where society takes three misguided steps
back in its interminable urgency to keep
moving forward.

That said, I will be the first to admit that
(70) the future livelihood of an industrialized
world most likely hinges on change, namely
the discovery of an effective, inexpensive
source of renewable energy. But, as the
federal government wastes billions here
(75) and billions there throwing money at hopeless companies with hapless executives
(Solyndra, for instance), I can't help but feel
like renewable energy is *New Coke*. Certainly,
we have not yet perfected our energetic ways
(80) and means, but why are we so obsessed with
discarding what we have now?

Principally, despite decades of apocalyptic
forecasting of peak oil, petroleum output is
as healthy as ever. In fact, petroleum compa-
(85) nies are leaving the industry not because oil
reserves are dwindling, but rather because
oil production is so massive that demand
is falling considerably. Case in point: oil is
currently selling at a third the cost of *bottled*
(90) *water.*

So, yes— the day most likely will come
when the wells run dry. But, until then, let us
celebrate our good fortune and be thankful
for what we have.

43. The author of passage 1 most strongly
implies in paragraph 1 (lines 1–6) that the
choice of whether to pursue alternative
energy is

(A) multi-faceted.
(B) obvious.
(C) ambiguous.
(D) premature.

44. As used in line 30, the word "breaking" most
closely means

(A) flouting.
(B) eliminating.
(C) separating.
(D) categorizing.

45. The author of Passage 1 suggests in lines
44–49 ("Our current . . . reach") that extensive
research into alternative energy resources
should begin

(A) in the coming centuries.
(B) in the coming decades.
(C) in the coming years.
(D) immediately.

GO ON TO THE NEXT PAGE

46. Lines 59–61 ("throw . . . accident") can best be paraphrased as

    (A) systematic, focused research will lead to a successful result.
    (B) amateur researchers should be put on equal footing with academic researchers.
    (C) nearly all useful recent innovations have come as the result of chaotic creativity.
    (D) if you try enough different things, something will eventually work.

47. As used in line 82, the word "apocalyptic" most closely means

    (A) pessimistic.
    (B) technical.
    (C) asymmetric.
    (D) deceitful.

48. The author of Passage 2 primarily uses the example in lines 88–90 ("Case in . . . *water*) to

    (A) show how water prices reflect relatively high demand for it.
    (B) illustrate how oil prices reflect relatively low demand for it.
    (C) explain how oil has come to be more plentiful than water.
    (D) demonstrate why consumers find fewer uses for oil than water.

49. The author of Passage 1 would most likely state that the author of Passage 2 needs to make what important clarification to his statement in lines 82–84 ("Principally . . . ever")?

    (A) To what extent this applies to just domestic petroleum production
    (B) Whether the petroleum produced is organic and renewable
    (C) If the petroleum production will generate greenhouse gases.
    (D) If the petroleum mentioned here will be more or less expensive than ethanol

50. Which option gives the best evidence for the answer to the previous question?

    (A) Lines 7–10 ("One promising . . . years")
    (B) Lines 19–21 ("Another . . . for it")
    (C) Lines 37–40 ("While . . . gasoline")
    (D) Lines 40–43 ("A couple . . . provide")

51. What evidence from Passage 1 would the author of Passage 2 most effectively use to support his statement in lines 78–81 ("Certainly . . . now")?

    (A) Lines 1–4 ("No one . . . eye")
    (B) Lines 15–19 ("One glucose . . . oil")
    (C) Lines 21–25 ("Unfortunately . . . prices")
    (D) Lines 29–32 ("The glycerol . . . biodiesel")

52. Which statement best summarizes the overall relationship between the two passages?

    (A) Passage 2 and Passage 1 are in direct opposition to each other when it comes to the question of the association of petroleum with greenhouse gas emissions
    (B) Passage 2 explores the association of petroleum with contemporary popular culture far more than does Passage 1
    (C) While both passages are concerned about petroleum depletion, Passage 1 advocates immediate action and Passage 2 calls for patience
    (D) While both passages are interested in alternative energy solutions, Passage 2 focuses on government funding and Passage 1 focuses on scientific innovation

STOP

If you finish before time is called, you may check your work on this section only. Do not turn to any other section.

Reading

1.	A	14.	C	27.	C	40.	D
2.	C	15.	C	28.	C	41.	B
3.	A	16.	C	29.	A	42.	C
4.	B	17.	C	30.	B	43.	B
5.	D	18.	C	31.	A	44.	C
6.	C	19.	A	32.	B	45.	D
7.	D	20.	A	33.	C	46.	D
8.	B	21.	C	34.	A	47.	A
9.	C	22.	C	35.	B	48.	B
10.	A	23.	A	36.	D	49.	A
11.	B	24.	D	37.	D	50.	B
12.	D	25.	D	38.	C	51.	C
13.	B	26.	B	39.	A	52.	C

Number Correct _____

Number Incorrect _____

SCORING APPROXIMATION

This table gives you an estimate of how your performance on the Reading section will contribute to your overall Evidence-Based Reading and Writing score. Keep in mind that each test *will be curved*, making the number of questions needed for a particular score dependent on the test that day. This is the best estimate we can give you based on (1) previous SAT curves and (2) the fact that guessing is now permitted on the SAT.

Questions out of 52 answered correctly	Estimated overall section score (between 200–800)
52	800
49	750
46	700
43	650
40	600
37	550
33	500
30	450
26	400
20	350
13	300
7	250
0	200

ANSWERS EXPLAINED

1. **(A)** This passage can be paraphrased best by choice (A). (B) is not supported since the running away has not yet happened. (C) is tempting, but ultimately incorrect because Mr. Shelby is not trying to make a profit, but to pay off a debt. (D) is a detail but not a summary.

2. **(C)** From the conversation between Haley and Mr. Shelby, it is clear that Haley is first and foremost a businessman. Moreover, he won't be persuaded to just accept Tom as payment for the debt, so (C) is an accurate depiction of his character. He is neither empathizing nor passive. In fact, he is nearly uncompromising. Finally, choice (B) won't work because we can infer by his negotiation skills that he is not an amateur.

3. **(A)** *Include* could be a substitute for *fling in* since this sentence refers to Haley's request that Mr. Shelby add the small boy to the deal. *Hurl* would incorrectly indicate the act of throwing. *Involve* is too weak for this context. And it would be nonsensical to say that Haley wanted Mr. Shelby to *relate* the boy.

4. **(B)** There is evidence in the passage that Mr. Shelby is reluctant to sell his slaves, and doesn't want to separate the child from his mother. Yet, his treatment of the boy in these particular lines is more fitting for an adored pet than a human child, making choice (B) correct. The passage does not support the idea that Mr. Shelby is dishonest or aggressive. And finally, choice (D) is contradictive since *impartial* means "neutral or disinterested."

5. **(D)** *Item* most closely fits the meaning of *article* in this line, since it refers to Eliza as an object. (A), (B), and (C) are not fitting since they do not refer to the woman as a commodity as intended by the speaker.

6. **(C)** Lines 84–86 indicate that upon hearing the news, Tom is shocked and dejected. *Despondency* refers to hopelessness and joylessness. His reaction is neither peaceful, relieved, nor playful so (A), (B), and (D) are incorrect.

7. **(D)** Tom "collapsed" and "sunk his head," so these lines provide direct evidence for the previous question. (A) and (C) refer to Mr. Shelby's wife's and Eliza's reactions, respectively. And (B) describes Tom's state before hearing the news, rather than after.

8. **(B)** As evidenced by lines 41–42, Mr. Shelby is clear and resolute that Eliza will not be sold. Since, he agrees—albeit grudgingly—to the sale of Tom and Eliza's son, it can be inferred that he places a higher value on Eliza. The passage does not provide evidence either way for his opinion of Chloe.

9. **(C)** Lines 37–42 give the most direct evidence of Mr. Shelby's determination to keep Eliza regardless of what Haley might offer. Choice (A) suggests a slight fondness for Tom, and choice (B) exhibits a sadistic affection for the child; but in both cases, Mr. Shelby still agrees to sell them. (D) is irrelevant as it just reveals Aunt Chloe's surprise at Eliza showing up at night unannounced.

10. **(A)** It is safe to assume that the "light tap" is indicative of Eliza's discretion, as she must be very secretive about her plans to run away. So, it is fitting to say that she is trying to avoid detection as in choice (A). (C) is incorrect because we know she risked visiting Tom specifically to share the news. Choice (B) wrongly assumes her caution is related to offending Tom and Chloe by visiting them so late. Finally, choice (D) inaccurately assumes she is worried more about breaking the law than being caught.

11. **(B)** Lines 13–19, lines 47–50, and lines 63–65 all suggest that the audience is unknowingly manipulated by advertising. The author appears to be speaking to a general audience, rather than a financially elite one as in (A). Likewise, there is no indication of what the audience might feel towards their children as in (D). (C) can be tempting because the author states that the audience thinks they are less inclined to foolery than previous generations, but not necessarily in regard to politics.

12. **(D)** The author begins conversationally, hinting at all the aspects of culture that are influenced by advertising before moving into a detailed analysis of advertising schemes. *Rapport* refers to a close relationship or a mutual understanding, making (D) correct. Neither the benefits nor the history of advertising is thoroughly addressed. And (B) is inaccurate because the terms are defined before they are used in context.

13. **(B)** These words are used to denote fashion subcultures that the author uses to introduce the manifestations of effective advertising in a consumerist society. They are not used to suggest a reformist agenda as in (A) or (C). And the author is actually implying that the labels are conventional, making (D) incorrect.

14. **(C)** Lines 110–113 serve as a warning to the readers to "use caution" and not to assume they are "unaffected." So, *distrustful* is indicative of how the author would advise consumers. (A) is too positive. (B) refers to the part of the mind one is not fully aware of, but does not describe an attitude. (D) means aggressive or hostile, and is too extremely negative.

15. **(C)** In these lines, the author urges the reader to be skeptical of advertising, giving clear evidence that one should not candidly trust whatever is said or depicted. (A) is a rhetorical device to appeal to the readers. (B) merely states how ubiquitous advertising is. (D) is an appealing choice because it describes how a particular scheme of advertising creates an attitude in a consumer, but the author would caution against this reaction.

16. **(C)** This is a statistic intended to prove that advertising is pervasive and successful, so (C) is correct. The other options don't consider the context around these lines in which the author tries to persuade the reader that advertising is effective despite common opinion that one is immune to influence.

17. **(C)** *Methods* fits the meaning best since this refers to other mechanisms used for advertising. Choices (A) and (D) refer to "a midway point," while (B) means "a span," or "the variation between upper and lower limits or values."

18. **(C)** This is a percentage-of-change problem. To calculate percent change, you find the difference between the values and then divide by the original value. Here, the combination of personal and psychological factors makes up 40%, compared to the 60% of cultural factors. $60 - 40 = 20$ and 20 divided by the original 40% gives 0.5. This is equivalent to 50%.

19. **(A)** From the graph, we know that cultural factors are most effective in persuading consumers. From the passage, lines 92–109, we know that affective conditioning associates positive feelings through appealing imagery with products. Therefore, we can assume that a car advertisement would use feel–good, culturally relevant images to transfer those feelings to the car itself, making (A) correct. (D) is an example of logical persuasion rather than affective conditioning. And choices (B) and (C) fail to transfer feelings through pleasant scenes.

20. **(A)** These lines give direct evidence of images that an advertisement might deploy when hoping to influence consumers through affective conditioning. Choices (B) and (C) refer to an authoritative source used by the author to illustrate the effects of affective conditioning, but do not discuss how it works. And (D) is incorrect because it simply concludes the passage with a warning from the author.

21. **(C)** If a consulting firm were advising a range of industries on advertising, it would be important that this graph be more specific to each particular industry. For instance, an entertainment firm might use these factors differently than a corporate banking firm. Additionally, psychological factors might influence an educational firm's consumers to a greater extent than a clothing firm's. (C) is the only choice that addresses the graph's ambiguity toward different industries. Although precision is needed, (A) fails to give any new information. (B) might be helpful if the industries were targeting certain social classes, but there is no evidence for that. And (D) would only be helpful if the industries were targeting certain locations and if there was research to prove geography significantly alters a person's consumer behavior, both of which are not supported.

22. **(C)** It might be said that the purpose of this passage is to inform, making (C) correct. After introducing hemoglobin, the author relays information about its vital role in the human and then discusses the disorders that arise when its production goes awry. The author does not take a position or appeal for change, making (A) and (D) incorrect. Similarly, the style is informative without raising questions, as in (B).

23. **(A)** *Notoriety* refers to fame, so it is the correct choice. *Infamy* is a close synonym, but is more associated with being well known for a bad deed, which makes it incorrect; although the disorders associated with erroneous hemoglobin may be infamous, hemoglobin itself is not. *Personage* refers specifically to a famous person. *Festivity* refers to a celebration.

24. **(D)** Lines 20–22 state that a combination of polypeptide chains accounts for the varieties of hemoglobin. Choices (A) and (B) refer to characteristics of the *heme* that each type of hemoglobin has in common. And choice (C) is imprecise because metalloprotein refers to collective heme, not to the distinct chains associated with the globin.

25. **(D)** Globin, the variable part of hemoglobin, is defined in these lines and attributed to each type's "unique characteristics," giving direct evidence for the previous question. Choice (A) is tempting, but it defines hemoglobin's parts more generally. (B) and (C) both refer to the heme, metalloprotein, which all types share.

26. **(B)** Lines 44–53 state that because of hemoglobin's importance, it is not surprising that its malfunctions cause serious disorders. Yet, it is surprising that its errors are so common and occur in so many people. Therefore, choice (B) is correct. (A), although tempting, is wrong because the author is not surprised that the disorders are caused by hemoglobin, but that they are so frequent. The disorders are inherited, not contagious as in (C). And the passage does not give evidence for (D).

27. **(C)** *Widespread* makes the most sense here. The author states that the errors "are among the most common," and follows the statement with empirical evidence of the prevalence of these disorders. Hence, he/she is referring to how recurrent and extensive they are. *Communal* means "to have in common" or "share." *Lowly* indicates "inferiority or baseness." And *famous* refers to "being well known."

28. **(C)** Lines 60–72 consider the geographical specificity of thalassemia disorders and explain that it is not coincidental but linked to evolution's defense against malaria, making (C) accurate. The distribution is not linked to migration as in (A), or related to cultural phenomena as in (B). Finally, (D) is incorrect because there is no connection made to medical innovation in these lines.

29. **(A)** These lines contend that the range of effects associated with thalassemia is so broad because there is a redundancy, namely, four copies of the α globin gene. So, we can infer that the disorder would be more uniform, or consistent, if there were fewer copies. The paragraph even states that the severity is based on how many copies of the gene are defective. (B) would not change the scope of intensity. (C) would likely increase the variation. (D) can be ruled out because not enough evidence is given to infer what might decrease the dissimilarity.

30. **(B)** According to the paragraph, one deletion causes subtle symptoms while four deletions are lethal. Hence, we can say that as the number of deleted genes increases, so does the severity of the disease. This relationship is *proportional*. *Inverse* would imply that as one increases, the other decreases. And (C) and (D) don't accurately describe a corresponding relationship.

31. **(A)** The *x*-axis of the graph begins long before birth, with the very first weeks of pregnancy, so we are looking for evidence to support the idea that hemoglobin develops right away. Lines 5–7 are appropriate because they refer to its appearance "within the very first week of embryogenesis." Neither hemoglobin's characteristics (B) nor the prevalence (C) and severity (D) of its associated genetic disorders can account for the graph's gestational tracing of it.

32. **(B)** To find the clearest indication that a child was born two months premature, we would want to determine the level of a particular hemoglobin protein that had an easily measureable and unique value at 7 months of gestation—beta is approximately 20% at this point, and this is the only time that it meets the level. It is not (A) because the alpha maintains its 7 month percent for some time. It is not (C) because gamma is at its 7 month percent both at 7 months *and* at 5 months. It is not (D) because zeta ceases to be a factor after 3 and half months of gestation.

33. **(C)** John Muir is very passionate in his argument to save the forests. He is not merely telling a story or describing nature. Additionally, he does not make a point to examine current knowledge other than to consider the expertise of other countries.

34. **(A)** Lines 89–91 best illustrate Muir's tone of urgency. He is neither *arrogant* nor *cheerful*. And while the current ignorance surrounding environmental conservation may make him *depressed*, his passage is a call to action rather than a *hopeless* rant.

35. **(B)** Lines 17–19 states that the white man's axe *sealed* the fate of the trees, so *settled* is most appropriate. This use of *sealed* refers to "concluding or guaranteeing a fate," rather than "a fastening or closing," as in (A). Likewise, it is not precise to say that the white man *authenticated* or *killed* the doom of the trees.

36. **(D)** According to the passage, the East and Midwest regions of the U.S. had already been plundered, so (D), *The Pacific Region*, is what is left unharvested.

37. **(D)** Lines 49–55 indicate that the harvesting has "entered the last of the great aboriginal forests on the shores of the Pacific." As such, these lines give evidence of which region is still abundant in forests and provide the answer for the previous question. Choices (A), (B), and (C) illustrate which areas have been harvested, but do not address the region which has not.

38. **(C)** Lines 59–62 specifically state possible consequences of overharvesting in the form of "scarce" timber without nature "left to rest in or pray in." Thus, the narrator appeals to *economics, leisure, and religion.* No other choice encapsulates all three of his appeals.

39. **(A)** According to Muir, the government has been ineffective in conserving its forests. Hence, we can assume it has not taken measures to create legislation, or intervene in any productive or liberal manner.

40. **(D)** Lines 81–84 address Muir's evaluation of the government as a "foolish spendthrift" that has left its forests "to be sold and plundered and wasted at will." Therefore, these lines specifically describe his understanding of the government's role in forest management up to this point. (A) affirms Muir's opinion that the United States had the best forests. (B) refers to the land that has been deforested recklessly. And (C) conveys an effort by citizens and conservationists to stop the irresponsible destruction of the forests.

41. **(B)** Lines 70–80 contend that other nations have taken more responsible approaches to nature. Specifically, Muir references Prussia which "has learned that the forest plays an important part in human progress." (A) and (C) are nations that Muir calls barren, or bleak and unproductive. And (D) is not a separate country, but a state within the U.S.

42. **(C)** *Devastation* is the precise choice, since lines 89–91 refer to desperate measures that must be taken to avoid *ruin.* He is advocating that we avoid *devastation* of the national forests, rather than the *hostility* or *ignorance* of them. *Undoing* is a tempting choice, but usually refers to a person's downfall.

43. **(B)** The question is asking for the first author's opinion on alternative energy. According to lines 1–6, the author believes oil will be gone shortly, and we must stop relying on it or witness complete chaos. Thus, the author advocates clearly for a pursuit of alternative energy. (A) would imply that the author is uncertain because the choice is complex. (C) would infer a similar inexactness. (D) is the opinion of author 2 rather than author 1.

44. **(C)** Lines 30–31 refers to the "breaking of fat into three separate chains," so *separating* is the closest word meaning. *Flouting* means defying. *Elimination* would imply that the fat was removed instead of divided. And *categorizing* is a close synonym, but indicates a classifying of parts.

45. **(D)** Lines 44–49 call for immediate action, making (D) correct. Specifically, the passage states, "The time for alternative fuel exploration is now."

46. **(D)** Lines 59–61 metaphorically suggest that a great number of attempts ensures eventual success, so (D) is correct. (A) is the opposite of this suggestion. Choices (B) and (C) fail to capture the author's idea that even the most haphazard efforts will occasionally result in a win.

47. **(A)** Lines 82–83 refer to "apocalyptic forecasting of peak oil," and contrast it with the current healthy output. So, we can infer the author is saying that even though people have been predicting the depletion of oil for a long time, it is still going strong. Hence,

pessimistic is the best choice. Choices (B), (C), and (D) do not account for expectation of a bad outcome. Furthermore, (D) would imply that the predictions were purposely insincere.

48. **(B)** By comparing oil prices to water prices, the author is attempting to show how low the demand for oil is in regard to its supply, making (B) right. Passage 2 is not concerned with the demand for water as in (A). (C) is false and unsupported. (D) is incorrect because the author doesn't attempt to compare utility, just price.

49. **(A)** You should work backwards on these. First, lines 83–84 state that "petroleum output is healthy." Now, consider how the first author might respond. Choices (B), (C), and (D) are not variable: petroleum is not renewable, always generates greenhouse gases, and is less expensive than ethanol. (A) works because the first author would want to consider how much oil is available domestically since it impacts our self-sufficiency.

50. **(B)** Lines 19–21 specifically indicate that the author of Passage 1 is interested in energy that is not only renewable, but also domestically made. (A) introduces ethanol, while (C) declares alternative energies more expensive than gasoline. (D) is a tempting choice because it references self-sufficiency as a desirable quality, but these lines serve as more of an evaluation of risks than to show specifically what kind of fuel that most interests the author.

51. **(C)** Again, work backwards. In lines 78–81, Passage 2 questions why we are so adamant about replacing something that we still have. Now, consider what lines in Passage 1 could support the idea that we should stick to oil for the time being. Lines 21–25 affirm that ethanol would not only be more expensive than gasoline, but also raise food prices. So, these lines serve as effective reasoning of why we might consider sticking with oil until we don't have a choice but to use an alternative.

52. **(C)** Passage 1 believes that oil will be gone soon and argues for an immediate pursuit of alternative fuels. Passage 2 acknowledges that we will have to replace oil eventually, but says there is no hurry. Hence, (C) is the appropriate choice. The passages are not mainly concerned with arguing about emissions or funding. (B) is not mentioned in either.

ANSWER SHEET
Practice Test 2

Reading

1. Ⓐ Ⓑ Ⓒ Ⓓ	14. Ⓐ Ⓑ Ⓒ Ⓓ	27. Ⓐ Ⓑ Ⓒ Ⓓ	40. Ⓐ Ⓑ Ⓒ Ⓓ
2. Ⓐ Ⓑ Ⓒ Ⓓ	15. Ⓐ Ⓑ Ⓒ Ⓓ	28. Ⓐ Ⓑ Ⓒ Ⓓ	41. Ⓐ Ⓑ Ⓒ Ⓓ
3. Ⓐ Ⓑ Ⓒ Ⓓ	16. Ⓐ Ⓑ Ⓒ Ⓓ	29. Ⓐ Ⓑ Ⓒ Ⓓ	42. Ⓐ Ⓑ Ⓒ Ⓓ
4. Ⓐ Ⓑ Ⓒ Ⓓ	17. Ⓐ Ⓑ Ⓒ Ⓓ	30. Ⓐ Ⓑ Ⓒ Ⓓ	43. Ⓐ Ⓑ Ⓒ Ⓓ
5. Ⓐ Ⓑ Ⓒ Ⓓ	18. Ⓐ Ⓑ Ⓒ Ⓓ	31. Ⓐ Ⓑ Ⓒ Ⓓ	44. Ⓐ Ⓑ Ⓒ Ⓓ
6. Ⓐ Ⓑ Ⓒ Ⓓ	19. Ⓐ Ⓑ Ⓒ Ⓓ	32. Ⓐ Ⓑ Ⓒ Ⓓ	45. Ⓐ Ⓑ Ⓒ Ⓓ
7. Ⓐ Ⓑ Ⓒ Ⓓ	20. Ⓐ Ⓑ Ⓒ Ⓓ	33. Ⓐ Ⓑ Ⓒ Ⓓ	46. Ⓐ Ⓑ Ⓒ Ⓓ
8. Ⓐ Ⓑ Ⓒ Ⓓ	21. Ⓐ Ⓑ Ⓒ Ⓓ	34. Ⓐ Ⓑ Ⓒ Ⓓ	47. Ⓐ Ⓑ Ⓒ Ⓓ
9. Ⓐ Ⓑ Ⓒ Ⓓ	22. Ⓐ Ⓑ Ⓒ Ⓓ	35. Ⓐ Ⓑ Ⓒ Ⓓ	48. Ⓐ Ⓑ Ⓒ Ⓓ
10. Ⓐ Ⓑ Ⓒ Ⓓ	23. Ⓐ Ⓑ Ⓒ Ⓓ	36. Ⓐ Ⓑ Ⓒ Ⓓ	49. Ⓐ Ⓑ Ⓒ Ⓓ
11. Ⓐ Ⓑ Ⓒ Ⓓ	24. Ⓐ Ⓑ Ⓒ Ⓓ	37. Ⓐ Ⓑ Ⓒ Ⓓ	50. Ⓐ Ⓑ Ⓒ Ⓓ
12. Ⓐ Ⓑ Ⓒ Ⓓ	25. Ⓐ Ⓑ Ⓒ Ⓓ	38. Ⓐ Ⓑ Ⓒ Ⓓ	51. Ⓐ Ⓑ Ⓒ Ⓓ
13. Ⓐ Ⓑ Ⓒ Ⓓ	26. Ⓐ Ⓑ Ⓒ Ⓓ	39. Ⓐ Ⓑ Ⓒ Ⓓ	52. Ⓐ Ⓑ Ⓒ Ⓓ

Practice Test 2

65 MINUTES, 52 QUESTIONS

Directions: Each passage or pair of passages is accompanied by several questions. After reading the passage(s), choose the best answer to each question based on what is indicated explicitly or implicitly in the passage(s) or in the associated graphics.

Questions 1–10 are based on the following reading selection.

This excerpt is the beginning of F. Scott Fitzgerald's This Side of Paradise, *published in 1920. The book opens up with the following character introduction of Fitzgerald's semi-autobiographical protagonist, Amory Blaine.*

Amory Blaine inherited from his mother every trait, except the stray inexpressible few, that made him worth while. His father,
Line an ineffectual, inarticulate man with a taste
(5) for Byron and a habit of drowsing over the *Encyclopedia Britannica*, grew wealthy at thirty through the death of two elder brothers, successful Chicago brokers, and in the first flush of feeling that the world was his,
(10) went to Bar Harbor and met Beatrice O'Hara. In consequence, Stephen Blaine handed down to posterity his height of just under six feet and his tendency to waver at crucial moments, these two abstractions appearing
(15) in his son Amory. For many years he hovered in the background of his family's life, an unassertive figure with a face half-obliterated by lifeless, silky hair, continually occupied in "taking care" of his wife, continually harassed

(20) by the idea that he didn't and couldn't understand her.

But Beatrice Blaine! There was a woman! Early pictures taken on her father's estate at Lake Geneva, Wisconsin, or in Rome
(25) at the Sacred Heart Convent—an educational extravagance that in her youth was only for the daughters of the exceptionally wealthy—showed the exquisite delicacy of her features, the consummate art and sim-
(30) plicity of her clothes. A brilliant education she had—her youth passed in renaissance glory, she was versed in the latest gossip of the Older Roman Families; known by name as a fabulously wealthy American girl to
(35) Cardinal Vitori and Queen Margherita and more subtle celebrities that one must have had some culture even to have heard of. She learned in England to prefer whiskey and soda to wine, and her small talk was broad-
(40) ened in two senses during a winter in Vienna. All in all Beatrice O'Hara absorbed the sort of education that will be quite impossible ever again; a tutelage measured by the number of things and people one could be contemptu-
(45) ous of and charming about; a culture rich in all arts and traditions, barren of all ideas, in the last of those days when the great gar-

GO ON TO THE NEXT PAGE

dener clipped the inferior roses to produce one perfect bud.

(50) In her less important moments she returned to America, met Stephen Blaine and married him—this almost entirely because she was a little bit weary, a little bit sad. Her only child was carried through a tiresome
(55) season and brought into the world on a spring day in ninety-six.

When Amory was five he was already a delightful companion for her. He was an auburn-haired boy, with great, handsome
(60) eyes which he would grow up to in time, a facile imaginative mind and a taste for fancy dress. From his fourth to his tenth year he did the country with his mother in her father's private car, from Coronado, where
(65) his mother became so bored that she had a nervous breakdown in a fashionable hotel, down to Mexico City, where she took a mild, almost epidemic consumption. This trouble pleased her, and later she made use of it as an
(70) intrinsic part of her atmosphere—especially after several astounding bracers.

So, while more or less fortunate little rich boys were defying governesses on the beach at Newport, or being spanked or tutored or
(75) read to from "Do and Dare," or "Frank on the Mississippi," Amory was biting acquiescent bell-boys in the Waldorf, outgrowing a natural repugnance to chamber music and symphonies, and deriving a highly special-
(80) ized education from his mother.

"Amory."

"Yes, Beatrice." (Such a quaint name for his mother; she encouraged it.)

"Dear, don't *think* of getting out of bed yet.
(85) I've always suspected that early rising in early life makes one nervous. Clothilde is having your breakfast brought up."

"All right."

"I am feeling very old to-day, Amory," she
(90) would sigh, her face a rare cameo of pathos, her voice exquisitely modulated, her hands as facile as Bernhardt's. "My nerves are on edge—on edge. We must leave this terrify-

ing place to-morrow and go searching for
(95) sunshine."

Amory's penetrating green eyes would look out through tangled hair at his mother. Even at this age he had no illusions about her.

1. Beatrice is best characterized as

   (A) privileged and eccentric.
   (B) mean-spirited and haughty.
   (C) wealthy and industrious.
   (D) misanthropic and itinerant.

2. Lines 1–3 ("Amory . . . while") most strongly suggest that

   (A) Amory and his mother share many unfavorable qualities.
   (B) Amory's best characteristics came from his mother.
   (C) Amory's great intellect and personality came from his father.
   (D) Amory has a striking interest in genetics.

3. The style of the second paragraph (lines 22–49) is generally

   (A) educational and morose.
   (B) intellectual and nebulous.
   (C) idealistic and optimistic.
   (D) emphatic and descriptive.

4. As used in line 31, the word "passed" most closely means

   (A) spent.
   (B) gave up.
   (C) tossed.
   (D) agreed.

GO ON TO THE NEXT PAGE

5. The passage implies that Beatrice married Stephen for what reason?

   (A) True love
   (B) Because she settled
   (C) Because she was forced
   (D) Because of vengeance

6. Which option gives the best evidence for the answer to the previous question?

   (A) Lines 3–10 ("His father . . . O'Hara")
   (B) Lines 15–21 ("For many . . . her")
   (C) Lines 50–53 ("In her . . . sad")
   (D) Lines 84–87 ("Dear . . . up")

7. Amory's upbringing and education can best be described as

   (A) demanding.
   (B) scholarly.
   (C) exhausting.
   (D) unique.

8. Which option gives the best evidence for the answer to the previous question?

   (A) Lines 15–21 ("For . . . her")
   (B) Lines 41–49 ("All in . . . bud")
   (C) Lines 72–80 ("So . . . mother")
   (D) Lines 84–87 ("Dear . . . up")

9. As used in line 63, the word "did" most closely means

   (A) made.
   (B) traveled.
   (C) caused.
   (D) organized.

10. Amory's relationship with his mother is

    (A) traditionally pious.
    (B) unusually friendly.
    (C) blatantly disrespectful.
    (D) cold and distant.

Questions 11–21 are based on the following reading selection and accompanying material.

What's Not to "Like"?

Eliza Jennings is excited to be a part of her company's first ever community event. Come get your face painted and try Zing—

Line *the new eight-hour energy shot! #zing*

(5) *#LawrenceCoFieldDay #lovemyjob*

Tom Willis has a position open for administrative secretary—2 years of experience preferred. Message with any inquiries.

Sherry Swanson needs help with the new

(10) *software program. Alert: Technophobia! Can anybody explain?*

If the eruption of smart phones has been the vanguard of anything, it is the near societal takeover of social media. Within the

(15) workplace, most supervisors quickly block sites like Facebook, Twitter, and Instagram from company computers, and for good reason. Productivity is likely to decrease if three hours of an eight-hour workday are spent

(20) "liking" and "tweeting" and "pinning." Then there is company bad-mouthing to consider. In the digital age, nothing one says or does or records online is private—*nothing.* It takes only a few incidents to realize that a social

(25) media page is not the best place to post one's aggravation with company policies, to share confidential business plans, or to announce one's forthcoming resignation. And with even the most responsible staff, there is the

(30) heightened possibility of viruses or hacking. Simply put, many employers decide the cons outweigh the pros.

Many of these same administrative boards agree that social media outside of work is

(35) just as harmful and make addendums to employee contracts outlawing all mention of work and/or colleagues via online social

GO ON TO THE NEXT PAGE

outlets. Other jobs go farther, demanding that one's social media personalities align (40) with the corporate values maintained in the workplace. One may face disciplinary action and even termination if a page appears indecent or offensive. Still, when bringing in new hires, employers violate their own embargo (45) and check out prospective employees' pages, quickly disqualifying applicants who may not seem to fit the company culture. Social media has certainly altered today's workforce, and many would argue that the change (50) hasn't been for the best.

Yet, the examples above paint another picture—one where the workforce is actually improved by the open communication, wider network, free advertising, and increased (55) accessibility of social media. In fact, there are many reasons why an employer should hesitate to ban all social networking. For some, the unique ability of social media to market company services and extend company repu- (60) tation is indispensable. Many startup businesses find that they simply cannot compete without a social media page to deliver their mission and broaden their contacts. It can simply be the best tool available for adver- (65) tising, marketing, expansion, and customer feedback. Likewise, it provides an unrivaled medium for market research.

Networking expansion isn't the only plus. While it is possible that social media could (70) create discord, it is just as likely to promote collaboration and solidarity within company culture. Never before has it been as easy for colleagues to link up, interact, and initiate friendships. The benefits of hav- (75) ing employees who know one another and develop respect for one another are endless. A congenial icebreaker, Facebook and Twitter pages are known for bringing together former strangers and allowing acquaintances to real- (80) ize similar interests. A corporate culture that embraces affinity and breaks down barriers

to allow open and constructive discussion is in a far better situation than one that doesn't.

Surprisingly, social media has also been (85) connected to better company retention. Some technologically savvy employers have created company pages where staff can make announcements, share ideas, discuss problems, and congratulate one another on excel- (90) lent work. The page becomes a space where colleagues can support one another, but also where the company itself can show appreciation. Feelings of openness, teamwork, and apt recognition keep good workers happy (95) and in their positions longer. More so, some offices report that employees who use social media are actually more productive, with occasional tweets and status updates providing a much-needed break in an otherwise (100) monotonous workday.

Social media in the workplace has gotten a bad rap; in many ways, it deserves it. But the role it can play—when embraced appropriately—in networking, collaboration, and (105) retention proves that it isn't as simple as that. Like any new and rapidly changing technology, it will take time and adaptability for its advantages and pitfalls to be clear. The smart company will find it necessary to consider (110) the implications social media presents for its future—is it really something that can just be ignored or banned altogether?

GO ON TO THE NEXT PAGE

Percentages of members of each demographic group who use social networking sites in 2014.

	All People who Use the Internet	74%
Gender	Men	72%
	Women	76%
Ages	Ages 18-29	89%
	Ages 30-49	82%
	Ages 50-64	65%
	Ages 65+	49%
Education Level	High school graduate or less	72%
	Some college	78%
	College graduate and beyond	73%
Yearly Salary	Less than $30,000 per year	79%
	Between $30,000 and $49,999	73%
	Between $50,000 and $74,999	70%
	Greater than $75,000	78%

Source: Pew Research Center

11. Which of the following statements best expresses the thesis of the passage?

(A) Social media has already proven to be one of the most valuable workplace tools.
(B) Social media should not be disregarded as a potentially valuable tool in the workplace.
(C) The risks of social media are far too great to allow it in the workplace.
(D) Employees should be able to decide for themselves how to best use social media while working.

12. Which option gives the best evidence for the answer to the previous question?

(A) Lines 12–21 ("If the . . . consider")
(B) Lines 33–43 ("Many . . . offensive")
(C) Lines 90–100 ("The page . . . workday")
(D) Lines 101–112 ("Social . . . altogether")

13. The structure of the essay is best described as a/an

(A) analysis of the pros and cons of an issue.
(B) argument in favor of a change from the mainstream.
(C) critique of the latest media research on a topic.
(D) a series of interesting anecdotes.

14. The most likely purpose of lines 1–11 is to

(A) introduce the thesis of the essay by giving three major points to be analyzed going forth.
(B) hook the reader's interest with concrete examples illustrating the applicability of the passage's topic.
(C) connect to the sentence that follows by providing instances of common smart phone language.
(D) draw upon the author's personal experiences to connect with similar experiences of the readers.

GO ON TO THE NEXT PAGE

15. Lines 51–55 ("Yet . . . media") primarily function to

(A) digress from the theme of the passage.
(B) challenge the argument that follows.
(C) explain how certain social media companies came to dominate the marketplace.
(D) provide a major transition.

16. The passage suggests that what type of business would most likely benefit from utilizing social media?

(A) A large, expanding business
(B) A well-established business
(C) A small, growing business
(D) A mid-sized, industrial business

17. Which option gives the best evidence for the answer to the previous question?

(A) Lines 23–28 ("It takes . . . resignation")
(B) Lines 33–41 ("Many of . . . workplace")
(C) Lines 51–57 ("Yet . . . networking")
(D) Lines 60–63 ("Many . . . contacts")

18. As used in line 67, the word "medium" most closely means

(A) best.
(B) means.
(C) middle.
(D) standard.

19. As used in line 90, the word "space" most closely means

(A) area.
(B) dimension.
(C) clearing.
(D) separation.

20. Based on the information in the table, a randomly selected person with which of the following characteristics would be most likely to use a social network website?

(A) A 45-year-old man who has an advanced graduate degree.
(B) A 35-year-old man who has a master's degree in engineering.
(C) A 25-year-old woman who left college without completing her degree.
(D) A 15-year-old girl who is a sophomore in high school.

21. What statement, if true, would best connect to the information in the graph to explain what the passage states about startup businesses in lines 60–66 ("Many startup . . . feedback")?

(A) Those in the age group 18–29 are by far the most likely to be interested in the products of startup businesses.
(B) As more consumers use social media sites, they develop "ad blindness," tuning out informational appeals that distract from their primary focus.
(C) Startup businesses typically have more young people as part of their workforce.
(D) Venture capital investors are interested in reviewing detailed financial statements of startups before making initial investments.

GO ON TO THE NEXT PAGE

Questions 22–31 are based on the following reading selections.

Two scientists present their views on vaccinations.

PASSAGE 1

Smoking tobacco causes cancer. It causes small cell and squamous cell cancers of the lung, as well as oral and nasopharyngeal
Line carcinoma, gastrointestinal carcinoma, and
(5) cancers of half a dozen additional tissues. It is highly correlated with the second leading cause of death in the United States, and the decision to not smoke reduces one's risk of lung cancer by more than half. This infor-
(10) mation will surprise no one. It is, therefore, baffling that 1 in 5 Americans continues to use tobacco. Yet there is one behavior on the rise that is still more contrary to human health than smoking—and perhaps more
(15) inexplicable as well, as it cannot be explained away by chemical dependence, nor by social custom. I speak, of course, of the decision to not vaccinate one's children.

There is apparently a belief among these
(20) erring individuals that the ailments against which the Centers for Disease Control rec- ommends we vaccinate are somehow less serious than we, as a society, have been led to believe. There is a belief, moreover, that
(25) because these diseases are easily preventable through modern medical science, they must, implicitly, be easily treatable as well. Let us clarify this matter.

Not long before it was eradicated by
(30) vaccination, smallpox virus erased entire cultures on two continents, where fatal- ity rates rose as high as 90%. For those who survived, it was a cause of permanent, often debilitating disfigurement. Prior to the HiB
(35) and DTaP vaccines, epiglottitis caused by *Haemophilus influenzae*, and diphtheria caused by *Corynebacterium diptheriae* were both exceedingly common causes of death in young children, largely because of their

(40) tendency to develop rapidly and obstruct the airway. Death typically occurs well before medical attention can be accessed, and thus, in spite of all our modern medical advances, these diseases remain just as dire as they
(45) were two hundred years earlier.

We could continue this list. In the past, for instance, rubella was the most common cause of congenital deafness, and mumps a major cause of sterility. Children who
(50) survived the measles, meanwhile, ran and still run the risk of the virus reemerging years later as subacute sclerosing panencephalitis, a frequently fatal infection of the brain. The point, however, is clear. Vaccination is neither
(55) a conspiracy, nor merely a matter of modern convenience; nor is it entirely without risk. But vaccination, plainly put, is the only effec- tive medical intervention to safeguard our children from some of the deadliest and most
(60) virulent diseases known to man.

PASSAGE 2

Let us dispense entirely with the fallacies and the delusions; there is not an analytically credible source on the planet that will defend a link between vaccines and autism spectrum
(65) disorder. But for many conscientious parents who choose not to vaccinate their children, the decision is based not on delusion, but upon a simple, mathematical reality.

Philosophically, medicine is premised on a
(70) balance between beneficence, and nonmalef- icence. That is to say, for a medical interven- tion to be deemed ethical and appropriate, the risks of not treating an individual must always outweigh the risks inherent in the
(75) treatment itself. Risk accompanies every medical intervention, and vaccination is no exception. Specifically, in a certain subset of individuals, exposure to either the gelatin or egg protein components used to stabi-
(80) lize vaccines can result in a life-threatening anaphylactic reaction. Additionally, so-called "live-attenuated vaccines", including those

GO ON TO THE NEXT PAGE

for varicella, rotavirus, and MMR, contain
living strains of their corresponding patho-
(85) gens that, through genetic modification,
have been rendered pathologically inert.
Rarely, these attenuated strains may undergo
mutation, and revert back to their pathogenic
forms. Immunocompromised individuals,
(90) such as those infected with HIV, are particularly at risk for this dangerous outcome.
    While it is true that adverse vaccine
events are uncommon, it is equally true
that, within the American population, most
(95) diseases against which vaccinations protect
are uncommon—more uncommon, in fact,
than the incidence of adverse vaccine events.
Thus, so long as the majority of the American
population remains vaccinated, an unvac-
(100) cinated individual will be well-protected
through a phenomenon described as "herd
immunity." The decision not to vaccinate,
therefore, hangs upon an appreciation of the
dynamic balance between beneficence and
(105) nonmaleficence as it pertains to the individual. While some may argue that taking
advantage of such a strategy violates an ethical obligation to society, one cannot help but
wonder: when presented with the numbers,
(110) will these individuals truly value the health
of society above that of their children? Their
math, I would wager, just doesn't add up.

22. With respect to the author's argument as a
     whole, lines 1–12 ("Smoking . . . tobacco")
     most strongly serve to

     (A) show the obvious absurdity of a personal
          decision to set up the argument that
          follows.
     (B) highlight the primary topic of the essay.
     (C) provide key statistics on both tobacco
          and vaccination research .
     (D) illustrate the irrationality of widespread
          tobacco use given the latest scientific
          research.

23. The primary purpose of lines 19–27 ("There
     is . . . as well") is to

     (A) cite scholarly evidence in support of the
          author's thesis.
     (B) present the alternative views that the
          author will later dissect.
     (C) underscore the author's fundamental
          respect for opposing viewpoints.
     (D) give a vital clarification to the author's
          argument.

24. As used in line 30, the word "erased" most
     closely means

     (A) transported.
     (B) eliminated.
     (C) fought.
     (D) affected.

25. The author of Passage 2 would most likely
     agree that an unvaccinated individual would
     be most likely to survive

     (A) under no circumstances.
     (B) if he or she took preventative measures
          based on alternative medicine.
     (C) if he or she were careful to remain
          immunocompromised.
     (D) in a society where virtually everyone else
          is vaccinated.

26. Which option gives the best evidence for the
     answer to the previous question?

     (A) Lines 61–65 ("Let us . . . disorder")
     (B) Lines 77–81 ("Specifically . . . reaction")
     (C) Lines 87–91 ("Rarely . . . outcome")
     (D) Lines 98–102 ("Thus . . . immunity")

27. As used in line 61, the phrase "dispense
     entirely with" most closely means

     (A) fundamentally understand.
     (B) physically remove.
     (C) somewhat ignore.
     (D) do away with.

GO ON TO THE NEXT PAGE

28. What is the overall relationship between the two passages?

    (A) Passage 1 strongly disagrees with the tolerance of non-vaccination in Passage 2.

    (B) Passage 1 uses a more scientific approach while Passage 2 is more mathematical.

    (C) Passage 2 advocates careful cost-benefit analysis while Passage 1 advocates decisive policies.

    (D) Passage 2 attempts to explain a phenomenon that Passage 1 deems inexplicable.

29. The author of Passage 2 would most likely respond to the final sentence of Passage 1 (lines 57–60) by stating that it

    (A) contradicts widespread thinking.

    (B) needs an important qualification.

    (C) is overly influenced by popular opinion.

    (D) is insufficiently paranoid.

30. Which option gives the best evidence for the answer to the previous question?

    (A) Lines 65–68 ("But for . . . reality")

    (B) Lines 71–75 ("That is . . . itself")

    (C) Lines 81–86 ("Additionally . . . inert")

    (D) Lines 92–97 ("While it . . . events")

31. The respective attitudes of the authors of Passage 1 and Passage 2 toward parents who choose not to vaccinate their children are best described as

    (A) hatred and appreciation.

    (B) forgiveness and intolerance.

    (C) loathing and gratitude.

    (D) contempt and understanding.

Questions 32–41 are based on the following reading selection.

In 1862, Ralph Waldo Emerson delivered the excerpt below as part of a lecture called "American Civilization" at the Smithsonian Institution in Washington, D.C.

At this moment in America the aspects of political society absorb attention. In every house, from Canada to the Gulf, the children
Line ask the serious father,—"What is the news of
(5) the war today? and when will there be better times?" The boys have no new clothes, no gifts, no journeys; the girls must go without new bonnets; boys and girls find their education, this year, less liberal and complete. All
(10) the little hopes that heretofore made the year pleasant are deferred. The state of the country fills us with anxiety and stern duties. We have attempted to hold together two states of civilization: a higher state, where labor and
(15) the tenure of land and the right of suffrage are democratical; and a lower state, in which the old military tenure of prisoners or slaves, and of power and land in a few hands, makes an oligarchy: we have attempted to hold
(20) these two states of society under one law. But the rude and early state of society does not work well with the later, nay, works badly, and has poisoned politics, public morals and social intercourse in the Republic, now for
(25) many years.

The times put this question,—Why cannot the best civilization be extended over the whole country, since the disorder of the less civilized portion menaces the existence of
(30) the country? Is this secular progress we have described, this evolution of man to the highest powers, only to give him sensibility, and not to bring duties with it? Is he not to make his knowledge practical? to stand and to
(35) withstand? Is not civilization heroic also? Is it not for action? has it not a will? … America is another word for Opportunity. Our whole

GO ON TO THE NEXT PAGE

history appears like a last effort of the Divine Providence on behalf of the human race;
(40) and a literal slavish following of precedents, as by a justice of the peace, is not for those who at this hour lead the destinies of this people. The evil you contend with has taken alarming proportions, and you still content
(45) yourself with parrying the blows it aims, but, as if enchanted, abstain from striking at the cause. [...]

Emancipation is the demand of civilization. That is a principle; everything else is an
(50) intrigue. This is a progressive policy;—puts the whole people in healthy, productive, amiable position,—puts every man in the South in just and natural relations with every man in the North, laborer with laborer.

(55) The power of Emancipation is this, that it alters the atomic social constitution of the Southern people. Now their interest is in keeping out white labor; then, when they must pay wages, their interest will be to let it
(60) in, to get the best labor, and, if they fear their blacks, to invite Irish, German, and American laborers. Thus, whilst Slavery makes and keeps disunion, Emancipation removes the whole objection to union. Emancipation
(65) at one stroke elevates the poor white of the South, and identifies his interest with that of the Northern laborer. [...]

The end of all political struggle is to establish morality as the basis of all legislation. It
(70) is not free institutions, 'tis not a republic, 'tis not a democracy, that is the end,—no, but only the means. Morality is the object of government. We want a state of things in which crime shall not pay. This is the consolation
(75) on which we rest in the darkness of the future and the afflictions of today, that the government of the world is moral, and does forever destroy what is not.

32. What is the general purpose of this passage?

(A) To argue in favor of emancipation
(B) To illustrate the evils of slavery
(C) To highlight the economic problems in the South
(D) To articulate a comprehensive theory of morality

33. What is Emerson's overall attitude toward politics?

(A) Its practice is his great passion
(B) It is merely a means to an end
(C) It takes on less importance in war
(D) It will ultimately settle the question of slavery

34. Which option gives the best evidence for the answer to the previous question?

(A) Lines 20–25 ("But the . . . years")
(B) Lines 37–39 ("Our . . . race")
(C) Lines 62–64 ("Thus . . . union")
(D) Lines 69–72 ("It is . . . means")

35. Lines 6–9 ("The boys . . . complete") most clearly indicate that

(A) interests in childhood entertainment changed greatly.
(B) war led to a focus on the bare necessities.
(C) children became less interested in stimulation.
(D) emancipation was not a priority for the young.

36. As used in line 12, the word "stern" most closely means

(A) playful.
(B) terrifying.
(C) serious.
(D) pointless.

GO ON TO THE NEXT PAGE

PRACTICE TEST 2

37. What is the purpose of the questions in lines 26–36?

   (A) To rhetorically emphasize a need for action
   (B) To encourage readers' intellectual curiosity
   (C) To critique the reasoning given in the previous paragraph
   (D) To summarize the thoughts of Emerson's mentor

38. Emerson frames the philosophical struggle underlying the nation's conflict as one between

   (A) geographical needs versus international recognition.
   (B) monetary concerns versus political considerations.
   (C) traditional precedent versus moral necessity.
   (D) skeptical questioning versus pious obedience.

39. Which option gives the best evidence for the answer to the previous question?

   (A) Lines 1–6 ("At this . . . times")
   (B) Lines 9–11 ("All . . . deferred")
   (C) Lines 37–43 ("Our whole . . . people")
   (D) Lines 57–62 ("Now . . . laborers")

40. As used in line 40, the word "following" most closely means

   (A) ensuing.
   (B) succeeding.
   (C) resulting.
   (D) obeying.

41. What option best summarizes the paragraph in lines 56–67?

   (A) Emancipation will lead to the political dominance of European immigrants.
   (B) Emancipation will ensure an equitable redistribution of income across the races.
   (C) An end to slavery will cause the Southern Constitution to be amended.
   (D) An end to slavery will realign Southern economic interests in favor of union.

GO ON TO THE NEXT PAGE

Questions 42–52 are based on the following reading selection and accompanying material.

Searching the Skies

In 1950, Enrico Fermi posited the question, "Where is everybody?" when considering the apparent contradiction between high
Line estimates of the likelihood of the existence
(5) of extraterrestrial life and mankind's lack of contact with, or evidence for, such civilizations. Later referred to as the Fermi Paradox, his provocative query was founded on the assumption that since the Sun is quite typi-
(10) cal, other Earth-like planets surely exist and have intelligent life, and by now, should have visited or contacted Earth. Extraterrestrial intelligence, or ETI, refers to hypothetical intelligent civilizations that are assumed to
(15) exist based on the existence of human intelligence and the vast size of the universe. While popular and scientific opinion on ETI varies greatly—from certainty to skepticism to downright incredulity—the search for alien
(20) intelligence is extensive and substantive.

Whether you anticipate the stringy worm guys with serious fire power in *Men In Black*; the eternally wise Jedi Master, Yoda; Stan Winston's nightmarish predators; or Steven
(25) Spielberg's sweet-loving E.T.; the search for intelligent life outside Earth is on. SETI, or "the search for extraterrestrial intelligence," is the collective name for activities undertaken to seek intelligent extraterrestrial
(30) life, and most recently involves constant monitoring of electromagnetic radiation with radio telescopes in hopes of detecting non-natural radio emissions or other signs of transmissions from civilizations on other
(35) worlds. In March 2014, UC Berkeley began an all-sky survey using the Arecibo radio telescope.

Although we have been listening for messages since the 1960s, there have also been
(40) recent efforts to communicate with and purposely send out our own messages. Active SETI is the attempt to send messages to intelligent extraterrestrial life via radio signals. CETI, on the other hand, is any number of
(45) efforts to communicate with ETI that focuses on composing and deciphering messages that, theoretically, could be understood by another technological civilization. And the pursuit of ETI contact is no longer limited to
(50) the few and far between. SETILive, launched in February 2012, uses data from the Allen

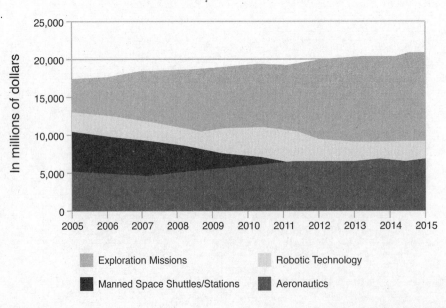

NASA Space Program Budget

In millions of dollars

- Exploration Missions
- Manned Space Shuttles/Stations
- Robotic Technology
- Aeronautics

GO ON TO THE NEXT PAGE

Telescope Array to allow the public to search radio signals themselves.

Many astronomers and physicists attribute the renewed efforts to establish contact with alien civilizations to the present-day escalation in the discovery of exoplanets, or planets that orbit a star other than our Sun. According to NASA's data, as of June 2015, there have been 1,838 confirmed exoplanets, where, just 20 years ago, it seemed that our solar system was destined to be the extent of our planetary discovery. A significant part of that escalation can be attributed to NASA's Kepler Mission, an unmanned space observatory craft launched in 2009 to find Earth-sized and smaller planets orbiting other stars. More than 800 systems like our own solar system with stars and orbiting planets have been identified.

So why is it, with a rejuvenated effort to find evidence of extraterrestrial intelligence, that Fermi's question is still so pertinent? Despite billions of dollars and years of research, SETI has nothing substantial to show for itself. In fact, the closest thing to ETI contact is the *Wow! Signal*: a strong narrowband radio signal detected in 1977 by Jerry R. Ehman of Ohio State University's Big Ear radio telescope project. Ehman was able to successfully observe the signal for a 72-second window, circling its non-natural waves and writing "Wow!" next to it—his enthusiasm led to its name, but not to any significant breakthrough. Since 1977, efforts to relocate the signal have failed again and again.

The theoretical explanations for Fermi's paradox differ greatly. Some simply believe that few, if any, other civilizations exist. The Rare Earth Hypothesis suggests that Earth is unique, and so, therefore, is intelligent life. Others theorize that intelligent life has a tendency of destroying itself quickly; they hypothesize that self-annihilation occurs before contact can be made. On the other hand, many postulate that ETI's do exist, but we see no evidence for a variety of reasons.

Perhaps we are too far apart in space or time. Perhaps humans, a relatively new species, haven't searched long enough. Or maybe we aren't listening properly. What if our distant neighbors are using different frequencies?

Regardless of how certain or uncertain you are that extraterrestrial intelligent life exists, the venture to solve Fermi's Paradox is prevailing, and many believe the stakes are high. Some argue that the enormous expense involved in such projects is only surpassed by the futility of seeking aliens when we have had decades without success; but, others counter that the discovery of 1,838 exoplanets is hardly unsuccessful.

42. What is the purpose of this passage?

(A) To advocate for a particular course of technological action
(B) To survey various attempts to resolve a scientific dilemma
(C) To detail the established consensus on an interesting problem
(D) To consider alternative approaches to a social issue

43. According to the passage, the general scientific attitude toward the existence of extraterrestrial intelligence is best described as

(A) deeply passionate and mostly certain.
(B) quite interested but currently unsettled.
(C) somewhat pessimistic and rather fearful.
(D) fundamentally skeptical but always dogmatic.

44. Which option gives the best evidence for the answer to the previous question?

(A) Lines 1–7 ("In 1950 . . . civilizations")
(B) Lines 16–20 ("While . . . substantive")
(C) Lines 21–26 ("Whether . . . on")
(D) Lines 38–41 ("Although . . . messages")

GO ON TO THE NEXT PAGE

45. Which of the following is the best paraphrase of the Fermi Paradox (line 7)?

(A) "It seems reasonable that there should be extraterrestrial intelligence, so why haven't we found it?"
(B) "It is contradictory that there is both concrete evidence in favor of alien life and direct evidence against their existence."
(C) "It is clear that aliens have made contact, so why won't the majority of humanity accept this obvious truth?"
(D) "The universe is so old and large that there should be extraterrestrial intelligence; why won't scientists make an effort to locate it?"

46. As used in line 19, the word "incredulity" most closely means

(A) curiosity.
(B) anticipation.
(C) wisdom.
(D) disbelief.

47. The example in lines 72–83 primarily serves to demonstrate that

(A) there is decisive evidence in favor of alien life.
(B) the search for extraterrestrial intelligence has been virtually fruitless.
(C) scientists are redoubling their efforts to build on Ehman's discovery.
(D) astronomers are notable for the enthusiasm with which they conduct their observations.

48. The purpose of lines 95–99 ("Perhaps we . . . frequencies") is to

(A) explain why the author is quite pessimistic about the possibility of finding ETI.
(B) offer suggestions that have not likely been considered by scientists.
(C) give a recommended course of action to solve a scientific problem.
(D) elaborate on possible reasons why we have not found evidence of ETI.

49. As used in line 102, the word "venture" most closely means

(A) endeavor.
(B) risk.
(C) business.
(D) speculation.

50. Based on the trends in the graph and the information in the passage, which of these best represents a logical next step in the search for extraterrestrial intelligence?

(A) A manned space station that will monitor radio waves
(B) An analysis of previous extraterrestrial communications
(C) An exploratory mission to an Earth-like exoplanet
(D) A space shuttle delivery of an advanced outer-space telescope

GO ON TO THE NEXT PAGE

51. According to the graph, between the years 2008–2015, the growth in which of these budget components most closely mirrored the growth of NASA's entire budget?

(A) Exploration Missions
(B) Robotic Technology
(C) Space shuttles/Stations
(D) Aeronautics

52. Suppose that a scientist wants evidence that would support NASA's funding decisions with respect to space stations and space shuttles as outlined in the graph. Which option gives the best evidence from the passage?

(A) Lines 38–41 ("Although . . . messages")
(B) Lines 50–53 ("SETILive . . . themselves")
(C) Lines 63–66 ("A significant . . . identified")
(D) Lines 72–76 ("In fact . . . project")

If you finish before time is called, you may check your work on this section only. Do not turn to any other section.

Reading

1.	A	14.	B	27.	D	40.	D
2.	B	15.	D	28.	D	41.	D
3.	D	16.	C	29.	B	42.	B
4.	A	17.	D	30.	D	43.	B
5.	B	18.	B	31.	D	44.	B
6.	C	19.	A	32.	A	45.	A
7.	D	20.	C	33.	B	46.	D
8.	C	21.	A	34.	D	47.	B
9.	B	22.	A	35.	B	48.	D
10.	B	23.	B	36.	C	49.	A
11.	B	24.	B	37.	A	50.	C
12.	D	25.	D	38.	C	51.	D
13.	A	26.	D	39.	C	52.	C

Number Correct _____

Number Incorrect _____

SCORING APPROXIMATION

This table gives you an estimate of how your performance on the Reading section will contribute to your overall Evidence-Based Reading and Writing score. Keep in mind that each test *will be curved*, making the number of questions needed for a particular score dependent on the test that day. This is the best estimate we can give you based on (1) previous SAT curves and (2) the fact that guessing is now permitted on the SAT.

Questions out of 52 answered correctly	Estimated overall section score (between 200-800)
52	800
49	750
46	700
43	650
40	600
37	550
33	500
30	450
26	400
20	350
13	300
7	250
0	200

ANSWERS EXPLAINED

1. **(A)** Beatrice is described as exceptionally wealthy, charming, and cultured; yet, the author makes sure to depict her as superficial and idiosyncratic. *Eccentric* means "unconventional" or "unusual," so (A) accurately expresses her character. Beatrice is certainly *haughty* or "arrogant," but she is not *mean-spirited* or hateful. She is *wealthy*, but not hard-working. And *itinerant*, meaning traveling, describes Beatrice, while *misanthropic*, meaning "unsociable," does not.

2. **(B)** The opening lines state that the traits that have made Amory worthwhile came from his mother. (A) is incorrect because the narrator asserts that Amory's best qualities are those that he received from Beatrice, i.e., his mom. (C) is incorrect because Stephen passed down only his height and indecisiveness according to lines 11–15. (D) is not supported within the passage at all.

3. **(D)** The second paragraph is a compelling description of Amory's mother, Beatrice. *Emphatic* means "forceful or done with emphasis," so it exemplifies the paragraph's style. It is not gloomy and *educational* as in (A), vague and *intellectual* as in (B), or naïve and hopeful as in (C).

4. **(A)** Lines 30–49 refer to how Beatrice's youth is *passed*, so *spent* is the appropriate choice. It is not correct usage to say she *gave up*, *tossed*, or *agreed* her youth.

5. **(B)** Lines 50–53 claim that Beatrice married Stephen because she was "weary" and "sad," making (B) the correct answer. There is no evidence that she fell in love with or was forced to marry him. Likewise, *vengeance* implies retaliation or a punishment for a wrongdoing, which is not mentioned.

6. **(C)** These lines provide the most direct evidence for Beatrice's marital motivations. (A) refers to Amory's father's choices rather than his mother's. (B) describes the relationship of Amory's parents after they are married. And choice (D) is unrelated as it is a dialogue between Beatrice and Amory regarding the merits of inactivity.

7. **(D)** Lines 72–80 indicate that Amory's upbringing is unlike other "little rich boys" and that his education is "highly specialized," making choice (D) correct. Choices (A) and (C) are not supported since the passage describes Amory's youth as one of advantage and leisure. And while Amory was certainly educated, his knowledge came from atypical experiences rather than the more conventional scholarly methods.

8. **(C)** Lines 72–80 provide the best evidence for Amory's one-of-a-kind childhood. The narrator differentiates him from even those children of his same social and economic class, making it clear that Amory's experience is anomalous. Choice (A) refers to Stephen's role in the family. (B) is incorrect because it addresses Beatrice's education rather than her son's. Finally, (D) is an example of Beatrice's quirky morality that she attempts to pass on to her son, but is not reflective of his upbringing or education more generally.

9. **(B)** In this context, the narrator is referring to the fact that Amory and his mother wandered the country for several years of his childhood, so *traveled* makes the most sense here. It is not accurate to say they *made*, *caused*, or *organized* the country in her father's private car. The following sentences refer to a couple of the locations they visited during their travels.

10. **(B)** Amory's relationship with his mother can be best seen through their dialogue at the end of the passage. Amory's use of his mother's first name indicates that their affiliation is unceremonious, while her anxiety over him rising too early shows that it is a kindly relationship. So, (B) works best here, where *friendly* refers to "approachable and informal." Using his mother's first name is far from traditional, as in (A). And since she finds it agreeable, there is no evidence that Amory is disrespectful as in (C). Choice (D) can be tempting because Amory not only uses Beatrice's first name in addressing her, but the narrator also tells us that Amory holds no illusions about his vain mother. However, *cold* or *distant* is too negative.

11. **(B)** The passage argues that the advantages of social media need to be considered in the workplace, so (B) is the correct choice. The author provides evidence of (A) to support the thesis, but it is not the thesis itself. (C) represents a general argument that the passage questions. And (D) is not discussed.

12. **(D)** Lines 101–112 make up the conclusion paragraph where the author argues that "it isn't as simple" as a comprehensive prohibition of all social media, and support the author's argument that social media can be very useful in the workplace. Choices (A) and (B) indicate the standard negative view of social media at work, while choice (D) merely gives one example of its utility.

13. **(A)** The author is interested in showing both sides of the social media conflict, and does so without advocating for change, but instead encouraging an inclusive approach to the decision. Choice (A) is the only choice that addresses both the benefits and disadvantages, while staying true to the author's informative caution.

14. **(B)** Lines 1–11 provide examples of social media use in the workplace that could be potentially valuable to the company, so (B) is correct. These lines do not provide points to be later analyzed, examples to align the reader with smart phone language, or personal experiences of the author.

15. **(D)** These lines provide a transition from the common arguments against social media to the discussion of the prefaced examples that pose its possible perks. (A), (B), and (C) don't account for that transition.

16. **(C)** The author's number one advantage to social media use is network expansion, so we can infer that a growing company that needs to extend its professional networking and marketing would benefit the most from social media. While the author would support the idea that the other choices could benefit as well, the impact is not as clear.

17. **(D)** Lines 60–63 state that "startup businesses" specifically find social media useful, and therefore, support the previous question. Choices (A) and (B) refer to undesirable social networking. Finally, (C) supplies the transition to the pros of social media, but does not suggest a particular business that could profit from it.

18. **(B)** Line 67 states that social media can be "an unrivaled medium for market research," making (B) the precise word meaning. It is nonsensical to say social media provides an unrivaled *best* or *middle*. And while *standard* is the next best choice, it refers more to what is accepted as best, rather than an avenue for doing something.

19. **(A)** *Area* is the correct choice. Here, the passage presents a situation where a company uses a social media page as a "space" for staff support and appreciation. It is inaccurate

to say that a *clearing* or *separation* is created. And while *dimension* is a tempting choice, it imprecisely refers to "measurement" or "a level of existence."

20. **(C)** The graph indicates that women, those in the age group of 18–29, and those who have completed some college are the most likely categorizations to use social networking sites—choice (C) is the only option that fits all these criteria. Choices (A) and (B) both have males, and choice (D) uses an age group that is outside the range given by the graph.

21. **(A)** The passage uses these lines to express that a social media presence is essential for startup companies to grow. Since the graph indicates that those in the age group between 18–29 are the most likely age group to use social media sites, it is reasonable to conclude that if startups want to reach the customers most likely to purchase their products, they must have a social media presence. It is not (B) because this would make creating social media appeals far less promising as a marketing strategy. It is not (C) or (D) because there is no indication about the demographics of these groups, making it impossible to use the information in the graph to connect to them.

22. **(A)** Lines 1–12 do not particularly speak toward the author's argument, but instead are used to show how a personal choice can put one at very serious health risks. Since the author wages that the decision to not vaccinate is even more ridiculous than the decision to smoke, these lines are effective at setting up the argument. Lung cancer is not the primary topic nor do these lines give statistics for vaccination research. And while choice (D) is true, it does not show how the lines contribute to the author's argument as a whole.

23. **(B)** Lines 19–27 express the perceived views of those who do not vaccinate, so that the author can go on to refute these views, making (B) correct. These lines do not support or clarify the passage argument, nor are they connected with a respect for opposition. In fact, the author is passionately against the choice to not vaccinate.

24. **(B)** Here, the author states that smallpox virus was extremely dangerous "before it was eradicated by vaccination," resulting in entire cultures being *eliminated* in the Americas. The context doesn't support that the virus was *transported* in any way. Similarly, while it may be accurate to say vaccinations *fought* and *affected* cultures, neither word choice indicates the destruction of whole cultures.

25. **(D)** According to Passage 2, unvaccinated persons are particularly safe in a vaccinated population because they are protected from the viruses themselves through "herd immunity" and from adverse vaccine events.

26. **(D)** Lines 98–102 state that as long as Americans in general are vaccinated, the "unvaccinated individual will be well-protected," making (D) the correct choice. Choice (A) rules out what the author sees as a delusional reason for not vaccinating. And choices (B) and (C) discuss the rare risks of vaccinating, but don't allude to the circumstances under which the unvaccinated are safer.

27. **(D)** *Do away with* works best here because the line is saying that the author wants to rule out "fallacies" and "delusions." The author is not spending time trying to understand the delusions as in (A). (B) is too literal. (C) is too lukewarm.

28. **(D)** To approach this question, consider that the first author finds no excuse for avoiding vaccinations. On the other hand, the second author shows that choosing not to vaccinate one's children can be an even safer choice in a place like America where the majority of the population is vaccinated. Thus, (D) is the only choice that describes a relationship where Passage 2 explains an unforgivable instance in Passage 1.

29. **(B)** The final sentence of the first passage suggests that vaccinations are the only option to protect our children. Passage 2 acknowledges the need for general vaccination, but ultimately understands that in a vaccinated population, a parent can actually protect a child from more common risks via the choice to not vaccinate. So, (B) is right here. Both agree that vaccination is more widespread than not. And the author of Passage 2 still recognizes the need for the general population to be vaccinated, ruling out the other options.

30. **(D)** Lines 92–97 refer to the second author's acknowledgement that the risks of vaccines are actually more common than the diseases they protect against in America. Therefore, these lines provide evidence for how the author might respond to the statement that unvaccinated children are less protected. (A) introduces the foundation for a parent's choice to not vaccinate but doesn't give detail. (B) broadly considers risks, but again doesn't address the risks of vaccination. And (C) is a description of one vaccination risk that does not include its prevalence in comparison to the virus it vaccinates against.

31. **(D)** Passage 1 sees no reason for a parent to not vaccinate. Passage 2 acknowledges a valid reason for a parent to not vaccinate. *Hatred* and *loathing* are too strong for the first author's disdain, but surely he or she doesn't make room for *forgiveness*. Likewise, *appreciation* or *gratitude* would be too positive for the mere comprehension of author 2, while *intolerance* is more descriptive of author 1.

32. **(A)** Emerson's purpose is to present support for Emancipation as in (A). While slavery is obviously related, this passage doesn't work to illustrate its evils as in (B). Likewise, choice (C) is a detail used to argue for Emancipation, but is not the objective. And finally, morality is the basis for Emancipation according to Emerson, but again, is related to his general purpose as a thinker rather than the purpose of the passage itself.

33. **(B)** This can best be seen in lines 68–72, which state that political struggle is not the end, "but only the means." Thus, (B) is the correct choice. There is no evidence for choice (A). Emerson would disagree with choice (C) according to lines 1–2. And finally, as for (D), Emerson believes a moral government would settle the question of slavery, but not necessarily any political body.

34. **(D)** Lines 69–72 indicate that, for Emerson, American democracy is not important in and of itself, but only useful in achieving a bigger aim. That aim, he contends, is morality; and in this specific instance, emancipation represents the moral choice. Therefore, these lines best express his overall attitude toward the role of politics. (A) and (C) give detailed support for emancipation, while (B) suggests that America is a divine power's last chance at getting humanity right.

35. **(B)** In the context of the first passage, these lines serve to illustrate the effects of the Civil War. We learn that the atmosphere is one of "anxiety" and "stern duties." Choice (B) is the only option that focuses on the misfortunes of children as being caused by the war.

36. **(C)** According to lines 11–12, the state of the country induces "stern duties," so *serious* is the correct choice. A country at war would not connect to anything *playful*. (B) is too negative. Choice (D) would inaccurately indicate that what's at stake is *pointless*.

37. **(A)** The questions in lines 26–36 rhetorically appeal to a sense of duty and justice associated with American democracy, making choice (A) correct. Words in these lines like *practical, heroic, action,* and *will* emphasize the author's urgency. Choice (C) is incorrect because the questions expand on the previous paragraph's reasoning rather than critique it. And (B) and (D) are nonsensical because this device is reflecting on the application of democracy and calling for action, not arousing curiosity or summarizing another's thoughts.

38. **(C)** To approach this question, consider how Emerson introduces the conflict of American Civilization as the incompatibility between "two states of society under one law." He, then, makes the case that democracy has a responsibility, that following the tradition of slavery is not the American destiny, and that "emancipation is the demand of civilization." Hence, we can say that he frames the conflict between what is long-established and what is ethical. (A) is incorrect because international relations are not thoroughly discussed. According to Emerson, both aspects of (B) would be solved by emancipation. (D) uses details of Emerson's argument, but does not consider the underlying aspects.

39. **(C)** Choices (A) and (B) introduce the nation's state of restless disillusionment. Choice (D) gives an example of how emancipation will solidify the North and South. None of these options provides evidence of a philosophical struggle framing the nation's decision. (C) is the only answer that addresses how Emerson understands the fundamental conflict—an opportunity for morality that diverges from "a literal slavish following of precedents"—and thus, affirms the previous question.

40. **(D)** *Obeying* is appropriate here since Emerson is arguing that a "following of precedents," or a repeating of history, isn't befitting of American civilization. *Ensuing* means "to happen as a result." *Succeeding* refers to coming after something in time. Likewise, *resulting* is a synonym of *following* that doesn't indicate a conforming to past tradition.

41. **(D)** To paraphrase lines 55–56, emancipation will change Southern culture in ways that will unify the nation. Thus, (D) best captures this idea. Emerson only mentions immigrants to argue that emancipation opens up labor options. Choice (B) is a distorted exaggeration. A Southern Constitution, as in (C), was never mentioned.

42. **(B)** Consider that the author poses a question and then talks about various ways science is attempting to answer this question. So, (B) accurately describes the author's purpose. The author does not argue one way or the other as in (A). There is not an established consensus—in fact, opinions differ greatly, ruling out (C). And the issue itself is much more scientific than social as in (D); furthermore, he doesn't consider any alternative approaches.

43. **(B)** The author allows that the search is extensive, but that opinion varies "from certainty to skepticism to downright incredulity," giving evidence for (B). The other options inaccurately indicate that there is a scientific agreement of some sort.

44. **(B)** Lines 16–20 provide direct evidence of an unsettled attitude toward a question that is being explored intensely. Hence, they work to support the previous question. (A) is where the author poses the question concerning ETI. (C) consists of the irregular imaginings of what ETI could look and act like. Finally, (D) refers to new methods of ETI research.

45. **(A)** Line 7 refers to the phenomenon described in the preceding lines, namely the inconsistency in not having any proof whatsoever of other intelligent life in a universe so vast. (A) accurately paraphrases the Fermi Paradox. Choices (B) and (C) imply that we have already had contact with alien life. Meanwhile, choice (D) proposes that we are not searching.

46. **(D)** *Incredulity* is the inability to believe something. However, even if you didn't know that, this line is a spectrum of opinion around the existence of alien life. So, if the spectrum starts at *certainty*, we can infer the word we are looking for has the opposite meaning. Hence, (D) is correct. (A) is too mild, and (B) is not an opposite of *certainty*. (C) is not an attitude toward something, but implies good judgment and intelligence.

47. **(B)** Lines 72–83 provide evidence for the statement directly above: "SETI has nothing substantial to show for itself." These lines go on to show how a 72-second anomaly in 1977 that was never relocated is the closest thing we have to evidence of outside life. Hence, (B) is correct. (A) implies that this evidence proved alien existence, which is false. And we have no evidence for (C); we only know that efforts have failed in the past. (D) is wrong because it assumes that the significance of this example is Ehman's "Wow!" rather than its feeble rank as the closest we've come to proof.

48. **(D)** Lines 95–99 give possible explanations for why we have not come into contact with ETI's even if they do exist. There is no evidence as to the author's opinion, as in (A). Choices (B) and (C) are incorrect because neither a recommendation nor suggestion is given in these lines.

49. **(A)** *Endeavor* works best here, since the context refers to "the venture to solve Fermi's Paradox." The line is saying that the attempt to solve the question is ongoing, so the other choices are imprecise. (B) and (D) imply bias toward the undertaking. Choice (C) could only be logical if we were saying "the business of solving," not "the business to solve."

50. **(C)** Since the graph shows more and more of the budget being designated to exploration missions, we can assume the next step would be (C). We know "exoplanets" are being discovered on an almost weekly basis from the passage information, so this represents a logical inference. Funding is decreasing for (A) and (D). And we know from the passage that (B) does not exist.

51. **(D)** The sum of the four curves will give the entire budget, so the budget went from about 18 million to 21 million. We can rule out (B) and (C) since these components show a decrease. Finally, the graph indicates that exploration missions doubled from about 5 million (18–13) to 10 million (21–11), which is not representative of the more gradual increase in the program budget. Aeronautics, on the other hand, went from about 5 to 8 million, and maintained about a third of the entire budget consistently, so it is closely mirrored with the budget itself.

52. **(C)** To approach this question, consider that funding for manned space shuttles and stations has declined dramatically. So, we are looking for evidence to explain that drop. Lines 63–66 offer possible support, since they detail an escalation in "unmanned" space observatories. It is plausible to infer that NASA doesn't have to devote spending to manned stations when unmanned stations are now more common. (A) references initiatives toward sending our own messages. (B) focuses on telescopes and radio research. And choice (D) occurred in 1977, so it wouldn't be helpful with the given graph data.

ANSWER SHEET
Practice Test 3

Reading

1. Ⓐ Ⓑ Ⓒ Ⓓ	14. Ⓐ Ⓑ Ⓒ Ⓓ	27. Ⓐ Ⓑ Ⓒ Ⓓ	40. Ⓐ Ⓑ Ⓒ Ⓓ
2. Ⓐ Ⓑ Ⓒ Ⓓ	15. Ⓐ Ⓑ Ⓒ Ⓓ	28. Ⓐ Ⓑ Ⓒ Ⓓ	41. Ⓐ Ⓑ Ⓒ Ⓓ
3. Ⓐ Ⓑ Ⓒ Ⓓ	16. Ⓐ Ⓑ Ⓒ Ⓓ	29. Ⓐ Ⓑ Ⓒ Ⓓ	42. Ⓐ Ⓑ Ⓒ Ⓓ
4. Ⓐ Ⓑ Ⓒ Ⓓ	17. Ⓐ Ⓑ Ⓒ Ⓓ	30. Ⓐ Ⓑ Ⓒ Ⓓ	43. Ⓐ Ⓑ Ⓒ Ⓓ
5. Ⓐ Ⓑ Ⓒ Ⓓ	18. Ⓐ Ⓑ Ⓒ Ⓓ	31. Ⓐ Ⓑ Ⓒ Ⓓ	44. Ⓐ Ⓑ Ⓒ Ⓓ
6. Ⓐ Ⓑ Ⓒ Ⓓ	19. Ⓐ Ⓑ Ⓒ Ⓓ	32. Ⓐ Ⓑ Ⓒ Ⓓ	45. Ⓐ Ⓑ Ⓒ Ⓓ
7. Ⓐ Ⓑ Ⓒ Ⓓ	20. Ⓐ Ⓑ Ⓒ Ⓓ	33. Ⓐ Ⓑ Ⓒ Ⓓ	46. Ⓐ Ⓑ Ⓒ Ⓓ
8. Ⓐ Ⓑ Ⓒ Ⓓ	21. Ⓐ Ⓑ Ⓒ Ⓓ	34. Ⓐ Ⓑ Ⓒ Ⓓ	47. Ⓐ Ⓑ Ⓒ Ⓓ
9. Ⓐ Ⓑ Ⓒ Ⓓ	22. Ⓐ Ⓑ Ⓒ Ⓓ	35. Ⓐ Ⓑ Ⓒ Ⓓ	48. Ⓐ Ⓑ Ⓒ Ⓓ
10. Ⓐ Ⓑ Ⓒ Ⓓ	23. Ⓐ Ⓑ Ⓒ Ⓓ	36. Ⓐ Ⓑ Ⓒ Ⓓ	49. Ⓐ Ⓑ Ⓒ Ⓓ
11. Ⓐ Ⓑ Ⓒ Ⓓ	24. Ⓐ Ⓑ Ⓒ Ⓓ	37. Ⓐ Ⓑ Ⓒ Ⓓ	50. Ⓐ Ⓑ Ⓒ Ⓓ
12. Ⓐ Ⓑ Ⓒ Ⓓ	25. Ⓐ Ⓑ Ⓒ Ⓓ	38. Ⓐ Ⓑ Ⓒ Ⓓ	51. Ⓐ Ⓑ Ⓒ Ⓓ
13. Ⓐ Ⓑ Ⓒ Ⓓ	26. Ⓐ Ⓑ Ⓒ Ⓓ	39. Ⓐ Ⓑ Ⓒ Ⓓ	52. Ⓐ Ⓑ Ⓒ Ⓓ

Practice Test 3

65 MINUTES, 52 QUESTIONS

> **Directions:** Each passage or pair of passages is accompanied by several questions. After reading the passage(s), choose the best answer to each question based on what is indicated explicitly or implicitly in the passage(s) or in the associated graphics.

Questions 1–10 are based on the following reading selection.

Finnegan—A short story

David Benson was a timid boy born to parents who had long since stopped worrying
about having children. Willie and Louise had
Line three grown girls, the youngest was nineteen
(5) and leaving to cosmetology school the year
David was born. Louise had suspected an
arsenal of health issues before realizing she
was with child, and even then, she waited
another three weeks to tell her unsuspecting
(10) husband.

Long ago, when he had just taken over
the farm and his body was strong and his
dreams were considerable, Willie had wanted
a son more than anything else. He had hopes
(15) of expanding his property, becoming a rich
man, and gaining respect in town—these
were all things that never came which he
planned to pass on to the son who came far
too late. By the time David was born, more
(20) than half the farm had been divided and sold,
and Willie kept only a handful of hired hands
to tend his small share of the land while
he drove semi-trucks fifty hours a week to
supplement his meager income.

(25) David was an oversensitive, misunderstood boy. He learned quickly that his mother
was far too tired to love him as she had the
girls. His father, often absent, seemed distant
and begrudging around David. So it was
(30) that David, from the age of four on, often
wandered the farm alone, contemplating
the burly pigs or collecting berries and nuts
or simply doing his best to avoid the sinister
silence that was home.

(35) When David was ten, he felt that he would
have his first adventure. Mr. Harding, an old
friend of his father who had a boy just two
years older than David, offered to let David
stay with them in town. It'd be easier on
(40) Louise if she didn't have to drive the boy to
and from school, and David would be happier having Michael to keep him company.
David could spend weekends on the farm
and help Willie with the chores, of course.
(45) For the first time in his life, David felt that
whatever he was missing he was sure to find;
whatever was the void that lingered about the
farm it was sure to disappear in town.

But whatever it was that David was look-
(50) ing for, he didn't find it with the Hardings. Mr.
Harding was a boisterous banker who found
David's shyness unbearable. Mrs. Harding
was a rather large woman who spent nine-

GO ON TO THE NEXT PAGE

tenths of her day cooking and grew solemn
(55) when David refused second helpings. And
in Michael, David found only a combative
stranger who held a singular interest: riding
his bicycle around the town square in search
of the coveted Sara Ridenour.

(60)   David had just turned fourteen when walk-
ing back from school, he heard the pathetic
whimper. The puppy was small—obviously
malnourished and feeble—and much too
young to be away from its mother. David
(65) removed his jacket and coddled the pup
against his chest as he walked briskly back to
the Hardings rehearsing what he might say.
To his surprise, Mr. Harding's only requests
were that David keep the frail animal in his
(70) own room and dispose of it once it was either
healthy enough to live on its own or dead.

These conditions seemed quite fair to
David; and day and night, he dedicated
himself to restoring the health of Finnegan,
(75) the boy's very first friend. The puppy slept
on his chest, suckled milk from a bottle, and
moaned softly when David wiped his failing body. In the end, David's devotion was
not nearly enough, and just six days after his
(80) rescue, the puppy's underdeveloped organs
failed him. David's anguish was palpable, and
Mrs. Harding, in a rare moment of compas-
sion, suggested that Michael help David bury
the poor animal in a proper manner.

(85)   A half-mile into the woods on the west
side of town, Michael dug a hole while David
wept inconsolably, clutching the tiny shoe-
box made coffin. When the hole was plenty
deep, Michael, embarrassed, excused himself
(90) to allow David a minute alone to dispose of
his beloved companion. After fifteen minutes—long after Michael had expected David
to trudge back out of the woods, muddy and
sobbing—Michael walked annoyingly back to
(95) the burial site. He planned on telling David
frankly that this was no way to act about a
silly dog. Instead, Michael found the hole still
empty and David nowhere to be found. Later,
the police would make him repeat the story
(100) again and again.

1. Which choice best summarizes the passage?

    (A) A boy is upset over his dog's death and
        goes missing.
    (B) Two parents contemplate their regrets
        and unfilled dreams.
    (C) A misunderstood boy finds purpose and
        joy only to lose it.
    (D) It illustrates the differences between life
        on a farm and life in town.

2. The primary purpose of the first sentence of
    the passage is to

    (A) demonstrate the age difference between
        David and his siblings.
    (B) scientifically explain how David was
        genetically predisposed towards having a
        more introverted personality.
    (C) give a reason for why David went to live
        with the Harding family.
    (D) give insight into David's personality and
        his parents' state of mind.

3. The passage indicates that when David went
    to live with the Hardings, he thought Michael
    was

    (A) helpful and friendly.
    (B) distant and quarrelsome.
    (C) embarrassed and unemotional.
    (D) athletic and observant.

4. Which option gives the best evidence for the
    answer to the previous question?

    (A) Lines 39–42 ("It'd be . . . company")
    (B) Lines 55–59 ("And in . . . Ridenour")
    (C) Lines 81–84 ("David's . . . manner")
    (D) Lines 85–88 ("A half-mile . . . coffin")

5. In line 65 "coddled" most nearly means

    (A) spoiled.
    (B) humored.
    (C) cosseted.
    (D) indulged.

GO ON TO THE NEXT PAGE

6. The primary purpose of paragraphs six and seven (lines 60–84) is to

   (A) demonstrate that Mr. Harding is fair and just.
   (B) provide a justification for David's "oversensitive" mindset.
   (C) give reasons as to why David is so upset after the puppy's death.
   (D) show that David initially misjudged Mrs. Harding's personality.

7. Based on the information in the passage, what is the best description of what David was looking for at the beginning of paragraph 5 (lines 49–59)?

   (A) A home in town
   (B) A new friend
   (C) A prosperous family
   (D) A pet of his own

8. Which option gives the best evidence for the answer to the previous question?

   (A) Lines 45–48 ("For the . . . town")
   (B) Lines 49–52 ("But . . . unbearable")
   (C) Lines 68–71 ("To his . . . dead")
   (D) Lines 72–75 ("These . . . friend")

9. The information in paragraph two most clearly implies that Willie

   (A) is a much better semi-truck driver than a farmer.
   (B) sold too much of his farm to pass any to his family.
   (C) would have accomplished his dreams if David was born earlier.
   (D) has not been successful in expanding the farm's size.

10. As used in line 81, the word "palpable" most closely means

    (A) concealed.
    (B) credible.
    (C) noticeable.
    (D) believable.

Questions 11–20 are based on the following reading selection and accompanying material.

A Democratic Duel

If one were to set out to form a nation based on democratic principles, there would be essentially two paths to take: presiden-
Line tial or parliamentary. Both hold their own
(5) in terms of advantages and disadvantages, and both possess the endorsement of great prosperous nations. Parliamentary is the far more common order, but many attribute its prevalence to the legacy of the British Empire
(10) rather than to its superiority.

The disparity between the two is hardly subtle. In a presidential system, the executive and legislative branches of government are completely independent of one another,
(15) such as in the United States of America. The President, elected directly by the people, is a national figure that is at once the head of government and state, but is separate and distinct from Congress, the lawmaking
(20) body. On the other hand, a parliamentary system is a fusion of executive and legisla- tive powers with the executive, most often called Prime Minister, being a member of Parliament. In the latter arrangement, mem-
(25) bers of Parliament, the legislative assembly, are elected by the people, but then choose amongst themselves the most fit to be execu- tive. Most often, a monarch, like in Great Britain, is given the responsibility of head-
(30) ing the state and being the icon of national ceremony.

Other divergence occurs in the term limits and standards of accountability in which the executive is held to. For instance, the
(35) presidential model allows for fixed terms and scheduled elections. As such, the President enjoys the assurance of a secure term in which he or she can work to establish and meet goals for the nation's advance. Only in
(40) situations where the President is found guilty of serious crimes will he or she be removed

GO ON TO THE NEXT PAGE

from office before the end of the term. Conversely, the Prime Minister is subject to much more scrutiny and job insecurity.
(45) Legislatures within this model of government are expected to question the Prime Minister directly on a weekly basis and are able to remove the executive any time confidence is lost in his or her ability, character, or judg-
(50) ment. Hence, parliamentary systems are subject to random elections that can more easily replace an unfit leader.

Advocates of the presidential model posit that it is more democratic because the people
(55) themselves choose their executive. They contend that the fixed terms even allow for some stability that the parliamentary organization does not allow. Likewise, a further benefit lies in the separation of powers subject to
(60) checks and balances, in which the executive and legislative bodies are able to monitor one another and assure that power is not centralized. Yet, critics of the system allow that the President's national status affords tenden-
(65) cies toward authoritarianism. Furthermore, as a rule, deadlocks or stalemates are much more common within a system that often has executive and legislative bodies under the control of different parties. Cynics therefore
(70) suggest that the presidential model is privy to discord and inefficiency—not to mention, presidents are difficult to remove when thought to be unfit.

Those in favor of the parliamentary model
(75) believe that the fused government allows for unity and harmony that is all but alien within the former. Not only is it faster and easier to pass legislation, but more often than not, the government operates more cooperatively.
(80) Since it is very unlikely that the ruling party will choose a Prime Minister from another party, the executive and legislative bodies are almost always working in accord. Moreover, when a Prime Minister is decided unfit, he or
(85) she can be removed and replaced right away. This system, they argue, is much more efficient and less prone to corruption. Yet, not

everyone agrees. With the legislature holding supreme power, critics contend that "tyranny
(90) of the majority" is all too likely. Not only are the people not directly electing their leader, but there is also nobody to oppose or veto legislation passed by Parliament. The minority parties have virtually no say and the ruling
(95) party of the assembly can easily manipulate when the Prime Minister will be replaced and when elections will be held.

The two systems represent very different approaches to democracy, and as such, oper-
(100) ate so. One must consider both democratic ideals and effectiveness in deciding the best way to select a leader. While presidential elections can become feeble popularity contests, centralized power is a real concern.

11. What statement best summarizes the passage?

(A) A survey of two governmental forms that focuses primarily on the differences between them
(B) A survey of two governmental forms that focuses primarily on the similarities between them
(C) An analysis of whether a parliamentary or presidential system is a better fit for a particular country
(D) An analysis of whether a parliamentary or presidential system is a better fit for several different countries

12. The approach of the author is best described as

(A) neutral and pessimistic.
(B) passionate and strong-willed.
(C) analytical and objective.
(D) technical and predisposed.

GO ON TO THE NEXT PAGE

13. The author states that a possible reason for the greater practice of parliamentary than presidential democracy is

(A) majority rule.
(B) historical inheritance.
(C) legislative-executive unity.
(D) centralized authority.

14. Which option gives the best evidence for the answer to the previous question?

(A) Lines 7–10 ("Parliamentary . . . superiority")
(B) Lines 20–24 ("On the . . . parliament")
(C) Lines 58–63 ("Likewise . . . centralized")
(D) Lines 88–93 ("With the . . . Parliament")

15. Suppose a country with a parliamentary system and a country with a presidential system were choosing representatives to a global sports competition like the Olympics. Based on the paragraph in lines 11–31, which respective governmental officials from the parliamentary and the presidential system would be the most desirable and fitting representatives?

(A) Prime Minister, Congressperson
(B) Judge, Military General
(C) King, President
(D) Queen, Senator

16. As used in line 39, the word "advance" most closely means

(A) payment.
(B) progress.
(C) spread.
(D) increase.

17. The paragraph in lines 53–73 primarily serves to

(A) explore the pros and cons of the presidential model.
(B) compare and contrast the presidential and parliamentary models.
(C) highlight the superior aspects of the presidential model.
(D) give specific examples of countries that practice presidential politics.

18. As used in line 70, the word "privy" most closely means

(A) susceptible.
(B) privileged.
(C) concealed.
(D) open.

19. It is most reasonable to infer that those concerned about a "tyranny of the majority," as described in lines 89–90, are afraid that what would be likely to occur in such a situation?

(A) A dictator will emerge.
(B) The rights of most citizens will be respected.
(C) Government will stop functioning efficiently.
(D) Minority interests will be ignored.

20. Which option gives the best evidence for the answer to the previous question?

(A) Lines 45–50 ("Legislatures . . . judgment")
(B) Lines 80–85 ("Since it . . . away")
(C) Lines 93–97 ("The minority . . . held")
(D) Lines 98–104 ("The two . . . concern")

GO ON TO THE NEXT PAGE

Questions 21–30 are based on the following reading selection and accompanying material.

Humanity's Code

A protein is a large, complex macromolecule composed of one or more long chains of amino acids. Proteins are 15–25% nitrogen
Line and an equal amount of oxygen, and are
(5) present in and vital to every living cell. They are essential for the structure, function, and regulation of the body's tissues and organs. As a matter of fact, proteins hold together, protect, and provide structure to the body of
(10) a multi-celled organism. Furthermore, they are responsible for catalyzing and regulating the body chemistry. Yet, before Frederick Sanger—one of only two people to ever receive two Nobel Prizes in the same cat-
(15) egory—little was known about proteins and the sequence of their amino acid chains.

Frederick Sanger graduated with a doctorate in biochemistry from St. John's College in 1943, where he had spent three years
(20) researching the metabolism of the amino acid lysine. Yet, it wasn't until his work with insulin that Sanger differentiated himself in the field of chemistry. His first true accomplishment occurred when he success-
(25) fully determined the complete amino acid sequence of the two polypeptide chains of bovine insulin A and B in the early 1950s. His research proved that proteins have a defined chemical composition, and he ultimately
(30) concluded that every protein had a unique sequence. In 1958, Sanger was awarded the Nobel Prize in Chemistry for showing how amino acids link together to form insulin, and, therefore, providing the tools for scien-
(35) tists to analyze any protein in the body. Much later, after his retirement, he would describe himself as "just a chap who messed about in a lab."

Four years later, Sanger took a position as
(40) the head of the Protein Chemistry Division on the Medical Research Council, where he began to work on the sequencing of ribo-

nucleic acid. He developed methods for separating ribonucleotide fragments gener-
(45) ated with specific nucleases which triggered the discovery of formylmethionine tRNA, responsible for initiating protein synthesis in bacteria. Yet his earlier work with insulin helped him to form and deliberate on
(50) ideas of how DNA codes for proteins. When he turned to sequencing DNA—the blueprint-like molecule that carries the genetic instructions for all living organisms—Sanger collaborated with Alan Coulson to publish
(55) the "Plus and Minus Technique," a sequencing procedure he developed to determine the order of the chemical bases adenine, thymine, guanine, and cytosine which spell out the genetic code for all living things.

(60) When he devised a more efficient method for reading the molecular letters that make up the genetic code in 1977, he christened it the "Sanger Method." The "Sanger Method" allows long stretches of DNA to be rapidly
(65) and accurately sequenced, which earned him his second Nobel Prize in Chemistry in 1980. He employed his invention to decipher the sixteen thousand letters of mitochondria. More significantly, this method eventually
(70) allowed scientists to decode the three billion letters of the human genetic code, giving science the ability to distinguish between normal and abnormal genes. In the same way, Sanger's work directly contributed to
(75) the development of biotechnology drugs like human growth hormone.

In 1986, the celebrated chemist accepted an Order of Merit. Shortly after, he helped open the Sanger Institute outside of
(80) Cambridge, which is now one of the world's largest genomic research centers. Sanger died in November 2013; his obituary documented his supreme modesty in an autobiographical account of himself as "academically not
(85) brilliant." At any rate, Sanger's research prompted the decoding of the human genome.

GO ON TO THE NEXT PAGE

Nobel Prize Winners as of 2013

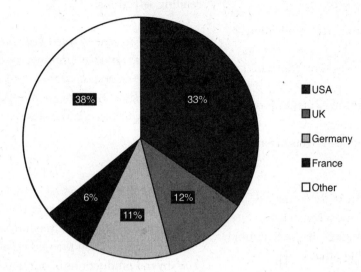

21. The organization of the passage is

    (A) somewhat chronological.
    (B) mostly chronological.
    (C) somewhat argumentatively sequenced.
    (D) mostly argumentatively sequenced.

22. As used in line 5, the word "vital" most closely means

    (A) vibrant.
    (B) essential.
    (C) biological.
    (D) dynamic.

23. According to the passage, Sanger's attitude toward his own accomplishments could best be described as

    (A) humiliated.
    (B) humble.
    (C) confident.
    (D) arrogant.

24. Which option gives the best evidence for the answer to the previous question?

    (A) Lines 12–16 ("Yet . . . chains")
    (B) Lines 31–35 ("In 1958 . . . body")
    (C) Lines 73–76 ("In the . . . hormone")
    (D) Lines 81–85 ("Sanger . . . brilliant")

25. Which option could best be cited as evidence in support of the claim that Sanger was confident in the significance of his research?

    (A) Lines 23–27 ("His first . . . 1950s")
    (B) Lines 39–43 ("Four . . . acid")
    (C) Lines 60–63 ("When he . . . Method")
    (D) Lines 73–76 ("In the . . . hormone")

26. Sanger's quote in lines 37–38 ("just . . . lab") has a tone best described as

    (A) playful.
    (B) somber.
    (C) bombastic.
    (D) careless.

27. As used in line 67, the word "employed" most closely means

    (A) tried.
    (B) hired.
    (C) created.
    (D) utilized.

GO ON TO THE NEXT PAGE

28. The primary purpose of lines 69–76 ("More . . . hormone") is to

(A) elaborate on the practical applications of a discovery.
(B) anticipate and address objections to the author's thesis.
(C) explain Sanger's primary methods of research.
(D) show the negative side effects of Sanger's findings.

29. It is most likely that one of the "other" countries that has the most Nobel Prize winners has a percentage of the total number of prize winners in what range?

(A) Between 12% and 33%
(B) Between 11% and 12%
(C) Between 6% and 11%
(D) Between 0% and 6%

30. What is the probability that a randomly selected Nobel Prize winner from the set of winners from Germany and the United States will be from Germany?

(A) 33
(B) 0.33
(C) 11
(D) 0.25

Questions 31–41 are based on the following reading selections.

Below is an excerpt adapted from Booker T. Washington's notable "Atlanta Exposition Speech" in 1895. The second is part of a 1903 response, titled "Of Mr. Booker T. Washington and Others," by W.E.B. DuBois. (As historical texts, these use antiquated language.)

PASSAGE 1

Our greatest danger is, that in the great leap from slavery to freedom we may over-look the fact that the masses of us are to live
Line by the productions of our hands, and fail to
(5) keep in mind that we shall prosper in propor-tion as we learn to dignify and glorify com-mon labor and put brains and skill into the common occupations of life… No race can prosper till it learns that there is as much dig-
(10) nity in tilling a field as in writing a poem. It is at the bottom of life we must begin and not the top. Nor should we permit our grievances to overshadow our opportunities.

To those of the white race who look to
(15) the incoming of those of foreign birth and strange tongue and habits for the prosperity of the South, were I permitted, I would repeat what I say to my own race. "Cast down your bucket where you are." Cast it down among
(20) the 8,000,000 Negroes whose habits you know, whose loyalty and love you have tested in days when to have proved treacherous [meant] the ruin of your firesides.
[…]
(25) While doing this you can be sure in the future, as you have been in the past, that you and your families will be surrounded by the most patient, faithful, law-abiding and unresentful people that the world has seen.
(30) As we have proven our loyalty to you in the past, in nursing your children, watching by the sick bed of your mothers and fathers, and often following them with tear dimmed eyes

GO ON TO THE NEXT PAGE

to their graves, so in the future in our humble
(35) way, we shall stand by you with a devotion
that no foreigner can approach, ready to
lay down our lives, if need be, in defense of
yours, interlacing our industrial, commercial,
civil and religious life with yours in a way that
(40) shall make the interests of both races one. In
all things that are purely social we can be as
separate as the fingers, yet one as the hand in
all things essential to mutual progress.

PASSAGE 2

... Booker T. Washington arose as essen-
(45) tially the leader not of one race but of
two—a compromiser between the South, the
North, and the Negro. Naturally the Negroes
resented, at first bitterly, signs of compromise
which surrendered their civil and political
(50) rights, even though this was to be exchanged
for larger chances of economic development.
The rich and dominating North, however,
was not only weary of the race problem, but
was investing largely in Southern enterprises,
(55) and welcomed any method of peaceful
cooperation. Thus, by national opinion, the
Negroes began to recognize Mr. Washington's
leadership; and the voice of criticism was
hushed.
(60) Mr. Washington represents in Negro
thought the old attitude of adjustment and
submission, but adjustment at such a pecu-
liar time as to make his programme unique.
This is an age of unusual economic devel-
(65) opment, and Mr. Washington's programme
naturally takes an economic cast, becoming a
gospel of work and money to such an extent
as apparently almost completely to overshadow the higher aims of life. Moreover, this
(70) is an age when the more advanced races are
coming in closer contact with the less developed races, and the race-feeling is therefore
intensified; and Mr. Washington's programme
practically accepts the alleged inferiority
(75) of the Negro races. Again, in our own land,
the reaction from the sentiment of war time
has given impetus to race prejudice against

Negroes, and Mr. Washington withdraws
many of the high demands of Negroes as
(80) men and American citizens. In other peri-
ods of intensified prejudice all the Negro's
tendency to self-assertion has been called
forth; at this period a policy of submission is
advocated.
(85)   [...]
Mr. Washington distinctly asks that black
people give up, at least for the present, three
things—First, political power, Second, insistence on civil rights, Third, higher education
(90) of Negro youth—and concentrate all their
energies on industrial education, the accu-
mulation of wealth, and the conciliation of
the South.

31. As used in line 8, the word "common" most
closely means

(A) shared.
(B) public.
(C) ordinary.
(D) universal.

32. Lines 14–17 most precisely refer to

(A) invaders.
(B) foreigners.
(C) immigrants.
(D) travelers.

33. The general purpose of the paragraph in lines
25–43 is to argue in favor of

(A) foreign hostility coupled with a strong
defense.
(B) immigration restrictions coupled with
educational opportunities.
(C) national unity coupled with racial
separation.
(D) ethnic loyalty coupled with better care
for the sick.

GO ON TO THE NEXT PAGE

34. Lines 52–56 most strongly imply that the North was most concerned with

    (A) ethical considerations.
    (B) commercial advancement.
    (C) religious truth.
    (D) geographical awareness.

35. Passage 2 most strongly suggests that Washington encourages African-Americans to

    (A) fight for universal equality between the races.
    (B) settle for less than they rightfully should.
    (C) ignore economic goals in favor of moral ones.
    (D) deceive others with respect to their true loyalties.

36. Which option gives the best evidence for the answer to the previous question?

    (A) Lines 47–51 ("Naturally . . . development")
    (B) Lines 56–59 ("Thus . . . hushed")
    (C) Lines 69–73 ("Moreover . . . intensified")
    (D) Lines 78–84 ("Mr. . . . advocated")

37. As used in line 66, the word "cast" most closely means

    (A) event.
    (B) constraint.
    (C) throw.
    (D) direction.

38. Which sentence best summarizes the relationship between the passages?

    (A) Passage 1 advocates a course of action that Passage 2 expresses as insufficient.
    (B) Passage 1 presents empirical data that Passage 2 attempts to refute.
    (C) Passage 1 argues against the eventual goals laid out in Passage 2.
    (D) Passage 1 is more idealistic while Passage 2 is more pragmatic.

39. Based on the passages, what Washington would most likely define as African-American "compromise," Dubois would most likely define as

    (A) obedience.
    (B) negotiation.
    (C) treason.
    (D) persistence.

40. Which option gives the best evidence for the answer to the previous question?

    (A) Lines 14–18 ("To . . . race")
    (B) Lines 25–29 ("While . . . seen")
    (C) Lines 44–47 ("Booker . . . Negro")
    (D) Lines 60–63 ("Mr. . . . unique")

41. Which selection from Passage 1 gives the most direct response to the last paragraph of Passage 2 (lines 86–93)?

    (A) Lines 8–13 ("No race . . . opportunities")
    (B) Lines 19–23 ("Cast it . . . firesides")
    (C) Lines 30–32 ("As we . . . fathers")
    (D) Lines 40–43 ("In all . . . progress")

GO ON TO THE NEXT PAGE

Questions 42–52 are based on the following reading selection and accompanying material.

Influenza

It is a pestilence that has harried civilizations since at least the time of Homer. What's more, it has done so with such routine
Line periodicity that, in our modern age of annual
(5) inoculations, the enduring danger of this disease has grown all too easy to take for granted. Influenza owes its name to physicians of the Italian renaissance, who believed it was caused by inauspicious astrological
(10) "influences." Today, of course, we know it to be the result of infection by one of several closely related strains of virus. However, unlike other viruses for which vaccines are available—several of which, through
(15) tenacious public health efforts, have been eradicated worldwide—influenza remains a perennial menace, and due to the unique nature of its genome, is unlikely to ever be completely conquered.
(20) Traditionally, outbreaks of influenza are classified as either "epidemic," in which the incidence of the disease increases significantly within a given community, or "pandemic," in which the incidence increases
(25) over a much larger region, such as a continent. While superficially the distinction may seem arbitrary, in fact it reflects two well-delineated facets of the influenza virus replication process. In the Northern hemi-
(30) sphere, "flu season" spans from November to April, and represents an annual recurrence of influenza epidemics among communities situated in this part of the world. Pandemic outbreaks, though not nearly as common,
(35) also seem to follow an approximate epidemiological pattern, typically occurring about three times per century. In the 20th century, these outbreaks included Spanish Flu in 1918, Asian Flu in 1957, and Hong Kong Flu
(40) in 1968. Of the three, Spanish Flu was by far the most devastating. With an estimated

mortality as high as 100 million, its deadliness was on par with that of the infamous Black Plague, which ravaged Eurasia in the
(45) Middle Ages.

"Antigenic drift" and "antigenic shift" are the two chief processes through which influenza circumvents our adaptive immunity, and are thought to be the causes of epidemic
(50) and pandemic influenza, respectively. To understand these two processes, it is necessary to have a working knowledge of the virus itself. There are three known species of influenza virus—influenza A, B, and C—each
(55) of which consists of eight segments of RNA contained within a protein capsid, which in turn is surrounded by a lipid envelope. Collectively, these RNA segments code for eleven proteins; two of which, upon synthe-
(60) sis, are expressed on the envelope's exterior. These two proteins are known as hemagglutinin (HA), and neuraminidase (NA). In terms of the viral life cycle, HA is responsible for attaching to sugar residues that coat the
(65) cells of our respiratory tracts. Once the virus has infected a cell and replicated within its nucleus, NA cleaves these residues, allowing the virus to spread further throughout the body.
(70) Because HA and NA are the outermost viral proteins, it is specifically against these two "antigens" that our white blood cells create antibodies. Furthermore, among the diverse strains of influenza, genetically
(75) encoded differences exist in the types of HA or NA expressed. This allows scientists to sub-classify strains based on the specific antibodies produced against them. For instance, the H1N1 strain was responsible
(80) for both Spanish Flu, as well as the Swine Flu pandemic of 2009, while H5N1 caused the Avian Flu epidemic of 2004.

Random point mutation to the genes encoding HA and NA is one way in which
(85) these subtypes evolve, and can, moreover, interfere with the efficacy of our antibodies. The aggregation of many point mutations

GO ON TO THE NEXT PAGE

over time is referred to as antigenic drift, and eventually results in renewed vulnerability (90) to viral strains against which an individual was previously immune. Notably, influenza A lacks the ability to proofread and correct its genetic material during replication, and as a result, is prone to a much higher rate of (95) mutation than other species of influenza. For this reason in particular, influenza A is responsible for the vast majority of annual epidemics.

To date, 16 HA and 9 NA subtypes have (100) been identified, only a fraction of which are currently infectious to humans. However, because the influenza genome is split into segments, when an animal—a bird, for instance—is co-infected with a strain spe- (105) cific to its species, as well as one capable of infecting humans, the segments may become intermixed during replication in a process called "viral reassortment." When the genes implicated in reassortment include either HA (110) or NA, antigenic shift occurs, and the resulting viral particles will express novel proteins to which the entire human race is vulnerable.

The table shows, for each human outbreak of influenza, relevant epidemiological data, and the viral subtype involved.

Human Influenza Outbreaks

Name	Year	Subtype	Reservoir	Geography	Estimated cases	Estimated fatality rate (%)
Russian Flu	1889	Unknown	Unknown	Global	6.6 million	0.15
Spanish Flu	1918	H1N1	Humans, pigs, birds	Global	500 million	2.0
Asian Flu	1957	H2N2	Birds	Global	9.5 million	0.12
Hong Kong Flu	1968	H3N2	Pigs	Global	8 million	<0.1
Avian Flu	2005	H5N1	Birds	Asia	840	60
Swine Flu	2009	H1N1	Humans, pigs, birds	Global	89 million	2.5
N/A	2013	H7N9	Birds	China	220	25

GO ON TO THE NEXT PAGE

42. The structure of the passage is best described as a

   (A) broad survey followed by a technical analysis.
   (B) historical overview followed by a logical argument.
   (C) general critique followed by experimental summaries.
   (D) persuasive presentation followed by a research summary.

43. Lines 12–19 ("However . . . conquered") most strongly suggest that influenza

   (A) will continue to be a threat despite scientific advances.
   (B) can be fully eradicated with sufficient research funding.
   (C) is unique among diseases in the severity of its symptoms.
   (D) has been eliminated as a pervasive threat to humanity.

44. As used in line 21, the word "epidemic" would best describe which of the flu outbreaks in the table?

   (A) 1889
   (B) 1957
   (C) 2009
   (D) 2013

45. Based on the passage, would antigenic drift or antigenic shift result in greater fundamental changes to genetic structure?

   (A) Antigenic drift because it results in increasing vulnerability to viruses
   (B) Antigenic drift because it can easily spread throughout the body
   (C) Antigenic shift because it entails genetic replication
   (D) Antigenic shift because it involves interspecies genome exchange

46. Which option gives the best evidence for the answer to the previous question?

   (A) Lines 61–65 ("These . . . tracts")
   (B) Lines 65–69 ("Once . . . body")
   (C) Lines 83–91 ("Random . . . immune")
   (D) Lines 101–108 ("However . . . reassortment")

47. The primary purpose of the paragraph in lines 83–98 is to

   (A) explain how HA and NA antibodies lead to genetic mutations resulting in flu.
   (B) contrast the process of antigenic drift with that of antigenic shift.
   (C) describe the mechanism whereby a particular flu type becomes quite harmful.
   (D) critically respond to widespread misconceptions about flu vaccines.

48. As used in line 92, the word "ability" most closely means

   (A) aptitude.
   (B) capacity.
   (C) skill.
   (D) talent.

49. Given the data in the table, which of these flu outbreaks most likely resulted in the greatest number of deaths?

   (A) Russian
   (B) Asian
   (C) Hong Kong
   (D) Avian

GO ON TO THE NEXT PAGE

50. Based on the table and the passage, which flu outbreaks (given by year of occurrence) would most likely result in the human body producing similar chemicals to fight them?

(A) 1889 and 1957
(B) 1918 and 2009
(C) 1968 and 2013
(D) 2005 and 2013

51. Which option gives the best evidence for the answer to the previous question?

(A) Lines 37–45 ("In the . . . Ages")
(B) Lines 53–57 ("There are . . . envelope")
(C) Lines 78–82 ("For instance . . . 2004")
(D) Lines 108–112 ("When . . . vulnerable")

52. According to the information in the table, which of these options gives the most logical possible reason that the flus of 2005 and 2013 resulted in relatively few cases?

(A) These strains of flu are transmitted via blood rather than through the more contagious respiratory method.
(B) Asia, and particularly China, have lower population density than the global norm.
(C) Those humans infected were more likely to die before they could transmit the disease.
(D) The reservoir of the human influenza outbreak had birds as its source.

STOP

If you finish before time is called, you may check your work on this section only. Do not turn to any other section.

ANSWER KEY
Practice Test 3

Reading

1.	C	14.	A	27.	D	40.	D
2.	D	15.	C	28.	A	41.	A
3.	B	16.	B	29.	D	42.	A
4.	B	17.	A	30.	D	43.	A
5.	C	18.	A	31.	C	44.	D
6.	C	19.	D	32.	C	45.	D
7.	B	20.	C	33.	C	46.	D
8.	D	21.	B	34.	B	47.	C
9.	D	22.	B	35.	B	48.	B
10.	C	23.	B	36.	D	49.	B
11.	A	24.	D	37.	D	50.	B
12.	C	25.	C	38.	A	51.	C
13.	B	26.	A	39.	A	52.	C

Number Correct   _____

Number Incorrect   _____

SCORING APPROXIMATION

This table gives you an estimate of how your performance on the Reading section will contribute to your overall Evidence-Based Reading and Writing score. Keep in mind that each test *will be curved*, making the number of questions needed for a particular score dependent on the test that day. This is the best estimate we can give you based on (1) previous SAT curves and (2) the fact that guessing is now permitted on the SAT.

Questions out of 52 answered correctly	Estimated overall section score (between 200–800)
52	800
49	750
46	700
43	650
40	600
37	550
33	500
30	450
26	400
20	350
13	300
7	250
0	200

ANSWERS EXPLAINED

1. **(C)** The short story traces the lonely childhood of a timid boy who fails to fit in or feel loved until he finds a friend in an ill puppy. When the puppy tragically dies, the boy mysteriously disappears. (B) and (D) relate to details of the story, but are not main ideas. And although (A) is true, it fails to capture the gist of the entire passage.

2. **(D)** Lines 1–3 provide exposition that explains why David and his parents are the way they are, so (D) is the best choice. His siblings are not introduced until the following sentence, making (A) incorrect. (B) states that he is timid, but the lines do not offer a scientific explanation of the genetic reasons behind this. Choice (C) moving in with the Hardings, refers to an outcome of David's personality and his parents' state of mind, rather than a cause.

3. **(B)** Lines 56–57 refer to David's opinion of Michael as a "combative stranger" who doesn't share his interests. Therefore, *distant and quarrelsome* describe his impression most accurately. (A) is the opposite of this impression. It is true that Michael is momentarily *embarrassed* and doesn't show the affection for the dog that David does, but these are not representative of his personality as a whole. And there is no evidence for (D).

4. **(B)** These lines best support the claim that David finds Michael overall *distant and quarrelsome.* (A) gives justifications for David's move to town. (C) refers to the reaction to the dog's death. (D) describes the one instance that Michael is recruited to help David. Hence, (A), (C), and (D) do not indicate David's general impression of Michael.

5. **(C)** *Cosseted* makes the most sense here since one of its definitions is "to cuddle or caress lovingly." Choices (A), (B), and (D) can be eliminated because, although they are ways David may treat the dog, they are not reflective of his hugging the animal to his chest as in line 65.

6. **(C)** Paragraph 6 refers to David's discovery of the unhealthy animal that quickly becomes his friend and the sole focus of an otherwise empty life. Paragraph 7 describes his devotion to the pup, and his agony over its death. So, choice (C) is the best option. (A) and (D) are details, but are unrelated to the primary purpose. (B) is incorrect because David's actions are an effect of his sensitivity, rather than a cause of it.

7. **(B)** Lines 49–59 express that despite David's new arrangement, he is still unhappy and misunderstood. It makes sense to infer that because he did not find a companion in Mr. Harding, Mrs. Harding, or Michael, that what he wanted most was a friend. (A) and (C) are incorrect because these are both things he does get with his move, but that do not fill his void. Finally, although the pup becomes a friend and allows him to experience the companionship he is missing, it is not essential that the intimacy be formed with a pet.

8. **(D)** These lines give direct evidence that whatever David was looking for is fulfilled through the friendship with his new pet. (A) expresses his unfulfilled hope that moving to town would somehow help give his life meaning and happiness, but does not define how or what might do that. (B) reiterates that his hopes were unfulfilled. (C) explains Mr. Harding's reaction to David's new pet, but fails to provide support for the previous question.

9. **(D)** The author describes Willie's failed dreams for a prosperous farm in paragraph 2, so choice (D) is correct. (A), (B), and (C) use details within the paragraph to make unsupported assumptions.

10. **(C)** *Noticeable* makes the most sense in describing David's anguish since this use of *palpable* means "obvious and tangible." Choice (A) means the opposite. (B) and (D) are other possible meanings of *palpable*, but don't fit this context.

11. **(A)** This passage maintains an informative and objective tone, analyzing both forms of democracy without taking sides, ruling out (C) and (D). (A) is a more accurate choice than (B) because the author focuses on the differences, stating that, "The disparity between the two is hardly subtle."

12. **(C)** Since the author sustains an attitude that is both informative and impartial, (C) is the correct answer. While the author is certainly *neutral*, he or she is not *pessimistic, passionate*, or *predisposed* about either system of government.

13. **(B)** The passage states that the prevalence of parliamentary rule is connected to "the legacy of the British Empire," so the answer is (B). Choice (A) is an aspect of presidential rule. (C) and (D), although features of a parliamentary system, are not stated as reasons for its popularity.

14. **(A)** In lines 7–10, the passage gives its only mention of which system is more common, along with a possible explanation. Accordingly, (A) is correct. (B) gives a detail of how parliamentary systems are run. (C) actually refers to a benefit of the presidential system. And (D) provides a critique of parliamentary rule.

15. **(C)** From the context, we know that presidential systems expect the President to be both government leader and national figure. Contrastingly, a parliamentary system has a government executive separate from the national icon, most commonly a monarch. So, (C) is the correct choice.

16. **(B)** Line 39 refers to the nation's *advance*, so *progress* is the only appropriate answer. The passage is not indicating that the President is working toward a monetary or an imperialistic goal.

17. **(A)** The indicated paragraph addresses the pros and cons of the presidential model, making (A) correct. (B) is not accurate because the parliamentary model is not mentioned until the next paragraph. (C) is imprecise because it provides details of the aforementioned paragraph but does not encompass the perceived disadvantages as well as the benefits. (D) is wrong because it doesn't give specific examples of countries following this system in the paragraph.

18. **(A)** In line 70, *privy* refers to the presidential model's predisposition to discord and inefficiency. Hence, we could say the system is *susceptible*, meaning "vulnerable." Choice (D) is a near synonym, but not as precise a word choice.

19. **(D)** Lines 88–97 depict some negative features of the parliamentary model, stating that since power is centralized, "tyranny of the majority" is probable. This concern is related to the absence of a checks-and-balances system and according to lines 92–97 can result in minority parties being ignored. This concern refers to the majority party rather than a sole ruler as in (A). It is nonsensical to say critics would be concerned when human

rights are respected as in (B). Finally, (C) is related to productivity; a majority could be both productive and unjust.

20. **(C)** These lines give direct evidence of what might happen under the "tyranny of the majority." Choices (A) and (B) give strong points rather than concerns of the parliamentary system. And (D) refers to the author's neutral conclusion.

21. **(B)** Other than to provide definitions and refer to Sanger's own retrospect, this passage is structured chronologically, moving sequentially through time in regard to Sanger's accomplishments. This can be categorized as (B), *mostly chronological*.

22. **(B)** Lines 4–5 states that proteins "are present in and vital to every living cell." The line is indicating that proteins are necessary or fundamental, hence, *essential* is the correct word. It is not appropriate to say proteins are *vibrant*, *biological*, or *dynamic* to every cell.

23. **(B)** Sanger's own attitude is referenced twice within the passage: once in reference to his first Nobel Prize and once in his obituary. Both sentiments indicate modesty or humility, making (B) correct. (A) is not evidenced. (C) is a near antonym, and (D) is a definite antonym.

24. **(D)** Lines 81–85 document Sanger's account of himself as "academically not brilliant," and therefore, provide direct evidence for his humble nature. (A) introduces Sanger. (B) explains why he received his first Nobel Prize, but not his reaction to it. And (C) refers to the impact his work had on future discoveries.

25. **(C)** This question is asking for lines that indicate Sanger was optimistic or assured in his work. Lines 60–63 are the best evidence as these lines refer to the fact that he named his more efficient sequencing method after himself. We can assume he wanted it to be associated with his name because he knew it had great implications for chemistry. The other options give facts about Sanger but do not reflect any of his own feelings toward his work.

26. **(A)** Lines 37–38 is Sanger's self-reflection regarding the work that earned him a Nobel Prize in 1958. He is humorous and humble, so the only adjective that is accurate is (A), *playful. Somber* means "grave," while *bombastic* is "pompous." Sanger's quote is perhaps "carefree," but not *careless*, which means "indifferent or unworried to the point of negligence."

27. **(D)** Line 67 says that Sanger *employed* or "used" his method to decode mitochondria. Thus, (D) is the precise word choice. He succeeded, so (A) is imprecise. The method was already created, so (C) is misleading. And (B) is another meaning for *employed* that refers to employment in a workforce.

28. **(A)** Lines 69–76 outline some of the ways the Sanger Method crucially impacted the field of chemistry. Here, the author shows how Sanger used his method, how other scientists used his method, and the eventual outcomes of that combined research. Thus, (A) is correct. These lines don't address objections or negative consequence. So (B) and (D) are wrong. Choice (C) is also incorrect because the lines don't refer to his methodology as much as to the implications of his discoveries.

29. **(D)** This question refers to the graph. Since the graph has specific categories for the United States, United Kingdom, Germany, and France, we can infer these are the coun-

tries with the largest numbers of winners. Therefore, to be put in the "other" category, the country would have to have a percentage lower than that of 6%. So, (D) is correct.

30. **(D)** To approach this question, find the ratio of Germany to Germany plus the United States. Together, Germany and the United States make up 44% of the graph, so the ratio would be 11:44 or 1:4. The ratio 1:4 is the same as ¼ or 0.25, as in (D).

31. **(C)** This line refers to Washington's claim that economic gain will come as we "put brains and skill into the common occupations of life," so *ordinary* is the correct synonym. In the very next lines, we can see that Washington is comparing average duties to more elevated ambitions. As such, we can infer that he means typical, blue-collared work. The other choices give synonyms to *common*, but suggest communality.

32. **(C)** Lines 14–17 point to "the incoming of those of foreign birth and strange tongue and habits," meaning foreign immigrants. (A), (B), and (D) do not address the permanence of the persons coming to live and work in another country.

33. **(C)** To paraphrase, Washington suggests that historical loyalty is a good reason for whites to trust blacks, and then goes on to insinuate that social separation is fine if it is accompanied with economic unity. So, (C) accurately depicts the general purpose of these lines. He is not arguing for hostility or suppression toward foreigners. Nor is his argument founded on caring for the sick.

34. **(B)** Lines 52–56 state that the North yearned for "peaceful cooperation" because they were "weary of the race problem" and "investing largely in Southern enterprises." Thus, we can infer the North is concerned with *commercial advancement* instead of morality as in (A) or truth (C). Additionally, there is no evidence that the concern lay with locational distinction as in (D).

35. **(B)** DuBois states that Washington represents "adjustment and submission," and "accepts the alleged inferiority of the Negro races." Hence, (B) is correct. DuBois finds Washington's argument flawed because of its neglect for (A). Similarly, (C) is incorrect because DuBois believes that Washington is yielding morality in favor of economic advancement. There is no evidence for choice (D).

36. **(D)** Lines 78–84 specifically state that Washington "withdraws many of the high demands," advocating for a "policy of submission." These lines provide direct evidence of DuBois' perspective on Washington's efforts, and so support the previous question. Choices (A) and (B) communicate varying public response to Washington, rather than DuBois' own view. And (C) implies that the current time is a pivotal moment in history, making Washington's menial pursuits that much more inexcusable.

37. **(D)** *Direction* is the appropriate word choice. Here, DuBois argues that Washington's method takes an economic *cast*. The line is not referring to an economic *event, constraint*, or *throw*, but instead refers to an inclination or path.

38. **(A)** Washington is concerned with advocating for a way forward, while DuBois is interested in criticizing what he sees as Washington's immoral compromise. So, (A) is right. Passage 1 doesn't rely on statistics making (B) incorrect. (C) and (D) have the relationship reversed.

39. **(A)** To approach this question, consider that what Washington considers advancement, DuBois labels compromise. Thus, we can infer that a level down for Washington would

even be a further repression according to DuBois, so (A) is correct. (B) is a synonym for *compromise*, and clearly the authors don't have the same opinion. (C) is too extreme. (D) inaccurately indicates that Washington is more progressive than DuBois.

40. **(D)** These lines give DuBois' opinion of Washington's disposition as "the old attitude of adjustment and submission," and so can be used to support the idea that Washington is less liberal-minded. His more conservative demeanor gives us the evidence to answer the previous question. Choices (A) and (B) give details of Washington's argument, but don't give the reader a clear idea of how the two authors differ. And (C) is how Passage 2 introduces Washington, but does not provide insight of DuBois' attitude.

41. **(A)** Lines 86–93 state that Washington asks blacks to give up "political power," "civil rights," and "higher education" in favor of far less lofty goals. If Washington were to respond to DuBois, he might respond with lines 8–13 where he argues that blacks will not prosper until they embrace common labor. (B) and (C) refer to Washington's plea for work on behalf of the African-American population. (D) proves DuBois' point rather than responding to it.

42. **(A)** This passage can be classified structurally as a move from a general summary of the influenza virus to a very scientific analysis of how it operates and evolves at the molecular level. Hence, (A) is the best answer, with *survey* meaning a "general examination" rather than "a group of questions given to a wide audience to gather information." The author is not arguing as in (B), or presenting research summaries as in (C) and (D).

43. **(A)** Lines 12–19 refer to the fact that influenza remains a viable threat, and because of its unique disposition, is likely to stay that way. Choices (B) and (D) state the opposite, arguing instead that the virus is likely to be killed off and is essentially harmless. (C) is not correct because influenza's inability to be conquered, not its severity is what makes it unique.

44. **(D)** The author defines *epidemic* as being contained to a given community, and differentiates it from *pandemic*, in which the incidences occurs over a much larger region. From the table, we can see that only the outbreaks in 2005 and 2013 were confined to a region, while the others went global.

45. **(D)** Lines 106–108 describe the genetic changes associated with antigenic shift, stating that via "viral reassortment" the particles will produce completely new proteins "to which the entire human race is vulnerable." While the antigenic drift can also result in renewed vulnerability, it is to viral strains of which one was previously immune. Therefore, the changes would not be as great as those associated with antigenic shift. (Another way to think about it is that genetic drift results from random point mutations, which are the smallest changes possible.) Likewise, the author uses the example of a genome split in a bird that is capable of infecting humans making (D), rather than (C), the correct choice.

46. **(D)** Lines 101–108 give the interspecies genome exchange example and explain "viral reassortment," successfully providing evidence for why the antigenic shift results in greater fundamental changes than antigenic drift. Choices (A) and (B) describe the outermost viral proteins, but do not address drift vs shift. And choice (C) is incorrect because it refers to antigenic drift only, which does not alter genetic structure as significantly.

47. **(C)** The indicated paragraph explains antigenic drift and suggests that influenza A is particularly dangerous because it "is prone to a much higher rate of mutation." Therefore, it can be said that the author's purpose is to explain the reasons why one species of influenza virus is especially damaging, as in (C). (A) incorrectly understands antigenic drift as resulting in flu, when in reality it is a viral strand that undergoes many point mutations to renew vulnerability. And this paragraph doesn't talk about antigenic shift or vaccinations, so (B) and (D) can be ruled out.

48. **(B)** *Capacity* fits here because the line refers to influenza A's lack of ability to correct its genetic material. This type of flu virus simply doesn't have the capability to do it. The other words, although synonyms of *ability*, refer to a tendency to perform well rather than actual ability to perform a task.

49. **(B)** Choices (C) and (D) can be eliminated because Hong Kong Flu resulted in only a less than 0.1% fatality rate, and Avian Flu consisted only of 840 cases. Since the remaining two choices have similar fatality rates, we can assume that the outbreak which affected more people resulted in the greater number of deaths. Asian Flu is estimated to have affected approximately 3.1 million more humans than Russian Flu.

50. **(B)** According to lines 76–82, scientists are able to classify strains of influenza based on the antibodies produced to fight them. So, we can infer that outbreaks classified as the same subtype would cause the same reaction in the human body. (It also says in lines 78–82 that both outbreaks were caused by H1N1). Within the table, the only outbreaks with matching subtypes occurred in 1918 and 2009.

51. **(C)** Lines 78–82 indicate that "Spanish Flu" and "Swine Flu" were caused by identical strands of the influenza virus. These lines can be used in tandem with the table to answer the previous question. (A) merely lists well-known flu outbreaks. (B) gives the three species of the flu virus. (D) refers to the implications of antigenic shift.

52. **(C)** The best way to approach this question is to look for anomalies in the table for the outbreaks of 2005 and 2013. These two instances were contained geographically and held very high fatality rates compared to the other outbreaks. Therefore, we can infer that high fatality rates allowed the disease to die out before reaching a global scale. There is no evidence for (A) or (B). And (D) is not accurate because the Asian Flu also had its source in birds, but affected colossal numbers.